DECISION SUPPORT IN PUBLIC ADMINISTRATION

IFIP Transactions A: Computer Science and Technology

International Federation for Information Processing

Technical Committees:

Software: Theory and Practice (TC2)
Education (TC3)
System Modelling and Optimization (TC7)
Information Systems (TC8)
Relationship between Computers and Society (TC9)
Computer Systems Technology (TC10)
Security and Protection in Information Processing Systems (TC11)
Artificial Intelligence (TC12)
Human-Computer Interaction (TC13)
Foundations of Computer Science (SG14)

IFIP Transactions Abstracted/Indexed in:
INSPEC Information Services

A-26

DECISION SUPPORT IN PUBLIC ADMINISTRATION

Proceedings of the IFIP TC8/WG8.3 Working Conference on
Decision Support in Public Administration
Noordwijkerhout, The Netherlands, 13-14 May, 1993

Edited by

P.W.G. BOTS
H.G. SOL
School of Engineering, Policy and Management
Delft University of Technology
Delft, The Netherlands

R. TRAUNMÜLLER
Institut für Informatik
Johannes-Kepler-Universität Linz
Linz, Austria

1993

NORTH-HOLLAND
AMSTERDAM • LONDON • NEW YORK • TOKYO

ELSEVIER SCIENCE PUBLISHERS B.V.
Sara Burgerhartstraat 25
P.O. Box 211, 1000 AE Amsterdam, The Netherlands

Keywords are chosen from the ACM Computing Reviews Classification System, ©1991, with permission.
Details of the full classification system are available from
ACM, 11 West 42nd St., New York, NY 10036, USA.

ISBN: 0 444 81485 X
ISSN: 0926-5473

Printed in The Netherlands

DECISION SUPPORT IN PUBLIC ADMINISTRATION

Over time, IFIP's TC8 *Information Systems* (IS) has evolved. Working groups have been formed to focus on specific aspects of IS such as design and evaluation (WG8.1) and the interaction with the organization (WG8.2), on specific types of IS such as decision support systems (WG8.3) and office systems (WG8.4), or on a particular sector in which IS are used such as public administration (WG8.5). Is this a sign of segregation, of research communities digging themselves in? No. Joint activities of TC8 working groups such as the 1991 WG8.3/8.4 working conference on Support Functionality in the Office Environment in Canterbury show that these research communities are indeed next of kin, with common interests, language *and* problems.

This 1993 joint conference of IFIP's working groups 8.3 and 8.5 underlines their complementary roles in the search for solutions. The problems faced by government and its agencies on all levels are many and diverse. The already vast flow of information to be considered by policy makers and decision makers in national and local governments is swelling, while tightened budgets allow for less staff to process this information. To truly increase decision making capability with limited resources, specialized knowledge from the decision support systems community must be paired to insight in and experience with the multi-faceted problems and continually changing contexts that characterize the field of public administration.

The WG8.3/8.5 joint working conference on Decision Support in Public Administration is intended to provide a platform on which problems in (inter)national as well as local governments can be presented and discussed from a decision making and information systems perspective. The aim is to increase our understanding of these problems in order to better focus the efforts of researchers and practitioners in applying information technology to increase the performance of decision makers in public administration.

To cover such a broad area of interest, the programme committee called for papers on several themes:

- design considerations and approaches for, and practical experiences with, communication and information processing infrastructure and applications at the workplace level;
- the design and implementation of support systems for individual or group decision making in governmental and municipal settings;
- modelling and model management techniques, preferably based on case reports of successful *and* unsuccessful modelling efforts.
- concepts, approaches and models for re-designing tasks and processes in public administration;
- issues and challenges in integrating the information systems of several governmental bodies.

The papers that are contained in this volume of conference proceedings reflect these topics. They have been arranged in two parts. The first part deals to a large extent with theoretical and conceptual issues. It reflects the intention for the first day of the conference to be one of idea sharing and discussion. The second part contains the papers with a stronger emphasis on systems, their functionality and experiences in their development and application.

Part I opens with a paper by Alfs Berztiss (University of Pittsburgh, U.S.A. and University of Stockholm, Sweden) in which he explains a model for information transfer in a distributed decision making setting that allows reduction of the amount of data to be transferred and effective use of centralized expertise at remote decision making sites. Next, Bengt Andersson and Peter Nilsson from the Swedish National Audit Bureau report on their analysis of the complexity of inter-organizational information systems, uncovering a number of challenging research questions in this area.

Dirk Vriens (University of Nijmegen, the Netherlands) investigates the need to support problem setting, stimulating decision makers and/or analysts to examine the problem at hand in a broader context. He then presents the use of goal matrices as a practical technique for such problem setting. The next paper addresses a similar issue from a different angle: Fran Ackermann and Colin Edin (Strathclyde Business School, Scotland) and Steve Cropper (University of Keele, Scotland) report on their experiences with computer-aided cognitive mapping as a modelling technique to better understand and improve the individual performance review process in the UK National Health Service. Within that same organization, Philip Baugh and David Walters (University of Central Lancashire, UK) investigated the development and use of a decision support system for case mix management, aimed at cost control in health care. In the context of this investigation they present a socio-technical framework for analysis.

The paper by Gary Dickson (University of Minnesota, U.S.A.) marks the transition from theory and concepts to systems design and implementation. His experiences with the development and use of four decision support systems within the government of the State of Minnesota show the potential benefits and pitfalls of decision support in public administration.

Part II starts with a paper by Michel Klein (HEC School of Management, France) in which he gives an overview of the functionality of a decision support system for financial management in French municipalities. Alfred Schramm (University of Graz, Austria) demonstrates a knowledge-based decision support system that is currently used by municipalities in their policy making and operational decision making processes concerning construction activities on municipal grounds.

Bin Nguyen (AIRMICS, Software Technology Branch of the Army Research Laboratory, U.S.A.) describes the Work-Time Measurement System that has been in use at the Army Research Laboratory since 1990: why it was developed, how it was implemented and how it supports work process redesign. Other experiences with information technology as a means for streamlining non-profit organizations are reported by Mirko Vintar (University of Ljubljana, Slovenia). Jean-Charles Pomerol, Michel Futtersack and Jean-Marc Labat

(University of Paris VI, France) give a detailed account of a decision support system for use within the French Employment Ministry. Their analysis of the reasons why this system eventually failed makes their paper especially worth reading.

The next two papers relate specifically to group decision making. Martin Smits and Cees Takkenberg (Tilburg University, the Netherlands) and Theo Postma and Simon Terpstra (Groningen University, the Netherlands) outline an approach to solving health care manpower planning problems. Their approach centers around interactive model building by a group of decision makers and uses ideas from both group decision support systems and the policy Delphi method. The paper by Dirk Kenis and Lucas Verhaegen (Free University of Brussels, Belgium) also builds on the policy Delphi method. It describes the functionality of their prototype support system for Delphi studies.

Åke Grönlund and Bai Guohua (Umeå University, Sweden) close this volume of conference proceedings with a paper on what they call participatory information systems. In this paper they contrast two views on information systems and how they should be designed, and extensively discuss why, particularly in the public sector, one of these views is to be preferred.

The authors' affiliations (17 organizations from 8 different countries) demonstrate IFIP's international nature. The ideas put forward in their papers show that research into supporting decision making in public administration is well on its way. They also show that this research area is vast with yet many hills to scale. We hope that this working conference and its proceedings will challenge you to venture more in it.

Pieter Bots　　　Henk Sol　　　Roland Traunmüller

PROGRAMME COMMITTEE:

Henk Sol } *co-chair*
Roland Traunmüller } *co-chair*
Pieter Bots
Ron Lee
Ron Stamper

TABLE OF CONTENTS

PART I

THEORY AND CONCEPTS

Decision Support in Public Administration (A-26)
P.W.G. Bots, H.G. Sol and R. Traunmüller (Editors)
Elsevier Science Publishers B.V. (North-Holland)
1993 IFIP.

Information Transfer for Decision Support in Distributed Administrative Systems

A. T. Berztiss

Department of Computer Science, University of Pittsburgh, Pittsburgh, PA 15260, USA
(e-mail: alpha@cs.pitt.edu; fax: +412-624-8854)

and

SYSLAB, University of Stockholm

Abstract

This paper addresses two issues. First, increased decentralization in some public sector organizations and large private enterprises puts emphasis on effective sharing of expertise within organizations. Second, even in decentralized organizations some macro-level decisions still need to be made, which means that information must be made available at the points of decision. Similarly, with European integration, the decision-making role of central EC agencies can be expected to increase, necessitating the transfer of information from individual countries to the EC agencies. The objective is to transfer information without moving large amounts of data. We present a model of information transfer based on the movement of filters, and of extensional and intensional representations of functions. Extensional representations are data, and the other information captures expertise. Such expertise leads to a reduction of the volume of data to be moved.

1. Introduction.

The role of a decision maker is to perform cost-benefit analyses, where costs relate to the consumption of resources, and benefits to the strategic goals of an organization, where both costs and benefits are to be given a very broad interpretation. Under Simon's three-phase model of decision making [1] an intelligence gathering phase provides inputs from an environment that indicate problems or opportunities, a design phase results in the development of several strategies for dealing with the problems or opportunities, and an effective strategy is chosen in a selection phase. A measure of effectiveness is the ratio of benefits to costs. In a commercial enterprise costs can be expressed for the most part in monetary terms, and benefits as some combination of profits and market share. The major distinction between commercial enterprises and public sector organizations is that neither costs nor benefits can be quantified in the latter context. Moreover, every decision maker is faced with the problem that the relationship of benefits to costs is hardly ever properly understood. Hence only a few strategy systems *make* decisions; most such systems merely *support* human decision making. The first kind of strategy systems are expert systems (ESs); the second are decision support systems (DSSs). However, as pointed out in [2-4], differences between various types of management systems (DSSs, ESs, MISs, etc.) are differences in degree rather than in basic structure.

In Section 2 we shall discuss a language for describing conceptual models of organizations in a way that indicates precisely where DSSs and ESs can be introduced into an organization. However, this is not our main purpose. We note that many organizations, particularly those in the public sector, are distributed over numerous sites, that a decision made at one site depends on data gathered at other sites, and that the staff expected to perform some decision support activity at a remote site may lack the required expertise. In Section 3 we introduce a case study, use it to outline a method for transferring expertise to remote sites, and show that application of this method can lead to greatly reduced flow of data between sites. Section 4 shows how the modeling language of Section 2 relates to our case study. In Section 5 we draw conclusions, some in the form of suggestions for further research.

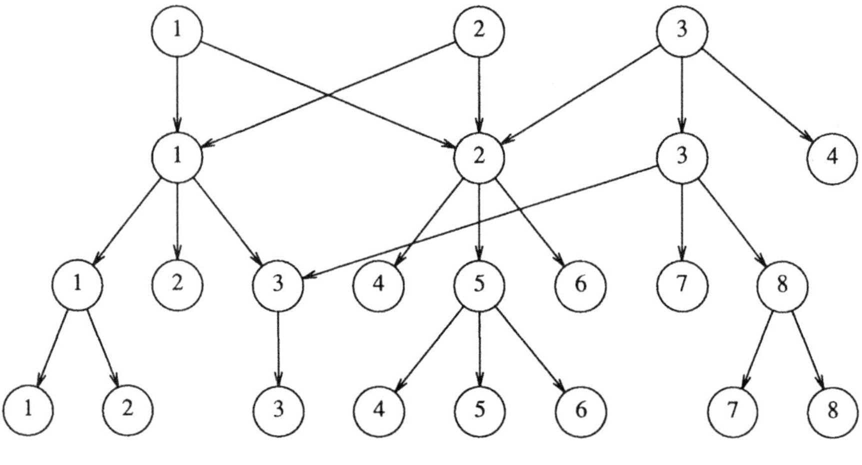

Fig. 1 – A distributed organization

The structural framework for our discussion is a distributed system of sites, represented by nodes in a tree-like directed acyclic graph. Sites do not necessarily have to be physically remote from each other – two sites may share the same building. The nodes occupy levels, and are connected by arcs representing communication links.

Figure 1 shows an example of such a structure in which the nodes are arranged in four levels. The levels are numbered 1, 2, 3, 4, and the nodes are numbered 1, 2, 3, ... at each level. The top level (level 1) contains "root nodes". A unique identifier for a node is obtained by joining its number to its level number, e.g., 1.3, 4.3, 3.8, and a path is defined by a sequence of such identifiers, e.g., <1.2, 2.2, 3.5, 4.3>. The level numbers are essential in the specification of a path, e.g., <1.3, 2.3, 3.3> and <2.3, 3.3, 4.3> are different paths. In Fig. 1 any two nodes are joined by at most one path. This means that there is always just one path along which information can flow from site to site. Such restriction of flows to unique paths is not essential.

2. A specification framework

Our framework is the SF (Set-Function) specification and prototyping language, which the author introduced in 1986 [5, 6], and is still refining and extending (a more recent outline can be found in [7]; for a full, but slightly dated, definition see [8]; examples of SF constructs can be found in our Appendix). An SF specification consists of segments, and each segment corresponds to a data type with three components. First, a schema describes the data base of an application in terms of sets and functions, where a function f is a mathematical object $f: A \longrightarrow B$ consisting of pairs $<a, b>$ with $a \in A$ and $b \in B$. Since SF functions may be set-valued, a relation can be freely converted into an SF function, and vice versa, so that there are no obstacles to the use of the relational model in the implementation of an SF data base.

An interesting feature of SF in the DSS context is that SF downplays implementation issues, and thus the conventional distinction between a data base and a model base (see, e.g., [9]) disappears. Consider a function that determines ideal weight given a person's height and sex. This function can be implemented as a table or as a computational rule, and we speak of an extensional or intensional representation, respectively. In one case the function would belong to the data base, in the other to the model base. This illustrates that the separation of the sources of information of a DSS into two components is arbitrary, at least at a sufficiently high level of abstraction.

Second, an SF specification defines events. Events are initiated by users or by the system itself, and generally they cause changes to the data base. For example, a user initiates an event in a library system by borrowing a book. In the data base the user is now listed as the borrower of the book, the status of the book becomes "out-on-loan", and the date of borrowing is entered into the data base as well. Events initiated by the system are called internal. An example of an internal event is the determination of whether or not a book is overdue – this event is initiated for each borrowed book at the close of each working day, and the status of books that are overdue is changed from "out-on-loan" to "overdue". Events can also raise signals, which are messages sent to a responder.

The responder is the third component of an SF specification. It consists of transactions that are activated by a clock, by one or more signals, or by a clock and signals in combination. A transaction can initiate an event on its own, prompt a user to initiate an event, or remind a user of an action to be performed. For example, the transaction that initiates events that are to change the status of overdue books is activated by a clock at the end of a working day. An example of a transaction initiated by a signal: a borrowing event in the segment relating to books raises a signal that is picked up by a transaction in another segment, one that relates to borrowers, and an event is initiated that increments the count of books held by our borrower. An example of a reminder that is issued by a transaction at a certain time, but only if a signal has been raised: at the end of day, an appropriate signal is raised for each book that has its status changed to "overdue"; next morning the clock activates for each such signal a transaction that reminds library staff to send out an overdue notice to the offending borrower.

Here our main interest is in transactions that issue prompts. A prompt is issued when the system has determined that an event is to be initiated, but the system cannot initiate the event on its own. Consider the arrival of a submission to a journal. Three referees are now to be selected, and there are three options: (i) an editor selects the referees without any support by the system; (ii) the system helps the editor select the referees, by supplying the editor with information that the system deems relevant, and we have a rudimentary DSS; (iii) an expert system is developed to do the selection, i.e., one function of the editor is now fully automated. Under the first two options the transaction continues to issue a prompt; under the third the system is made to initiate the referee selection event on its own, and the event becomes an internal event.

Our methodology has the attractive feature that in an SF model of an enterprise the transactions that issue prompts represent all opportunities for introducing a DSS or an ES, the cost-effectiveness of each prospective DSS or ES can be worked out, and these systems can be introduced incrementally, one DSS or ES at a time, according to the availability of resources. Our approach clarifies the distinction between a DSS and an ES – an ES makes a decision totally on its own, although it may request input of additional data; a DSS merely supports a human decision maker. The distinction is quite clear at the level of an individual "prompting" transaction – it either takes over the decision making, or it continues to issue a prompt. However, considering the system as a whole, some "prompted" events will now be initiated by ESs, others will receive support from DSSs, and still others will continue to require unsupported decision making by the user. In an unsystematic way DSS-ES hybrids have been discussed quite often (see, e.g., [10-12]). Here we have described a system with a single modularized data base that contains some distinct subsystems with an ES orientation and some with a DSS orientation.

3. A case study

For our case study we consider the structure shown in Fig. 2. The nodes represent a central health care authority (node 1.1), three regional centers (nodes 2.1, 2.2, 2.3), and seven district offices subordinated to the regional centers (nodes 3.1 through 3.7). Node 1.2 represents central school administration with which the health authority consults on matters relating to our case study. Each district health office maintains a data base on school children. We leave open the structure of this data base, but it must contain the following functions that map from the set of identifiers of the children (*ID*): *DofB* (birthdate), *S*(ex), *H*(eight), *W*(eight).

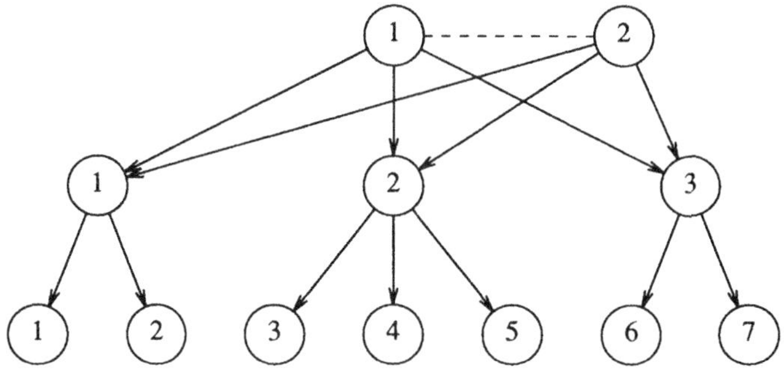

Fig. 2 – Site distribution for the case study

On June 30, 1993 the central health authority is beginning a study on nutritional improvements in school lunches. For this purpose it requires the height-weight relationship of female school children who are 12 years of age on June 30, 1993, i.e., were born between July 1, 1980 and June 30, 1981, inclusive. Each district office is to generate <*H*(*id*), *W*(*id*)> pairs for all 12-year old girls, and pass this information to its regional center. At the regional center the district data are to be combined, and a regression analysis carried out. The form of the regression curve has been determined by the central health authority. The authority also defines outliers by two functions $wmax_{girls}(height, f_{g1})$ and $wmin_{girls}(height, f_{g2})$, where f_{g1} and f_{g2} depend on the parameters of the regression curve. Both the central health and school authorities receive from each regional center the parameters of the regression curve and the set of <*height*, *weight*> pairs that lie outside the limits defined by functions $wmax_{girls}$ and $wmin_{girls}$.

Decisions are now made by the central authorities. The health authority determines whether the regional data are uniform by comparing the three regression curves. If there are significant differences, separate nutritional programs may have to be devised for individual regions, and the regional centers may be asked to do the regression analysis separately for each district. Assume that there are no significant differences between regions. The first step now is to repeat the study for boys. The health authority then submits a recommendation to the school administration, which considers budgetary aspects of the recommendation. After a few iterations the two authorities agree on the number of children to receive special lunches. These children are identified by functions $wmax^*_{girls}(height)$ and $wmin^*_{girls}(height)$, with a corresponding pair of functions for boys.

Consider now the information flows in the system. Node 1.1 sends to nodes 2.1, 2.2, 2.3 a message outlining the project, a filter to be applied to the data in district data bases, and the regression analysis program that also defines functions $wmax_{girls}$ and $wmin_{girls}$. The filter is the predicate

$$F_{girls}(id) = DofB(id) \geq 19800701 \wedge DofB(id) \leq 19810630 \wedge S(id) = \text{"female"}.$$

The idea is to generate at each district office the set of triples

$$S^*_{girls} = \{<id, H(id), W(id)> \mid F_{girls}(id)\}.$$

The filter is passed through regional centers to district offices as is. Each district office generates its set of triples S^*_{girls}, strips off the identifiers, and sends the resulting *<height, weight>* pairs to its regional center, where the regression analysis is undertaken, and its results passed to nodes 1.1 and 1.2. Then the central health authority sends down the filter for boys,

$$F_{boys}(id) = DofB(id) \geq 19800701 \wedge DofB(id) \leq 19810630 \wedge S(id) = \text{"male"},$$

regression analysis is performed on the data filtered through F_{boys}, and its results sent to nodes 1.1 and 1.2. We assume that the form of the regression curve and of functions *wmax* and *wmin* is the same for boys and girls. Consultation between the health and the school authorities now results in the definition of four cut-off functions (separate versions of $wmax^*$ and $wmin^*$ for girls and boys), which are sent to the district offices. Here they are used as filters on the two sets of triples of 12-year olds (S^*_{girls} and S^*_{boys}) to determine identifiers of children who are to receive special lunches. For girls the filters are

$$HI_{girls} = weight > wmax^*_{girls}(height); \quad LO_{girls} = weight < wmin^*_{girls}(height).$$

The filters restrict S^*_{girls} to

$$HIset_{girls} = \{<id, height, weight> \mid HI_{girls}\},$$

$$LOset_{girls} = \{<id, height, weight> \mid LO_{girls}\}.$$

Next the sets of identifiers $IDHI_{girls}$ and $IDLO_{girls}$ are extracted from the tuples in $HIset_{girls}$ and $LOset_{girls}$, respectively, and similarly for boys. Finally the identifiers are combined into two sets, $IDHI$ and $IDLO$.

It is easy to see that our system is a true DSS because human judgement is required in several instances. First, it has to be decided whether regional differences in the data are sufficiently minor to justify aggregation of the data. Next, the number of special lunches has to be fixed in consultation on budgetary matters with the school authority. Finally it has to be decided how this number is to be split between girls and boys, and between underweight and overweight children. All the decisions are made in just one place, represented by node 1.1 in Fig. 2. Nodes on lower levels merely provide raw data (level 3), process the raw data (level 2), and implement the final decision (level 3).

Although we have looked at just one example, and a somewhat contrived example at that, the example permits us to make several general observations:

- the flow of data in a distributed system can be reduced by use of appropriate filters – this is not a serious concern in our study, but flow reduction becomes important when very large volumes of data are in use and fast response times are required;

- the design of filters may be too difficult for non-specialists, but the design can be centralized at sites where specialists are available;
- similar remarks apply to methods for statistical analysis of data, e.g., the selection of an appropriate regression model;
- confidentiality is given automatic consideration in that identifiers of people are transmitted between sites only as needed.

4. The case study and SF

In [13] Sol emphasizes the importance of application domain models in decision making – organizational entities are to be viewed as loosely coupled systems in such conceptual models. A conceptual domain model defined in SF satisfies the requirement of loose coupling: data types define non-overlapping regions of a data base, and communication between SF segments is by signals alone – an event raises a signal, and the signal is picked up by a transaction in the same or some other segment. This becomes interesting when the transaction initiates another event (which must be in its own segment), this event raises another signal, the signal is picked up, and so forth. We have thus a facility for defining processes – SF processes correspond to Petri nets with events corresponding to places, transactions to transitions, and signaling to the movement of tokens.

But the initial design of an SF system cannot predict all the uses that will be made of the system – the number of sets and functions in the data base and the number of explicitly specified processes are severely limited. The functions that define a data type are *basic* functions, and functions derived from basic functions are *defined* functions. Thus, given basic function *DofB*, function *Age* can be defined in terms of *DofB* and today's date (*DateNow*):

$$Age(id) = (DateNow - DofB(id)) \text{ div } 10000,$$

where *DateNow* and *DofB* take the form year+month+day, e.g., May 9, 1945 is represented as 19450509, and, for the purposes of the arithmetic in the definition of function *Age*, the representations of data are interpreted as integers. The definition of functions such as *Age* is helped by a querying facility superimposed on SF. This is the visual language Vizla [14], which can also be used to construct filters [15].

The process of selection of children for special lunches would not have been part of the initial conceptual model either. We shall now define this process in a step by step manner, somewhat more formally than in Section 2.

Step 1. Denote the user at node 1.1 by U – U is to construct filter F_{girls} and send it to all level 3 nodes. Filters are essentially queries that have sets or functions for their answers. Hence U can use Vizla to define the set of triples

$$S^*_{girls} = \{<id, H(id), W(id)> \mid id \in ID \wedge F_{girls}(id)\},$$

and the bag of pairs (bag rather than set to allow for duplication)

$$S_{girls} = \{<coord(2, x), coord(3, x)> \mid x \in S^*_{girls}\},$$

where *coord*(*i*, *t*) extracts the *i*th coordinate from a tuple *t*. These definitions are sent to the level 3 nodes, where they are used to construct set S^*_{girls} and bag S_{girls} in a temporary data base.

Step 2. Bags S_{girls} are transferred to level 2 and combined: letting S^{ij}_{girls} denote the bag constructed at node j on level i, the combined bag S^{23}_{girls} is $S^{36}_{girls} \uplus S^{37}_{girls}$, where $\uplus$ is a "bag union" that allows for duplication.

Step 3. A regression analysis program (method in the terminology of object-oriented programming) that includes code for the computation of $wmin_{girls}$ and $wmax_{girls}$ is sent by U to level 2 nodes, where a regression analysis is performed on S^{21}_{girls}, S^{22}_{girls}, S^{23}_{girls}, respectively. This can be regarded as the determination of the value of a schematic regression function R, with functionality

$$R: \ (Ht \times Wt)\text{–set} \longrightarrow P^k \times (Ht \times Wt)\text{–set} \times (Ht \times Wt)\text{–set},$$

where X-set stands for the power set of X (here it is actually a "power bag"). The function takes a bag of pairs S^{2j}_{girls} (j = 1, 2, 3) for its argument, and the corresponding value is made up of k parameters of the regression equation and two bags of outliers. The latter are sub-bags of the argument.

Step 4. Values of R are sent from nodes 2.1, 2.2, 2.3 to nodes 1.1 and 1.2. At node 1.1 U makes the determination that there is insignificant variation between the three regression equations. Bags S_{girls} at level 2 are no longer needed.

Steps 5-8. Steps analogous to Steps 1 through 4 are carried out on data for boys.

Step 9. The budgetary analysis results in the definition of the set $IDHI_{girls}$,

$$IDHI_{girls} \ = \ \{coord(1,x) \mid x \in S^*_{girls} \wedge coord(3,x) > wmax^*_{girls}(coord(2,x))\},$$

and similarly for $IDHI_{boys}$, $IDLO_{girls}$, $IDLO_{boys}$. These definitions are combined by U to define the sets of identifiers

$$IDHI \ = \ IDHI_{girls} \uplus IDHI_{boys}; \quad IDLO \ = \ IDLO_{girls} \uplus IDLO_{boys}.$$

Definitions of *IDHI* and *IDLO* are sent to level 3 nodes, where they are used to identify the children who are to receive special lunches.

So far we have ignored validation, which for our example is the determination of the effectiveness of the diets. Assume that different diets are tried in different districts. This requires that validation data be obtained from each district individually. The simplified regression function R^*,

$$R^* \ : \ (Ht \times Wt)\text{–set} \longrightarrow P^k,$$

is to be applied separately to the heights and weights of children belonging to $IDLO_{girls}$, $IDLO_{boys}$, $IDHI_{girls}$, $IDHI_{boys}$ on June 30, 1993, and again on June 30, 1994. The districts obtain the form of R^* from regional centers, and the values of R^* for each set of data are sent to the central health authority.

Let us now look at the same problem from a slightly different angle. Suppose the special lunch program is not a once-only effort, but that every year on June 30 all children who turned 12 in the preceding year are to be considered. Now the selection of children for special lunches should become part of the conceptual model of the school system. Note that SF clocks can have different granularity, including a clock with resolution in days. Then the SF specification of a level 3 system contains the following:

(i) As part of the schema, set-valued zero-argument functions *IDHI* and *IDLO* (our purpose is to replace the sets of identifiers for the previous year with new sets of identifiers), and functions that incorporate $wmax^*_{girls}$, $wmax^*_{boys}$, $wmin^*_{girls}$, $wmin^*_{boys}$.

(ii) An event *SetNull* that makes *IDHI* and *IDLO* null sets, and raises signal *Search*.

(iii) An event *AddLunch* that determines whether a child identified by $id \in ID$ is to receive a special lunch, and, if so, adds *id* to set *IDHI* or *IDLO*.

(iv) A transaction, triggered on June 30, that initiates event *SetNull*.

(v) A transaction, triggered by signal *Search*, that initiates *AddLunch* for every element of the set *ID*.

The SF representation of this specification is shown in the Appendix.

5. Conclusions

We have developed a model of information transfer that (a) reduces the flow of data in support of decision making in an organization, and (b) allows effective use at remote sites of expertise concentrated at a central site. The model is based on intensional definitions of functions as expressions of expertise, where we regard filters as intensionally defined boolean functions. Such expertise is then easily made available at remote sites. Our detailed conclusions follow.

(1) Our model was developed within an SF framework, but our findings do not depend on SF. However, a functional data model such as SF has several advantages. First, it is sometimes feasible to convert an extensional representation of a function into an intensional representation. Second, in order to make use of the extensive theoretical knowledge relating to data types we have to assume that the main component of a data type is a set of functions free of side effects. Third, a natural modularization criterion is provided by a functional model: each entity type of a conceptual model is interpreted as a data type, and a module is made up of a set of entities together with functions that have this set for their domain. Fourth, a data model based on data types as modules can be given as much object orientation as is warranted in a given case.

(2) In a hierarchy of sites intensional definitions of functions are concentrated at higher levels, extensional definitions at lower levels. Although much thought has been given to software reuse (see, e.g., [16]), practical success with reusability has been limited. Functions that can be given intensional definitions have a better understood structure than those that cannot be intensionalized, and hence the former have a greater potential for reuse. The root nodes of a distributed organization thus naturally become repositories of reusable software

components. In our context, the reuse potential of functions such as *DofB*, *H*, and *W*, where, moreover, *H* and *W* keep changing, is close to non-existent. On the other hand, a generic regression analysis program can be used over and over again. Even filters F_{girls} and F_{boys} are unlikely to find further use, but their form can guide designers of other filters. A retrieval scheme for filters should therefore be devised. This could be based on similarity metrics analogous to the metrics used by Angehrn and Dutta [17] in the retrieval of cases from a case library for case-based reasoning.

(3) The investigation of the effects of a particular course of action that has been developed with the aid of a DSS often leads to the institutionalization of this course of action. The sequence of steps by which this course of action becomes a routine process in a conceptual model should be thoroughly studied, and standardized as far as possible. Research on disciplined approaches to the evolution of information systems has just begun [18]. Our particular interest here is the effect the institutionalization would have on information transfer in distributed information systems that support DSSs as subsystems.

(4) A structure such as Fig. 1 can serve as a model of a federated data base system [19], with nodes 1.1, 1.2, 1.3 representing federated data base management systems. If a DSS is to function in the context of a federated data base system, the classification problem of (2) assumes even greater significance.

(5) In the intelligence gathering phase of Simon's three-phase model, referred to at the start of Section 1, the environment is scanned for hints of opportunities for furthering the strategic goals of an organization, or even setting new goals. As far as we know, the only study of automatic acquisition of such hints is Lundberg's analysis of business news items [20]. Lundberg examines a stream of news items, and admits to the system items that pass through a filter, where the filter is based on a user profile. The accepted items are structured as a semantic net. We see the determination of the precise design principles for filters on the environment-system interface as a very important research topic.

References

1 Simon, H.A., *The New Science of Management Decision.* Harper and Row, New York, 1960.

2 Ariav, G., and Ginzberg, M.J., DSS design: a systemic view of decision support. *Comm. ACM* **28** (1985), 1045-1052.

3 Bots, P.W.G., *An Environment to Support Problem Solving.* Doctoral dissertation, Tech. University of Delft, 1989.

4 Alter, S., *Information Systems: A Management Perspective.* Addison-Wesley, Reading, MA, 1992.

5 Berztiss, A., The set-function approach to conceptual modeling. In *Information System Design Methodologies: Improving the Practice*, T.W.Olle, H.G.Sol, and A.A.Verrijn-Stuart (Eds.), North-Holland, Amsterdam, 1986, pp.107-144.

6 Berztiss, A.T., Data abstraction in the specification of information systems. *Proc. IFIP World Congress 86*, pp.83-90.

7 Berztiss, A., Formal specification methods and visualization. In *Principles of Visual Programming Systems*, S.-K.Chang (Ed.), Prentice-Hall, Englewood Cliffs, NJ, 1990, pp.231-290.

8 Berztiss, A.T., The specification and prototyping language SF. SYSLAB Report 78, University of Stockholm, 1990.

9 Sprague, R.H., and Carlson, E.D., *Building Effective Decision Support Systems*. Prentice-Hall, Englewood Cliffs, NJ, 1982.

10 Kurstedt, H.A., Responsive decision support systems: a broad view illustrates when to include expert systems. In *Expert Systems and Artificial Intelligence in Decision Support Systems*, H.Sol et al. (Eds.), D.Reidel, Dordrecht, Holland, 1987, pp.53-77.

11 Dzierzanowski, J.M., Christman, K.R., MacKinnon, G.J., and Klahr, P., The Authorizer's Assistant: a knowledge-based credit authorization system for American Express. *Proc. 1st Annual Conf. Innovative Appl. AI, 1989*, pp.168-172.

12 Bayad, R., and Pomerol, J.-Ch., An "intelligent" DSS for the reinforcement of urban electrical power networks. In *Decision Support Systems: Experiences and Expectations*, T.Jelassi, M.R.Klein, and W.M.Mayon-White (Eds.), North-Holland, Amsterdam, 1992, pp.153-165.

13 Sol, H.G., Expert systems for modelling of decision support and information systems. In *Modelling and Simulation Methodology in the Artificial Intelligence Era*, M.S.Elzas, T.I.Oren, and B.P.Zeigler (Eds.), North-Holland, Amsterdam, 1986, pp.353-363.

14 Berztiss, A.T., The query language Vizla. To appear in *IEEE Trans. Knowledge and Data Eng.*

15 Berztiss, A.T., Operational construction of integrity constraints. In *Proc. 4th Internat. Conf. Software Eng. Knowledge Eng., 1992*, pp.487-494.

16 Biggerstaff, T.J., and Perlis, A.J. (Eds.), *Software Reusability*. Addison-Wesley, Reading, MA, 1989 (two volumes).

17 Angehrn, A.A., and Dutta, S., Integrating case-based reasoning in multi-criteria decision support systems. In *Decision Support Systems: Experiences and Expectations*, T.Jelassi, M.R.Klein, and W.M.Mayon-White (Eds.), North-Holland, Amsterdam, 1992, pp.133-150.

18 Jarke, M., Mylopoulos, J., Schmidt, J.W., and Vassiliou, Y., DAIDA: An environment for evolving information systems. *ACM Trans. Inf. Systems* **10** (1992), 1-50.

19 Sheth, A., and Larson, J.A., Federated database systems for managing distributed, heterogeneous, and autonomous databases. *ACM Comp. Surveys* **22** (1990), 183-236.

20 Lundberg, B.G., On information support in decision making. In *Support Functionality in the Office Environment*, A.A.Verrijn-Stuart, P.Hammersley, and H.G.Sol (Eds.), North-Holland, Amsterdam, 1991.

Appendix: Examples of SF constructs

An SF segment comprises a schema, a set of events, and a set of transactions. Here we define these three components for our case study, which is the selection of school children who are to receive special lunches, where the process of selection takes place once a year. The specification is incomplete in that everything that does not directly relate to the case study has been left out.

I. Schema. The schema defines a type based on the set *ID*. SF secondary types correspond to the enumerated types found in some programming languages – no functions or events are associated with such types, and they do not therefore warrant implementation as separate segments. The specification of the defined boolean cut-off functions, e.g., *WGMax*, is incomplete – in a full specification they would be precisely defined.

TYPE *Student*;

SET *ID*;

SECONDARY TYPES *Sex* = {"male", "female"};

SIGNALS *Search*;

FUNCTIONS *DofB*: *ID* ⟶ *Date*;

S: *ID* ⟶ *Sex*;

H: *ID* ⟶ *Ht*;

W: *ID* ⟶ *Wt*;

IDHI: ⟶ *Student*–set;

IDLO: ⟶ *Student*–set;

FUNDEFS *Age* (*id*: *ID*): (*DateNow* – *DofB* (*id*)) div 10000;

WGMax (*id*: *ID*): *W* (*id*) > ······ ; (* an expression in *H* (*id*) *)

WGMin (*id*: *ID*): *W* (*id*) < ······ ; (* an expression in *H* (*id*) *)

WBMax (*id*: *ID*): *W* (*id*) > ······ ; (* an expression in *H* (*id*) *)

WBMin (*id*: *ID*): *W* (*id*) < ······ ; (* an expression in *H* (*id*) *)

ENDTYPE;

II. Events. In the specification of events, expressions containing the equals sign are not assignments, but are predicates to be satisfied. Primed quantities relate to the state of the system after the event; unprimed quantities to its state before the event. Thus $IDHI' = IDHI \cup \{id\}$ in the specification of an event asserts that after the event set *IDHI* contains element *id* in addition to all the elements it contained before the event. The data base is changed only by events: an event subjects it to the minimal change necessary to make all postconditions true, and to no more. An event takes place only if all its preconditions are true at the time it is initiated. Thus event *AddLunch* will take place only if *id* identifies a 12-year old.

EVENT *SetNull*; (* Internal event initiated by *Initialization* *)

DATACONDITIONS $IDHI' = Null$;

$IDLO' = Null$;

SIGCONDITIONS (*Search*)ON;

ENDEVENT;

EVENT *AddLunch*(*id*: *Student*); (* Internal event initiated by *Select* *)

PRECONDITIONS $Age(id) = 12$;

DATACONDITIONS $S(id) = \text{"female"} \wedge WGMax(id)$

$\vee \; S(id) = \text{"male"} \wedge WBMax(id)$

$\longrightarrow IDHI' = IDHI \cup \{id\}$;

$S(id) = \text{"female"} \wedge WGMin(id)$

$\vee \; S(id) = \text{"male"} \wedge WBMin(id)$

$\longrightarrow IDLO' = IDLO \cup \{id\}$;

ENDEVENT;

III. Transactions. Transaction *Initialization* is activated by a clock with resolution in days (the D in 0630D indicates that we are dealing with the date June 30). Transaction *Select* is activated by signal *Switch* with immediate effect. The FORALL is an iterator: the iteration is over all elements of *ID* in a nondeterministic manner, and for each element of *ID* the event *AddLunch* is initiated.

TRANSACTION *Initialization*;

@ (0630D): *SetNull*;

ENDTRANSACTION;

TRANSACTION *Select*;

@ ( ): ON(*Switch*)OFF: FORALL(*id*): $id \in ID$: *AddLunch*(*id*);

ENDTRANSACTION;

Decision Support in Public Administration (A-26)
P.W.G. Bots, H.G. Sol and R. Traunmüller (Editors)
Elsevier Science Publishers B.V. (North-Holland)

How to manage complexity in inter-organizational information systems (IOIS) - some preliminary conclusions

Bengt E. W. Andersson
Peter Nilsson

The Swedish National Audit Bureau

Summary

The current trend is towards the use of information systems involving a number of actors/organizations; so-called inter-organizational information systems (IOIS). This has created a higher degree of complexity, which must be controlled if we are to have effective and functional information systems. The Swedish National Audit Bureau (RRV) has come across this kind of system in a number of its audits. The RRV's conclusions are that there are substantial difficulties related to IOIS and that the government agencies have failed to deal satisfactorily with these difficulties.

It is essential that the boundaries of the systems are defined correctly, the definition being based on the purpose of the system. The basic EDP philosophy will then be that *one* information system should be linked to *one* operation carried out by *one* of the parties involved, and have *one* specific purpose in that operation (1:1:1:1). This philosophy may then form the basis for a discussion on changes.

Since IOIS boundaries are in no way related to organizational boundaries it is essential that the interfaces and responsibilities of the parties concerned are clearly defined. Further, common cooperation principles, strategies and contracts must be developed. The parties should also develop research and collaboration processes for the evolution and administration of IOIS.

1. Introduction

The RRV is the central state authority for accounting and auditing government administration. The RRV reports to the government and/or the agencies concerned. Its primary task is to promote effectiveness and efficiency in government administration. Since 1982 the RRV has been carrying out specific audits of the information technology (IT) and EDP systems used by central and local government.

This paper presents a brief description and analysis of recent IOIS audits carried out by the RRV. Discussions based upon shortcomings identified in the organization and management of IOIS point to a lack of clarity in, and the increasing complexity of IOIS as the main causes of the weaknesses observed.

The audits have produced some general conclusions on which are based a number of views on the way the issue of complexity in IOIS should be approached.

2. Auditing information systems

Sweden's government and municipal information systems are expanding rapidly, and the growing use of EDP support means that more and more actors are involved. Increasing attention is being devoted to the strategic importance of effective information support in public administration. There is also a growing need for agencies to use data from other agencies.

Starting a couple of years ago, RRV audits in this area have tended to focus on information systems (IS), i.e., the flow of information from the collection of data, through EDP systems, to the use of data. The perspective adopted involves cutting right across several agencies and other bodies, allowing problems relating to this cross-section of various interdependent activities to be tackled. The RRV tries to look at the situation in its entirety, while viewing the component parts in the context in which they are to function. When the approach is oriented towards information systems and not organizations or authorities, one often comes across systems that are in some respect IOIS.

In the last couple of years the RRV has studied a total of some twenty IOIS in two separate auditing programs. The aims of the audits were as follows.

- To be able to highlight problems with, or related to IOIS that concern public sector administration in general.
- To propose general steps to produce improvements in maintaining or developing IOIS.
- To produce specific proposals for the agencies that have been involved in IOIS audits.
- To check on the effects, both general and specific, of the measures taken.

3. IOIS audits - examples and conclusions

The two auditing programs had different perspectives. In auditing information quality in existing IOIS, the perspective was structural. The analysis concentrated on the relation between the various actors involved and the components within the system, and how the flow of information functioned and was controlled.

Audits of the development of IOIS concentrated on the various strategic decisions and necessary processes in the early stages of the development of an IOIS.

3.1 Information quality in existing IOIS

The starting-point here was that auditing had previously uncovered shortcomings in the ways the agencies handled the quality aspects of their information. There are also examples of the negative effects that arise from shortcomings in information quality.

The audit aimed to identify the general problems related to the agencies' work on information quality, and to suggest improvements. Three reports were produced (see under References, below).

The audit found the following.

- In many cases there had been no analysis of quality and risk.
- The organizational basis for dealing with quality aspects is often weak.
- Chains of responsibility were often ambiguous.
- As information systems often cross agency boundaries and overlap IOIS that are in process of being set up, there is often no overall view, which results in unjustifiable expense and inadequate checking.

An important observation in this program was that in certain respects many, if not most, information systems are IOIS. Such systems tend to provide some of their users with unchecked or insufficient information; the underlying problem being that the information quality is an unknown factor. As a general conclusion, a major reason for inadequate information quality is that the purpose for which the information is required has not been properly examined.

3.2 IOIS development collaboration projects

The starting-point for the audit was the review of EDP development projects that examine or develop IOIS based on interacting EDP systems. The audit aimed to identify strategic decisions in inter-agency collaboration, the contents of these decisions at different stages of the development process, and to produce supportive measures relating to them.

Two reports were produced (see under References below)

The audit found:
- shortcomings in the principles applied in configuring new information systems and in the designs of the EDP systems interacting at the local level,
- shortcomings in the principles and procedures used in the cooperation between the agencies involved in projects on developing IOIS.

An important conclusion was that there is a need for more efficient collaboration processes and better analyses of the basic premises for cooperation. This applies to both information collaboration and inter-agency cooperation. One therefore needs to clarify the underlying conditions affecting the agencies' ability to cooperate. Insufficient weight is often given to the question of why; what is the specific purpose of this collaboration.

3.3 General conclusions

As a rule it is difficult for the agencies to gain an overview and control of IOIS. This applies both to the operation and administration of existing IOIS and to the development and renewal of these systems. The audits under discussion here identified four general problem areas.

Shortcomings related to the system as a whole:
- the preconditions and principles that govern the design of IOIS are often unclear,
- a poor strategy for the supply of information between the actors concerned,
- too many, or unclear, aims (purposes).

Deficiencies at the information flow level:
- inadequate information quality, the issue of responsibility for information quality is unclear, resulting in confusion about the interfaces between actors in different parts of the IOIS,
- inadequate follow-up of information quality.

Shortcomings at the EDP system level:
- inexplicit strategies for the development and construction of EDP systems,
- inexplicit strategies for the development of technical infrastructures.

Weaknesses in the cooperation between actors in the development of IOIS:
- unsuitable project organization,
- management and influence relationships not clearly defined
- insufficient quality assurance in the development processes,
- difficulties in gaining an overview of development projects, that are also often far too cumbersome.

It may be seen from the above that the audits of these systems uncovered a large number of problems. The question to be addressed now is which causes of these problems are IOIS specific. Our hypothesis are that complexity IOIS is one important factor.

4. Complexity in IOIS, some theoretical comments

A common feature of the IOIS that were studied is that a number of associated parties were involved, and computer support was spread throughout the entire information system, resulting in a higher degree of complexity. Numerous new questions concerning IOIS arise because far more actors and system components etc. are involved than is the case with separate EDP systems.

4.1 A description of complexity

Complexity (in information systems) may be described in different ways. One way is to describe complexity as a function of four factors[1].

1) The number of objects/components such as agencies, sub-systems etc. that are included in the system.
2) The number of relations between these objects, i.e., the flow of information between them.
3) The characteristics of the objects, i.e., their function or work tasks.
4) The degree of organization in the system as a whole, i.e., the responsibility relations between the objects.

[1]*Schoderbek, Schoderbek, Kefalas. Management System, Conceptual Considerations. Business Publ., Plana, Texas 1985, 3rd ed.*

Two of these characteristics are quantitative and two are qualitative. The qualitative characteristics probably have the greatest effect on complexity.

4.2 Complexity in three basic IOIS models

With the IOIS examined under the two auditing programs as a starting point, three basic models have been developed for IOIS. These models represent the IOIS commonly found in Sweden's public sector. At the same time, the various stages in the development of IOIS - from relatively simple to more complex - are also represented. This development may be seen in the current ambition to decentralize operations and operational responsibility in Sweden's public sector. The following is a comparison of complexity in the three basic IOIS models.

1) IOIS with EDP-based system functions coordinated and located in a single agency.

These IOIS are often based on mainframe computer operations and usually process very large quantities of information or perform complicated data processing operations. Many of the larger (and older) EDP systems in government administration are to be found in this category. There is often a very high degree of data or processing dependency among the actors (agencies) involved.

As a whole, these IOIS are relatively simple, largely because the number of relations between the objects involved are minimized, often being limited to processing and the responsibility for these operations. Centralization produces simple responsibility relationships and less complex preconditions for the detailed definition of goals, and thereby the characteristics of the system.

2) IOIS with some EDP-based system functions located in the agencies concerned.

The technical design of this kind of IOIS is often based on cooperation between EDP systems in different operational environments (mainframe computers, microcomputers and PCs) at different agencies. However, some data processing essential to the agencies must be done in a coordinated system at the agency concerned. Central EDP systems with local subsystems are included in this category.

The complexity of these systems increases because the availability of better EDP support opens up wider possibilities for the existing objects, i.e., the agencies. These systems must then be maintained and refined. This places organizational demands on the agencies to be included in the systems administration. New relations between EDP systems may also arise.

Thus the local systems offer more user possibilities, but their complexity does not increase dramatically, because the functionality of the local systems is usually still under strong central control, and full use is therefore not made of the potential for variations between the local systems.

3) IOIS with all EDP-supported systems functions brought together in local EDP sys tems at each actor.

In this model the agencies' need for EDP support in a specific operational area, which is in some way common to all the agencies involved, is met entirely by utilizing EDP systems that collaborate at the local level. The IOIS technical design is based on an exchange of information between these local systems. The exchange of information may increase between operational parties based on small-scale computer technology.

Here, there is considerably greater complexity. There may be a large number of objects involved. Collaboration between local EDP systems means that the number of possible, and also actual relations (i.e., exchanges of messages) between the systems and agencies involved increases. Local requirements are met by means of variations in EDP support. There will therefore be some differences in this support and its characteristics from one agency to the next. Further, there may be no natural point for central systems development control. Instead, control is based upon discussions and collaboration contracts.

4.3 Main conclusions

The main conclusions drawn from comparing complexity in different IOIS is that complexity will increase as a result of the following.

- More actors and EDP systems are involved.
- More relations between actors and between EDP systems.
- A more dispersed information flow.
- More "own profile" in agencies' fields of activity, leading to more appropriate local EDP systems.
- More responsibilities distributed among the actors.

5.Some empirical remarks on complexity in IOIS.

5.1 The need for strategic decisions

If IOIS are to be developed and administrated effectively and efficiently, their complexity must be under control. This cannot be done immediately: the preconditions must be created first.

This makes the issue a strategic one.

According to our (preliminary) view, which is based upon earlier conclusions, the potential for the control of complexity is determined by the following five factors.

- The purpose the IOIS is to serve.
- The underlying ideology of the IOIS.
- The architecture of the IOIS.
- The organizational structure of the IOIS.
- The technical infrastructure of the IOIS.

1) The purpose of the IOIS
The purpose of the IOIS is possibly the most important complexity factor. The purpose states which activity the IOIS is a part of; its aim; and gives guidance in the selection and administration of data. The purpose also forms the basis on which an incentive structure is built.

2) The ideology of the IOIS
The ideology is an important factor, determining the underlying values applied to the choice of architecture, organizational structure and technical infrastructure.

3) The architecture of an IOIS comprises the following.
- The number of logical objects/components or actors included in the IOIS.
- The number of logical relations between these objects and components, i.e., the flow of information.
- The characteristics of the objects/components and their functions or work tasks.

Here, the architecture of a system is, in theory, the paths along which information flows between different actors or objects, and what takes place at each processing stage.

4) The organizational structure of an IOIS comprises the following.
- The responsibility among the objects (in the relationships) and for the system as a whole for ensuring that the IOIS runs smoothly.
- The responsibility for individual objects.

The organizational structure describes the allocation of responsibility and the interfaces between different actors in the IOIS.

5) The technical infrastructure of the IOIS comprises the following.
- The number of physical objects/components that make up the IOIS.
- The degree of standardization in the structure and function of the objects, compo nents and relations.
- The degree of standardization of models, methods, tools and work methods used to design and build the different parts of the IOIS.

The infrastructure describes the technical design of the system. In theory, a system can be distributed from the logical viewpoint. The technical design may, however, be central, i.e. all actors share a central computer because that happened to be a practical solution.

5.2 Weaknesses in managing complexity factors in an environmental data system

As part of a project, an IOIS system for environmental data was developed for a central agency, 24 regional and 285 local authorities. The system was to be based on an exchange of information between the agencies' EDP systems (model 3 in section 4.2). The collaborating systems were intended to replace an older terminal-based mainframe computer system (model 1) at the central agency.

The development project was run under the management of the central agency, which was also responsible for programming and technical development.

The agency had initially failed to have adequate discussions on which systems philosophy and system architecture, and which organizational structure would be used in the IOIS. It was therefore not clear whether it was a (1) information system in which the central agency was responsible for the entire system and in its distributed local collaborating EDP systems, or whether it was (2) a common information system where each respective agency owned its own EDP system. In the course of the project, the philosophy was changed from the former to the latter.

This confusion on fundamental points caused a number of serious problems as the project progressed. They were:

- cooperation problems because there was disagreement on, for example, the design and scope of the local EDP system,
- a lower level of ambition when it came to the production of separate local EDP systems
- the inability to make changes in project organization, decision-making processes etc. after changes in theoretical conditions,
- confusion about the roles in the collaboration project and about responsibility for, respectively, the systems and the exchange of information that evolved,
- failure to agree on a collaboration strategy and the frames and conditions that regulated the agencies' latitude in designing their own systems.

With the benefit of hindsight, one may say that in this case the actors did not realize the degree of complexity that the new information system actually produced. Since the com plexity of the system was unclear and above all underestimated, the project, and the design of the IOIS, was based on poorly-defined theoretical grounds. As the increasing degree of complexity became apparent, the problems listed above came to light.

5.3 The absence of strategic decisions on a government system for supplying addresses

The state has an IOIS for address information (SAIS), with three agencies as the main actors. They must collaborate if they are, in practice, to provide the entire Government administration and a large part of society in general with correct addresses.

A basic observation was that there was no overview of the SAIS. The three agencies involved did not act as though it was a system. Thus they were not coordinated efficiently, which results in shortcomings in controls and transfers between the bodies involved.

Each part of the system is in its turn dependent on other parts. Errors that occur may, for example, cause damage to a different part than the part that caused the error. This means that there is no direct incentive to correct the error. Errors in addresses also involve expenditure for the users of the addresses. Further, the lack of organization makes it impossible to clearly identify the person responsible. Thus the organizational structure is not an appropriate one.

SAIS was not deliberately developed, but evolved from a number of decisions, which failed to consider all the related conditions. This lack of strategic decisions, overview and a clearly-defined objective, resulted in the objective changing over time. The addresses were originally related to where a person was registered as resident for tax purposes, i.e., the data was designed to serve the purposes of the tax system. With time, the distribution of mail has become the main purpose. These two addresses are not necessarily the same; a person may be registered for taxation purposes at a different address than the address to which his mail should be sent. The system is designed to process an address. Since there are two purposes, one of them must become subordinate to the other. Thus, there are users which cannot obtain the type of address they wish to have, and moreover, with which they were originally supplied.

The lack of coordination in technical infrastructures has resulted in transfer problems, which have caused considerable delays in updating. One may also question whether the architecture and organizational structure are appropriate.

6. How to manage complexity in IOIS - some preliminary ideas

6.1 General assumptions

A general conclusion is that a lack of control of, or an unawareness of increasing complexity in IOIS is one of the main reasons for the shortcomings observed; i.e. the lack of control of the IOIS purpose, paradigm, architecture, organization structure and technical infrastructure.

A lack of control of these factors will in general have negative effects on the benefit and functionality of an IOIS. A more complex IOIS will probably degenerate quicker than a less complex IOIS. It will be harder to recognize shortcomings such as insufficient data quality.

The IOIS' ability to change and adapt to new requirements is weaker. It will probably be more difficult to manage, perform and control general system changes on the one hand, and local system components changes on the other.

There are greater difficulties in cooperating on IOIS development and maintenance projects than is normally the case. It will probably be more difficult to develop efficient collaboration processes and analyses of basic cooperation premises in, for example, the development of EDP supported inter-agency information collaboration based on interacting local EDP systems.

6.2 Coordinating the interests of several actors in IOIS

A system should reflect something, objects. The system will therefore be as complex as this object. Thus, complexity cannot be eliminated. It is, however, possible to identify and clarify complexity, reduce unnecessary complexity, avoid uncontrolled increases in complexity, and organize the management of the complexity that remains. However, we must differ between real complexity and perceived complexity. The way one perceives a system's complexity is dependent of the model one has of the system. Managing complexity therefore requires a good model.

An information system can be described as an ordinary input - process - output model. In our opinion it gives a framework for an overview of the information system. The model also applies to both an IOIS and a single-agency system. The question is, then, what else is there in an IOIS to make it so complex?

The difference is, in our opinion, that there are a number of organizations involved, bringing the additional problem of coordinating and managing a number of parties of equal value but with partly divergent interests. If these parties wish to use the system for different purposes, they will pull in different directions, and the actors may be unaware that this is happening.

The different parties will also act within different environments which may make different or even conflicting demands. Further, collaboration implies that the parties involved become dependent upon one another. Questions that must be asked here are: how can one deal with the changes within the system and in the environment; who has priority, and how should the dependency issue be dealt with if the parties' various purposes become too disparate?

Further, one must reduce the size of the information system in order to gain an overview of it. A common mistake is to mix different purposes in an IOIS but still regard it as being a single system. Our empirical studies indicate that this is the case with, for example, SAIS.

An information system should be defined on the basis of a clear and uniform, and preferably time-limited, purpose. If there are two (or more) purposes, there are by definition two (or more) information systems[2].

A basic EDP system philosophy will then be that one information system should be linked to one activity of one party involved and have one specific purpose in that activity (1:1:1:1). This may then form the basis for a discussion to determine if there are any restrictions or demands, e.g. of an economic or security nature, etc. that could impinge on the basic principle in a given situation.

The question of IOIS ownership will then become fundamental. If an information system is available in one agency alone, then the question of responsibility for information is relatively straightforward. However, the issue becomes more complicated where several central and local government agencies are interdependent. Principles are required to allow both the question of responsibility for EDP systems and the information to be handled effectively.

The interface between the different parties must be defined and regulated in agreements which cover the parties' rights and undertakings, the technical infrastructure and requirements for the information to be transferred. The information should, preferably, be quality-graded. If the quality of the information is not known, then the user cannot assume responsibility for his basic decision-making data.

The limits of an information system are not related to organizational limits; they are a function of the system's purpose. Technically speaking, where appropriate and rational a database can contain, and a program support, a number of information systems.

[2]If this line is taken to its ultimate conslusion it may be said that every user has his own information system, even if the information and the requirements are the same. In practice, one may not need to go as far as this.

Parties that jointly develop or administrate IOIS must also develop common investigation and collaboration processes concerning IOIS. Such processes should produce "contracts" between the actors concerning the development project and administrative measures. A feature of these processes is that the parties, before arriving at the "contract" stage for joint action, must discuss both theoretical and strategic issues. The theoretical issues are a matter of establishing consensus on IOIS issues. The strategy questions are a matter of agreeing on guidelines and restrictions for different activities.

6.3 Conclusions in summary

To summarize, if IOIS are to be properly developed and administrated, the actors involved must jointly:

- define clearly and unequivocally the purpose of the IOIS,
- gain an overview of, and insight into, the IOIS,
- Effectively monitor the organization's environment to observe significant changes good time,
- develop common principles, strategies and contracts
- define the responsibility relationships between the actors and the parts of the IOIS,
- develop effective investigatory and collaboration processes both in the development and administration of IOIS

References

Andersson, Bengt E W. Norström, Gunilla; Samverkande självständiga ADB-sy- stem - en möjlighet till omprövelse och förnyelse av myndigheters verksamhet. *NordDATA '90,* Göteborg 1990.

Andersson, Bengt E W; Samverkan, informationsutbyte och förnyelse av ADB-system. *NordDATA '92,* Tampere 1992.

Andersson, Bengt E W; Långsiktig förnyelse av informationssystem. *LISS92,* Linköping 21 May 1992.

Magoulas, T. Pessi, K. En studie om informationssystem, strategier. Gothenburg Studies in Information System Report 2, Chalmers University of Technology, Gothenburg February 1991.

Nilsson, Peter. Andersson, Bengt E W; Hur hantera komplexitet i ADB-system med flera intressenter? *Sundsvall V42,* Sundsvall 1990.

Nilsson, Peter. Andersson, Bengt E W; Auditing clients'EDP-systems - the life cycle approach. Swedish experiences. *Workshop of UNDTCD/INTOSAI on Government Auditing,* Vienna, Austria, 27 May - 4 June 1992.

Nilsson, Peter, Hägnemark, Göran; Informationskvalitet, din spegel mot verkligheten. *NordDATA '88,* Helsingfors-Esbo, 1988

Nilsson, Peter, Karlsson, Helena; Information, Beslutsstöd eller alibi. *NordDATA '90*, Göteborg 1990.

Nilsson, Peter, Lindström, Lena; Fel data kostar! *NordDATA '92*, Tamspere 1992.

Nilsson, Peter. Sparr, Eva; Data or Information quality. Report of the Invitational Workshop on Data Integrity. *NIST Special Publication 500-168.* Computer Systems Technology. US Department of Commerce, 1989.

Nilsson, Peter; Information Quality. An analysis of quality aspects of information used in decisionmaking. *Stockholm University & Royal Institute of Technology*, Stockholm 1990.

Nilsson, Peter; The distortion of information. In *The Information society: Evolving Landscapes. Report from Namur.* Jacques Berleur, Richard Sizer, Diane Whitehouse and Andrew Clements (eds). Springer Verlag, New York 1990.

RRV reports:
The collaboration project.

- Dnr 1988:1655. Revision av projektet KRUT vid Naturvårdsverket. 1989-06-29.
- Fg 1991:11. ADB i samverkan. 1991-06-14.

The information Quality project.

- Dnr 1987:1697. Informationskvalitet inom fiskeriområdet. 1988-11-16.
- Dnr 1989:393. Rätt data? 1990-11-30.
- F 1992:2. Fel data kostar! 1992-02-07.

Other reports.

- F 1992:21. IT/ADB-samverkan inom offentlig sektor.

Schoderbek, Schoderbek, Kefalas; *Management System, Conceptual Considerations.* Business Publ., Plana, Texas, 1985, 3rd ed.

SIS teknisk rapport. TR 322 *Informationssäkerhet och dataskydd - en begreppsapparat.* 1989-04-01.

Decision Support in Public Administration (A-26)
P.W.G. Bots, H.G. Sol and R. Traunmüller (Editors)
Elsevier Science Publishers B.V. (North-Holland)
1993 IFIP.

Problem-setting support

Dirk Vriens

Department of Business Administration, Faculty of Policy Sciences, University of Nijmegen. The Netherlands.

Abstract

Recent literature on decision-support shows a tendency to shift attention away from the choice-phase towards the definition (the setting) of the decision-problem. Moreover, the need for this shift is more strongly felt when the decision-problem gets less structured. When focusing on the choice-phase, the goal of the decision-process is to lay down several comparable alternatives and to choose one that is satisfactory. A different setting of the problem may, however, yield different alternatives which may have been unnoticed in the original setting. The important question is therefore how different problem-settings may emerge. Recent attempts to answer this question include "idea-generation" and the search for "generative metaphors". This paper will address an alternative answer, in which the goals of the decision-maker are taken as a means to seek alternatives beyond the original problem-setting. It is assumed that a problem-definition is connected to one or more goals a decision-maker seeks to realize. A thorough analysis of these goals may yield connected goals of a higher order for which realizations might be found that also (dis-)solve the problem. Looking at different levels may result in alternatives that were not considered at a lower level of (goal-) abstraction. If, moreover, several (hierarchically) independent goals are considered, one has to find a combination of realizations for the different goals that can be performed together. This may be done by means of a goal-matrix, which is the result of considering several goal-hierarchies at the same time. A central theme is, that when more alternatives with respect to one goal are found, the chance increases that a suitable combination for all the independent goals can be found. The goal-matrix is the vehicle to arrive at different problem-settings in which alternatives may be stipulated. In this approach, the traditional distinction between fixing goals, generating alternatives and choosing among them blurs and the whole process will be termed "problem-setting". Supporting this "setting of the problem" (and hence also the search for alternatives within these different settings) by means of the proposed method, is different from traditional decision support. Therefore, it must be outlined what this support amounts to. In the first part of this paper the need for the possibility of setting a problem in several distinct ways is given. Then, it is discussed how problems might be set differently by means of goal-matrices, and how alternatives courses of action are related to different problem-settings. Finally, attention will be paid to supporting problem-setting.

1. INTRODUCTION: THE NEED FOR SETTING PROBLEMS

In the design of decision support systems (DSS) one needs to have an idea of what the decision-process one is trying to support amounts to. Until now, most DSS-designs have been guided by a traditional account of the decision-process. This traditional view is captured by Winograd and Flores [1] in what they call the "rational tradition". Making a decision is considered to involve the following steps: after sensing some sort of conflict between the current situation and a desired situation, the "decision-environment" is decomposed into several alternatives, of which an (optimal or "satisficing") alternative is chosen. A dominating model within this tradition is that of Simon [2] which consists of three phases: an "intelligence phase" in which the problem is identified and formulated, a design phase in which the alternative courses of action are developed, and a choice-phase in which an alternative is chosen by means of some "decision-procedure". As Forgionne [3] points out, in terms of this model, support-attention has primarily been paid to the "choice-phase" of the decision-process. When dealing with structured problems (in which some procedure can give a solution to the problem; i.e. in which the characteristics of a problem (outcome, strategies etc.) can be tied together in such a way that the problem can be solved), this view of decision-making might suffice. Moreover, this gave way to a large amount of automated Operations-research-like support-facilities. Even where alternatives have not been outlined completely, techniques like Multi-Criteria Analysis help to construct and evaluate alternative courses of action. A common feature of the "choice-phase"-support is that somehow the alternatives have been generated with some goal(s) in mind in such a way that comparison between them is a mere procedural exercise. When the decision-process is less structured, however, it is doubtful that it could be moulded in the models just described. This is recognized by many researchers in the field of decision-making, and, lately, also by designers of support-systems. Young [4] notices that "...the newer approach of decision support systems has attempted to go further in enhancing the earlier stages of the decision-process described by Simon..." (p.23). This means that the "intelligence" and "design" phases, or, put differently: the identification and formulation of problems (the "setting of the problem") as well as the generation of alternatives comes within the scope of attention of the designers of support systems.

This change (or enlargement) in focus of attention in DSS-design is paralleled by a change in the conception of the decision-process. This new view, as expressed by e.g. Ackoff [5], Checkland [6] and Winograd and Flores [1], has as its key feature the "dynamic nature of the decision-process", in which "solving" problems can be regarded as a constant creation and re-creation of a context in which the problem gets its meaning and from which alternatives come and go as different conceptions of the problem come up. Because of the inherently unstructurable "mess" (that constitutes our social reality) we are facing when trying to make decisions, it is unlikely that a priori specifying alternatives among which to choose will help. Alternative courses of action will change in meaning and significance when viewed under different perspectives. Also, when more than one goal enter the process of solving problems, the relevance of a priori fixed alternatives can not be established on beforehand. As Ackoff [5] notices, decision-makers do not always realize the "full impact" of their problems. Therefore, the emphasis should be on trying to come to terms with the "true nature" of the problem, instead of rushing to the generation of alternatives. This sets the stage for a "problem-setting" view of decision-making, where the elements that characterize a problem are constantly monitored in order to account for new ways of looking at a problem. The changes in the definition of a problem may come about by considering new goals and/or realizations[1] (or reconsidering old ones). This alteration of the conception of the problem is thought to reflect actor- and context-specific changes. When this dynamic nature of defining a problem is taken into account, the decision-making process can be viewed as a kind of "continuous problem-setting". This is not to say that choosing among alternatives is of no importance, but that the relevance of choosing is relative on the setting of the problem. Changing the setting of a problem is changing the relevance of the alternatives. However, having outlined some courses of action might also influence thinking about the definition of the problem at hand. This cyclic process of setting and re-setting a problem, along with the possible courses of action is what is thought to be the "true nature" of the decision process. In fact, the traditional distinction between the different phases of the decision-making process gets blurred. It may even be argued that the distinction between "structured" and "unstructured" decisions might not be drawn sharply, because the structure of a problem can be thought of as imposed by choosing a setting. A different setting may yield a differently structured decision-problem. Of course, at some point of time, a decision has to be made, but this does not entail starting decision-making by imposing a structure. To describe the process of decision-making as a continuous setting of problems also includes generating alternatives and giving directions for choice among these alternatives. The emphasis is, however, on the dynamic (and hence changing) nature of the elements that constitute a decision-problem. The term problem-setting (as used here) extends its normal connotation in that it is meant to cover the whole process of decision-making.

These new ideas of what the decision-process amounts to, are different from "just" paying more attention to the first phases in the Simon-model: it emphasises the dynamic, recurrent, nature of decision-making, where -as noted- the traditional distinction between the phases more or less dissolves.

To appreciate the need to set problems, consider the following example. Suppose some friends want to spend an evening at the cinema. The question "which movie to go to" is posed and deliberated upon. In the traditional view this question constitutes the decision-problem (a structure may be "imposed" implicitly) and ways to spell out alternative courses of action easily come to mind. A multi-criteria approach would (as a rough sketch) propose to somehow list the possible cinemas/movies, identify salient criteria on which to score them, score them and integrate these scores in order to make a choice. Next to difficulties with defining the right criteria, the way to score them, how to properly integrate these into "wholes" and make a choice (in short: the "normal problems" with traditional modelling), more fundamental problems may arise. Suppose that the operation-researcher among these friends (because of his firm scientific reputation) persuades the others to perform the multi-criteria analysis as described. After a cinema has been chosen, however, some unease with the outcome may be felt. This may be because

[1] In this text, the term realization and the more common term "alternative" are used synonyms. (In spite of the risk of confusion, it is seems more appropriate to use "realization" when considering goals).

the "decision-makers" were forced to elaborate on the alternatives concerning a fixed goal. It might happen, then, that one poses the question: "why do we choose between cinemas in the first place?" This question may uncover (an) implicit function(s) of going to cinemas. One may e.g. notice that, although going to a cinema may serve functions like "enjoy oneself", or "spending an evening", it may not serve the function of "socializing", which may turn out to be another important function: these friends may not meet often. When these functions are considered together, it may be that an alternative can be found that serves all functions considered (e.g. going out for dinner -which serves even more functions). An objection might be that this is not a good example, because one had to suppose, that "some friends wanted to spend an evening at the cinema". With this fixed supposition in mind, (traditional) problem-solving procedures may be applied. It appeared that more goals were of importance and hence that the problem had to be restated in order to cover all the relevant goals. One might go on to object that one just didn't look hard enough and suggest to start the problem-solving methods once it is clear that all the relevant goals are known. This objection reaches the heart of the problem: how can one be sure that all relevant goals are known? or worse, how can the relevance of alternatives/goals be determined? Especially, when decision-making is thought to be a dynamic activity, where goals and/or realizations gain importance, or lose meaning as more/other aspects of the problem are considered. Therefore, setting problems (continuously) is thought to be a more appropriate way of looking at decision-making. With more/other perspectives, more/other ways to arrange the elements of decision-making may emerge.

It might be concluded, then, that the increased emphasis on the setting of problems has to do with the unstructured nature of many important decisions, which -it was felt- could not be moulded into the choice-oriented models of decision-making and -support. This led some researchers to turn to the earlier stages in the decision-process, as described by Simon, while others formulated different models of decision-making in which the setting of the problem was to be treated as the most important aspect.

As noted, the consequence for the design of DSS is that designers are to look for different ways of supporting the decision-process instead of the ones used in the choice-oriented support systems. In order to do this, one has to have a notion of what it means to set a problem and how this might be done. In the next section of this paper some answers to these questions will be presented, while, after this exploration, attention will be paid to the consequences for supporting the setting of problems.

2. SETTING AND RE-SETTING PROBLEMS

2.1. How to set problems

Setting a problem can be described as a kind of "ordering" of the elements that constitute it. Therefore there has to be some understanding of the nature of these elements. Young [4] proposes to reconsider the notion of "idea", which he wants to treat as conscious expressions of the interpretation of observations, which reflect both external and internal events (Chapter 8). He goes on to observe that the processing of these ideas plays a significant role in defining decision-problems: "idea processing [...] takes ideas as inputs and produces as outputs the contextual frameworks we identify as decision problems or as plans" (p. 244). During this processing new ideas might emerge, that, in turn, may re-enter the process. In a direct confrontation with decision-making, Young notices that "extensive idea processing is necessary in defining and constantly redefining the scope and components of complex decision problems" (p. 247). Idea processing can therefore be taken as a means to arrive at some problem setting. Moreover, different problem settings can be seen as the result of processing ideas differently.

The "only" thing that remains to be investigated is the nature of this processing. Unfortunately, this seems to be under the spell of hard-to-define notions as "intuition" and "creativity". Because creative thinking is thought to result in "synthesizing existing elements in interesting new ways" (Young [4], p.246), which seems to be constitutive for setting problems differently, it may be worthwhile to look at several attempts to describe recurrent themes in the process of creative thinking. Among these themes (see e.g. Majaro [7]; and Young [4]) are the emphasis on divergent thinking (finding many different solutions to a problem) instead of convergent thinking (focus on one solution), and, interestingly, the emphasis on the formulation of a problem instead of on its solution. These two "themes" are a kind of reformulation of the problem this paper addresses: Convergent thinking and problem-solving seem to be descriptive for the traditional way of tackling decision-problems, while divergent thinking and problem-formulation have to do with the change in emphasis as described in the introduction. Another theme is the role of metaphors in creative thinking (cf. [8, 9]).

From these general themes several methods for "fostering creativity" may be derived. Divergent thinking can be implemented by a method called "morphological analysis" (cf. Majaro [7], chapter 8). In this method, one first has to identify the relevant dimensions of the problem at hand and generate as many alternative states of these dimensions as possible. In the next step, these states are compared in order to investigate their combinational plausibility. In the example, Young gives of this method (pp.273), the problem is to "seek a new transportation system". Among the relevant dimensions of this problem he lists: "power-source", "container-vehicle", "control-mechanism" and "pathway/medium". For these dimensions possible states are generated. Among the dimensional states Young enumerates are those, listed in table 1.

Table 1
Dimensions and states in Youngs example

Dimensions	States
Power source:	"electric", "nuclear"
Container-vehicle:	"conveyer belt", "wheeled vehicle"
Control-mechanism:	"automated", "chauffeured"
Pathway/medium:	"paved road", "fixed track"

Next, a combination of these states must be formed in order to "solve" the original transportation problem. Not all combinations are feasible. A combination of dimensional states which includes e.g. "conveyer belt" and "chauffeured" may probably be dismissed as inadequate.

The emphasis on problem-formulation can be implemented by a method which "redefines and generalizes" aspects of the problem, i.e. it "...focuses on classifying and arranging ideas into logical hierarchies" ([4], p. 271). This method of "successive generalization" may be used to gain insight in the more abstract (or concrete) classes that encompass (or are encompassed by) the entity under investigation. Referring to the previous example, a conveyer belt, is an instance of a (semi-) automated transportation system, which belongs to the class of transportation systems. These broader classes may the be used to generate other instances.

Further, methods for metaphorical analysis have been investigated by Gordon [8].

The above mentioned themes and methods, then, are thought to be of importance in creative thinking and hence, because of its supposed dependence on creativity, also in the setting and resetting of problems. As might be clear from the examples, the emphasis in these methods is on the generation of alternatives which is thought take place in the first phases of the traditional decision-making account.

A different perception of setting problems is given by Schön [9] and Rein and Schön [10]. They share the concern of this paper, that the problem-solving paradigm is not sufficient for capturing (social policy) problem. Moreover, they argue for problem-setting in its stead. Setting problems is, in their vision, the application of a "frame" (a "way-of-seeing") to a set of problem-elements (worries). The frame (which is reminiscent of Kuhns paradigms) is an ordering-instrument with regard to the elements of a problematic situation. Different frames order problematic situations differently. The relevant question is: where do these frames come from? Although the authors try to pave the way toward a methodology for setting problems, (framing and reframing), they do not specify it. An important ingredient of such a method would be the idea of "generative metaphor". It is supposed, that "...frames contain generative metaphors that enable us to reason from the familiar to the unfamiliar" ([10], p.240).

Because of the relevance of these ideas, an attempt will be made to address them in a "framework", tailored to setting problems (not to be confused with the above-mentioned "frames"), that will be discussed in the next section.

2.2. A "dedicated" framework for setting problems

A problem with the methods, which were described in the previous section is that they lack "devotion" to decision-making. Although they are, no doubt, useful in generating creative thoughts, what misses is a framework; an integrating whole (in which -some of-these methods might find a place) which may yield (different) setting of problems. Such a framework might be called a "dedicated idea-processing system", which aims specifically at setting problems. In what follows, such a framework will be considered.

The proposed framework (as discussed in Vriens, [11,12]) represents thinking in the "newer" theories of decision-making, as described in the introduction. As such it rests on the assumption of decision-making as a dynamic creation and re-creation of the "decision-environment", from which alternatives are generated. The relevance of these alternatives is always determined against the background of the decision-maker and the context in which the decision is made. This background consists of the goals a decision-maker seeks to realize. Alternative courses of action are considered if they can realize these goals. When different alternatives can realize a goal, they are said to be functionally equivalent. Moreover, when more than one goal enters the decision-process, realizations for different goals might be in conflict. This conflict should be resolved by systematically looking for other, non-conflicting alternative realizations of the goals under consideration. The "decision-environment" (the goals and realizations) might be subject to change at any time: new goals and realizations may enter it, or may loose their meaning.

In short, this amounts to stating the problem (as conceived initially) in concrete goals, that serve as the rationales to generate different alternatives. With a concrete goal in mind, a functional class may be generated, that specifies the individuals that have in common that they can realize this goal; i.e. their membership of this class rests on their functional equivalence regarding the goal. If, e.g., a concrete goal is "get a car", then the functional class it specifies consists of alternatives that all somehow result in a car: e.g. "buy a car", "steal a car", "lend a car" etc. This class consists of a large number of members, which may be more or less specified. When this is done for all the goals that enter the decision-process at some point of time, from each class an alternative is taken in order to form a combination of alternatives. This combination is feasible if it simultaneously realizes all the goals that were thought to be constitutive of the problem at some point in time. Because not all the alternatives can be combined randomly (as in the "morphological analysis" example, see section 2.1), the classes should consist of as many members as possible. This increases the chance, that a feasible combination can be found. In essence, then, a decision-maker is thought to state some goal of interest and tries to enumerate as many (functional equivalent) alternative realizations for that goal as possible. When this is done for each goal, that enters the process, the chance increases that a combination of realizations can be found that realizes all the goals. When a change in the conception of the decision problem occurs, some goals and/or realizations will have to be altered, in order to reflect the changed situation. This "changing" of the network of connected goals and realizations yields a different "setting" of the problem, to which different kinds of alternative realizations are connected. Suppose, e.g., that the car (see above) is only used to "get to the office"; then the conception of the problem changes. The members of the functional class are now to "produce" realizations of the newly posed goal: e.g. "take a bike", "take bus", but also the old "car-producing" alternatives. Next to the reflection on these related goals, one also has to account for the compatibility with the realizations of other, (hierarchically) unrelated goals that also have to be realized. So, when it is important to be at work quickly (one may be a doctor), the realizations for this goal must match the realizations for the get-to-office goal. Considering both goals, a bike might not be a suitable alternative.

This framework is meant to yield methods for setting problems, that may help decision-makers to overcome their "exclusionary" bias towards a specific problem-setting, by enlarging their conception of the decision-problem in terms of goals and realizations. In the next section such a method will be presented.

2.3. A method for setting problems

Having discussed a framework in which goals and realizations are used in setting problems, it is now time to elaborate on a method that systematically applies these ideas, which, in turn, may be used as a starting-point for outlining support-facilities. In the previous section, a short description of this method has already been given. In this section, this description will be extended and the resulting method will be compared to its idea-generating relatives.

To set (and reset) problems, it is proposed to follow several steps. Having a notion of the problem, a decision-maker indicates, in the first step, the (initially perceived) relevant goals that must be realized. Next, per goal, as many realizations as possible are generated. This results in the functional classes, as discussed in 2.2. Generating these classes might be done in a way analogous to "morphological analysis", as described in section 2.1. In discussing "idealized design", Ackoff [5] gives two restrictions that can also be applied to the alternatives that are to be generated: they should be "viable" when implemented, and technologically feasible. The viability-criterion is important for our purposes, for it can be taken to mean: "a possible realization regarding the context/background, the decision-maker is bringing to the problem". A part of this background will be detailed (consisting of other goals that have to be realized and the concrete situation in which the problem is embedded). Most will, however, be left implicit which makes the decision-maker a vital part in determining the relevance of alternative courses of action (and therefore paves the way for support instead of mechanization of decision-making). These first steps results in a matrix in which the columns are the (classes of) realizations for some goal. Such a matrix is given in table 2.

Table 2
Matrix of goals and realizations

G1	G2	G3	...	Gn
r11	r21	r31	...	rn1
r12	r22	r32	...	rn2
...	...	...	...	...
...	...	...	...	...

rij : the jth realization of the ith goal. (Gi).

The next step is to combine realizations for different goals in such a way that these realizations (from different classes) can be performed in conjunction. When this is done, all the relevant goals are said to be realized. This amounts to taking a realization from each column, and conjunct them. Regarding the above matrix, a combination consists of: ($r1i_1$ AND $r2i_2$ AND $r3i_3$ AND ... AND rni_n) in which rij_i is the j_ith realization of the ith goal. Whether realizations from different columns conflict or not (i.e. are part of a feasible combination) is left to the decision-maker.

Once a matrix is build, it can be "worked" with, i.e., it can be changed in order to reset a problem. The state of a matrix can be said to correspond to the setting of a problem. Any change in the matrix yields -in principle- a different problem-setting. Changes in this setting can come about in several ways. First, realizations may be altered, added or removed. Dependent on the actor- and context-specific features, realizations may be stipulated. Furthermore, changes in these features may lead to changes in the relevance of realizations -which is source of their alteration. Second, goals may added, removed, or "extended". Extending goals is done by placing them in a hierarchy of goals. (As was done in the "get-car" example). In doing this, it may appear, that the higher-level goal yields other interesting realizations that are also relevant for the problem. Extending goals may therefore result in more and/or different realizations. When it is realized that the car is only used for work (getting to the office) a realization to be added may even be: "work at home", which dissolves the get-car problem. Each "G" in the matrix refers to a goal, that may be hierarchically analyzed (looking for super-goals), in order to arrive at different alternatives. This hierarchical analysis resembles the method of "successive generalization".

At each point in time a problem-setting "matrix" may result in several choice-options (suitable conjunctions of realizations from different columns). To focus upon these options is, however, not as relevant as trying to set the matrix differently, for these choice-options are clearly dependent on the state of the matrix; i.e. the setting of the problem. In essence, then, "working" with the matrix is actually a recurrence of the earlier steps: stating goals; defining realizations, and indicating feasible combinations. After an "initialization-phase"; in which a decision-maker states the initially perceived goals and realizations, an initial matrix is built (reflecting an initial problem-setting), that becomes, in turn, the starting-point for resetting the problem (changing the matrix). The steps in this method (with a short comment) are listed in table 3:

Table 3
Steps in the problem-setting method

step	comment
1. state goals	- decision-maker gives them directly; or explores goal-hierarchy
2. generate alternatives	- try to generate as many alternative realizations per goal as possible
3. identify feasible combination	- feasibility is left to user
4. go back to 1.	- the iteration is performed until "the decision has to be made"

A simple example may shed some light on the method. Suppose your car refuses to start. This may present a "breakdown" of the normal course of action. If it does, a goal that may enter the problem-setting, initially, could be: "get a working car". Realizations for this goal easily come to mind: "get car fixed", "buy new car" or "steal car". With these, a simple (one-column) matrix may be build. Each realization is, regarding this single goal, equally feasible. Suppose, it turns out that the car was used mainly for transportation to work. Then, the goal of "get a working car" could be "extended" in a goal like: "transportation to work"; for that was the main function of the car. This might then be considered a "super-goal" that is ordered, hierarchically, before the "get a working car"-goal. Of course, some realizations for this transportation-goal refer to some of the "get a working car"-realizations. What is more important, however, is that realizing a goal at a higher level may dissolve a goal at a lower level. The transportation-goal could also be extended if it appears that one could also be working at home (under certain conditions). Therefore "working at home" as a realization for "do work" might also dissolve the goal of "get a working car". Other goals may also enter the setting of the problem. It is possible that one also needs transportation for shopping purposes. Now, the "working-home"-realization is only valid when one states realizations for the "get food" goal where no car is needed (one may move near a shopping-centre, or take a bike). Now, in terms of the method, the initial goal brought to the setting was used to list an initial class of realizations. When this goal was extended, the conception of the problem changed and the class of realizations changed also. Next, other goals might also be considered (adding a new column to the matrix). These, too, can be extended when considering the hierarchies, of which they are part. As soon as more than one goal is considered, it is important to keep track of the feasible combinations. At some point of time a decision has to be made. This is where the "structure" of a problem setting is imposed, and from the set of feasible realizations one is chosen.

The above method can be compared to the methods of "morphological analysis" and "successive generalization". As noted, it bears resemblance with "morphological analysis", in that it lists several alternatives, regarding a goal, which was conceived to be of relevance to the problem. The resemblance with "successive generalization" has to do with the hierarchical ordering of the goals. When comparing the methods, however, several differences must be noted. An important difference is that the elements in the matrix are supposed to be constantly subject to change. Also, the emphasis should be on concrete problems. Problems derive their meaning in a specific situation. Stating a problem in a specific context makes them more susceptible to successive generalization. In the example of morphological analysis given in section 2.2, dimensions for the problem "seek a new transportation system" had to be found. Here, it is suggested, to place this in a specific situation in which the problem gets its meaning. Therefore, it might better be described as: "transportation of X to Y, under conditions ...". Not all conditions can be specified (see discussion above), but some specification is needed for the hierarchical ordering. When one takes the "seek a new transportation"-problem as a starting-point, there seems to be no restriction on the generation of alternative states. This may be fine when trying to arrive at "creative solutions" per se, it is problematic in a situation where the feasibility of the alternative states (as in the "problem-setting" matrix) are highly dependent on the specific situation. It is obvious that when transportation is sought for goods from the main production unit to some central store, which is 2 miles away, different alternatives may come up, than in the case where this distance is 200 miles. In the last case it may be realized that an alternative for transportation is "moving the plant to the central store". Going back even further might lead to question the function of a central store, which may, in turn, also result in alternatives for the transportation-problem. Furthermore, in generalizing, the focus is on the place of a goal within a hierarchy of other goals. This may be called: "functional generalization". The aim of this kind of generalization is to gain insight in the nature of alternatives at a higher level of abstraction. Each goal "defines" a class of alternatives. "Functional generalization", then, is used to investigate the relevance and usefulness of the alternatives of these higher-order classes.

The idea of framing and reframing problematic situations, resulting in different problem-settings, as discussed by Schön [9] and Rein and Schön [10] (see also section 2.1), can also be accounted for within the proposed method. To describe the setting of problems as the application of a frame (a "way of seeing") can be translated to the state of the matrix. One particular way of framing a problematic situation is reflected by the very goals (and realizations) that the decision-maker is considering (that enter the matrix). Changes always result in a different matrix, but do not necessarily mean a change in the frame. Adding one realization does probably not change the way of conceiving the problem. When, however, several goals are replaced by others (which may be done by means of the hierarchical restructuring of goals) it may be save to state that a different way of framing the problematic situation has been reached. It may be stated, then, that a change in the problem-frame results in a different matrix, but that changing the matrix does not necessarily change the frame. Mechanisms that are supposed to play a role in frame-changes (such as generative metaphor) can therefore also be linked to the method for setting problems as described here. The change of the matrix may account for more detailed differences between problem-settings then the frames.

To summarize, then, the proposed method consists of several steps. First, the "matrix" of goals and realizations is initialized to cover the initial setting of the problem. Then, this setting is used for further investigation. First, the question is posed, whether there can be found more realizations regarding some goal (in the matrix). Second, the goals may be abstracted (placed in a goal-hierarchy) in order to redefine the goal and/or enlarge/alter the set of alternatives towards that goal. Within each setting (as represented by a matrix), combinations of realizations for different goals may be given (as represented by a "way" through the matrix from "left to right", where from every column one realization is taken). The idea is that the more realizations per goal are given, the greater the chance of finding feasible combinations. And, the more feasible combinations can be indicated, the better the "setting of the problem" can account for changes in the problem-context. Every change in the conception of the problem, can/must be reflected in the matrix and is therefore supposed to yield a different matrix, and hence a different setting of the problem. In short, working with the proposed matrices is considered to be a way to model problem-setting.

3. SUPPORTING PROBLEM-SETTING

Shifting attention from the choice-phase to the earlier phases of the decision-process (as described by Simon) has already caused designers of DSS to change their minds about how to support decision-making. This has been noticed in earlier sections. In addition to these views of DSS-design, this section will deal with the specific nature of support-systems for continuous problem-setting, as modelled in the previous section.

In line with the general ideas of decision support (as opposed to decision "mechanization"), it is assumed that in supporting problem-setting a user-centred "shell-perspective" should be taken. This means that users are, as much as possible, constructing their "own decision-environment", in which one manipulates the elements of a problem-setting (which are believed to the goals and realizations). The support-system makes a "framework for setting problems" available, which may subsequently be "filled in" by a user who has the background to decide whether the elements (goals, realizations) are appropriate.

When specifically tailored to the support of continuous problem-setting as modelled above, several functions of such DSS may be outlined. The "matrix-idea" should be central. The system should be of help in listing (editing) the goals and their realizations in a way that may be comparable to the implementation of the method of morphological analysis by Young [4]. Next, regarding the goals, some zoom-function may be of help to investigate the hierarchical ordering and the realizations associated with higher goal-level. Furthermore, the usual "storage-retrieval"- and "edit"-functions must be available for all the relevant constructs. Also, the system might keep track of indicated feasible combinations and warn the user when there are only a few realizations for a specific goal. Functions may also be aimed at a comparison of different problem-settings. Regarding the discussion about frames, this can be most useful. Also, conflicts about different settings may be resolved better, when different users compare their problem-settings. Functions may e.g. be used to highlight differences. A complete list of functions that such a support-system may have is beyond the scope of this paper. Current research is focused on integrating these functions into a full-blown "continuous problem-setting"-support system. At this stage it is thought to be sufficient to have an intuitive grasp of what supporting problem-setting is thought to consist of here: specific features, tailored to the construction and reconstruction of the problem-setting-matrix.

4. SUMMARY AND CONCLUSION

This paper addressed the need for (continuously) setting problems in stead of solving them, and the consequences for designing DSS. It can be concluded that the need for setting problems is felt -not only because of the inherently unstructured nature of many of the decisions we face, but also because it reflects other ways of modelling decision-making. Setting problems continuously is proposed as a "model" for decision-making. When linked to idea-processing, several "schemes" may be proposed that may be applied to the setting of problems. This calls, however, for an integrative "problem-setting" framework. In short, in this framework, a decision-maker is thought to state the goals and realizations of these goals, that somehow describe the problematic situation. Then these elements are subject to reflection and changed, when different aspects of a problem gain importance. At any point of time several "ways" of realizing all the goals may be indicated. The feasibility of these "ways" is, because of the changes in the perceived relevance of the goals and realization, also subject to change. This framework yields a method for setting problems that can be said to encompass methods from idea-processing (notably: "morphological analysis" and "successive generalization"). It can however be concluded, that the way in which these methods are realized in the "problem-setting" method, differs from their original content. Furthermore, the framework (and method) can also account for a relevant aspect of problem-setting: the notion of framing problems. It may even be speculated that the method can give some insight in how different frames come into being. Last, some indications are given for functions that a DSS tailored to problem-setting may posses. The actual implementation of these functions is under current investigation.

5. REFERENCES

1 Winograd, T., & Flores, F., Understanding Computers and Cognition. Ablex: Norwood, 1986.

2 Simon, H.A., Administrative Behavior (3rd Edition). The Free Press: New York, 1976.

3 Forgionne, G.A., Decision Technology Systems. Information Systems Management, Fall, 1991.

4 Young, L.F., Decision Support and Idea Processing Systems. W.C. Brown: Dubuque, 1988.

5 Ackoff, R.L., The art of problem solving. Wiley: New York, 1978.

6 Checkland, P.B., Systems Thinking, Systems Practice, Wiley: Chichester, 1981

7 Majaro, S., The Creative Gap. Longman: London, 1988.

8 Gordon, W., Synectics: The development of creative activity. Harper & Row: New York, 1961.

9 Schön, D.A., Generative Metaphor: A Perspective on Problem-Setting in Social Policy. In: A. Ortony (Ed.), Metaphor and Thought, Cambridge University Press: Cambridge, 1979.

10 Rein, M. & Schön, D.A., Problem Setting in Social Research. In: C.H. Weiss (Ed.), Using Social Research in Public Policy Making. R.C. Heath: Lexington, 1977.

11 Vriens, D., Scenario Based Decision Making. In: R.E. Klosterman (Ed.), Proceedings of the Second International Conference on Computers in Urban Planning and Urban Management (Vol I)., University of Akron: Akron, 1991.

12 Vriens, D., A Scenario Based Decision Support System for Locational Decision making. Forthcoming in: A. Goethals (Ed.), Quantitative Geographical Methods, Applied in Demographic and Urban Planning Research. SISWO, Amsterdam, 1992.

Decision Support in Public Administration (A-26)
P.W.G. Bots, H.G. Sol and R. Traunmüller (Editors)
Elsevier Science Publishers B.V. (North-Holland)

The Role of Decision Support in Individual Performance Review

Fran Ackermann[b], Steve Cropper[a] and Colin Eden[b]

[a]Health Service Management Centre
University of Keele

[b]Strathclyde Business School
University of Strathclyde
26 Richmond Street
Glasgow G1 1XH
Scotland

E-mail: CIHS05@vaxa.strath.ac.uk

Abstract

This paper reports on the use of a Qualitative Decision Support System used within the National Health Service (NHS) in the UK. The system has been used to enable the Individual Performance Review (IPR) process to become more effective. One aim of IPR is to motivate managers. However the vision of the Unit General Manager was that the IPR DSS would help him a) understand how individually negotiated IPR objectives fitted together as a whole and related to corporate goals, b) monitor and control progress through the IPR year and c) build teams. Managers would be able to understand the impact each of their IPR objectives had upon one another and be able to identify what contribution their objectives made to the aims of the organization as a whole. The decision support system was based upon cognitive mapping as the modelling technique and COPE as the DSS software. The system was used by the General Manager for taking a composite view of the role of IPR in meeting the Strategy of the organization, and also as a method for monitoring progress of individual managers in relation to their personal IPR objectives. This paper reports on the development and implementation of the system within a specific NHS Hospitals Unit.

1. Introduction

Over the last ten years the UK National Health Service has been the subject of extensive change. In particular the devolution of responsibility for the total well-being of groups of hospitals and the services they provide has resulted in a shift in management style. For the "General Managers", who have roles similar to that of Chief Executive Officers, the "Individual Performance Review" (or IPR) can be a potent system for the motivation, control, and development of managerial and organizational performance (Wigley, 1989).

When this process is combined with the use team building activities designed to build a coherent strategy for the organization, it becomes possible for individual managers to see the links between their own contributions and the overall systemic behaviour and performance of the organization. This paper discusses an example of a General Manager developing a Decision Support System (DSS) which enabled him to keep track of the IPR process in relation to individuals but at the same time see each of them in relation to one another. The DSS was developed following the use of a Group Decision Support System (GDSS) by the top management team for the development of their overall strategy (Cropper et al, 1992).

2. The Individual Performance Review Process

One particular perspective of the IPR process is that it should be designed to recognise and establish a *system* of task-like objectives which takes the form of an hierarchy or "cascade". By so doing the review seeks to help both general manager and line manager negotiate an inter-weaved set of tasks and responsibilities that are internally coherent and related to one another in the form of a "means-ends" structure. In a parallel format these individual hierarchies can be knitted together to provide a cascade for the organization as a whole.

The overall cascade is seen ideally as working from the top down, dis-aggregating the organisation's *objectives* into *targets*, *tasks* and *objectives* for managers across each successive tier to the "lowest level of account". This standard Management by Objectives (MBO) approach either passes *objectives* down the hierarchy (for example "keep within agreed management budget") or it breaks broader objectives progressively into more concrete, specific, tasks (for example, a quality initiative might break down into implementing audits, designing training for quality and so on). Thus some of the objectives translate between several managers IPR and others are specific to a particular manager's IPR.

However, setting and agreeing the objectives with their associated interconnections for individual managers is non-trivial. The IPR process is not intended to focus solely on review, or on control, or future developments. If it is to act as a motivational tool then it must play to the competencies and style of individual managers. The other side of this focus on the individual manager however, is that the general manager wants to feel confident that the IPR's of all managers, taken as a whole, add up to something that will allow the organisation to move forward in as concerted and effective a way as possible (Nelson, 1989). It is important to find a way for the general manager and line manager to appreciate the IPR within the wider whole during the IPR meetings and to negotiate changes in the light of a systemic view of the individual's responsibilities and of the organisation's strategy.

Seeing responsibilities set out as an explicit hierarchy, where the nature of the individual's objectives can be seen graphically as a part of the organisation's interests may provide a powerful visual picture of the role of the individual manager within the grander scheme of things. However for such visual imagery to be useful the picture must be:

> i) capable of being changed interactively during IPR meetings, and changed with an appreciation of the full ramification of changes.

and

> ii) able to keep track of progress, so that the general manager can use the picture as a general control and review mechanism both for his own purposes on a day-to-day basis, and as a regular review process with management teams.

If these aims can be met then such an approach can be seen as a Decision Support System which supports team meetings, one on one meetings, and individual use (Ackermann et al 1992(a)).

Keeping track of progress is a complex task. The cascade "down" from any objective will often involve efforts from a number of managers; and a look "up" the cascade in setting IPR responsibilities may leave some managers wondering how their suggested tasks fit into the level above. This has been highlighted as a potential issue in the IHSM survey - "Few junior managers' objectives relate to the organisation" (Health Service Journal, 19th September, p 13). Whether this is actual or perceived commentary on progress must be recorded in an easily scanned manner so that junior managers are able to see where their objectives fit into the holistic picture, where "bottlenecks" can be spotted graphically, and the implications of fast progress toward strategic change fully appreciated.

In this paper we report on a case study involving a research collaboration between the General Manager of an Acute Hospital Unit in the Midlands of the UK and the authors. One of the objectives of the collaboration was to develop a computer based decision support system which would:

i) help the General Manager to manage the IPR process as a whole and in relation to the strategic direction of the Unit;
ii) hold all manager's IPR responsibilities, once agreed, in a single and readily accessible place;
iii) be useful in monitoring progress towards agreed objectives; and
iv) be capable of update and extension over time.

In general, decision support systems are expected to be "interactive computer based systems, which help decision makers utilize data and models to solve unstructured problems" (Scott Morton, 1971). This aged description of a DSS captures the aims set out above, however most DSS's are based upon an interpretation of data which is that it will be quantitative: in the reported collaboration, the data was essentially qualitative. Qualitative *data* is usually most appropriate when working with future managerial activities, activities that are designed to change the organisation. Whilst numerical data is sometimes used to target outcomes it is often inappropriate simply because the nature of the activities are, as yet, unspecified in any detail. The activities become clear as progress is made towards their completion. What defines an action or outcome is not its metrication but rather its means/ends context. Thus, it is defined qualitatively by the other activities that need to be undertaken to support it: the means of achieving it, and its intent: the reasons why it should be undertaken. The recurrent nature of the means/ends context forms the hierarchy which is the *model* of the data.

An effective DSS is also expected to: be made up of information *of potential use* to the decision maker (Turban 1990; Freyenfeld 1984); utilise modelling software to *hold the information*; provide facilities within the software for *exploration, analysis, update, and presentation* of the information and have the adaptability to accommodate changes in the environment (Sprague and Watson, 1986). Thus we see a good mapping between the demands of the General Manager set out earlier and the more abstract definitions commonly used in the literature as signals of good practice.

The base system used for the case reported here was a software package which is well established for use as a part of a Group Decision Support System for helping management teams resolve messy problems (Eden, 1989) and work on strategy development (Eden and Ackermann, 1992). The software, COPE, although originally designed for a mainframe and then IBM AT, now runs within a Windows 3.1[2] PC environment and is designed to display in a graphical format "chunks" of text which are related to one another by arrows. The software permits the user to move the text around the 'window'; categorize each chunk by colour, typeface, or formal set designation; edit it; ask the computer to redraw the interrelated text as a hierarchy; and conduct a large number of analyses both of the structure of the causal network or map, and of the categories (Ackermann, 1991; Cropper et al 1990).

3. IPR Aided by a DSS

3.1 Stage 1 - Strategy Influences IPR

The first part of the process of developing the DSS followed from the formulation and implementation of a strategy that had been developed using COPE as a GDSS. The General Manager had wanted to establish a Quality Assurance strategy for the hospitals Unit to help them cope with the quality initiatives. The strategy was developed independently of the existing IPR system and involved a number of ad hoc Quality Assurance Working Groups within the organisation.

The computer software was used in a similar manner to the SODA (Strategic Options Development and Analysis) process (Cropper et al 1992) except with a focus on developing quality assurance within the Unit rather than solving specific strategic problems. Nevertheless the process achieved more than producing outcomes for dealing with quality issues. It helped members of the working groups fashion a strategy of a more general nature, and with more wide reaching consequences and built a single unified team of senior managers to support the strategy.

The working groups managed to identify and agree a set of corporate objectives and the actions which were most likely to achieve them. In particular the groups found the ability, provided by the software, of exploring their aggregated understanding of the issues especially valuable. They were able to track the actions which were most "potent" in terms of tackling a number of objectives. Similarly powerful was the analytical help the software provided in assessing which strategic efforts were well resourced and which were being relatively neglected. The analysis, conducted in "real time" with the groups, aimed at achieving an appropriate *balance* of effort across the complete strategy (for a more detailed description of the role of balance see Eden and Cropper 1992). It was these potent actions and the resolution of balance that contributed to the strategic action plans.

Thus the series of Quality Assurance workshops using the model had helped the group keep track of how their ideas for future individual and departmental actions tied in consistently to a framework of organisational interests. Therefore the workshops, aided by a GDSS, influenced strategy which, in turn, influenced IPR responsibilities. The left part of figure 1 shows the role of the GDSS.

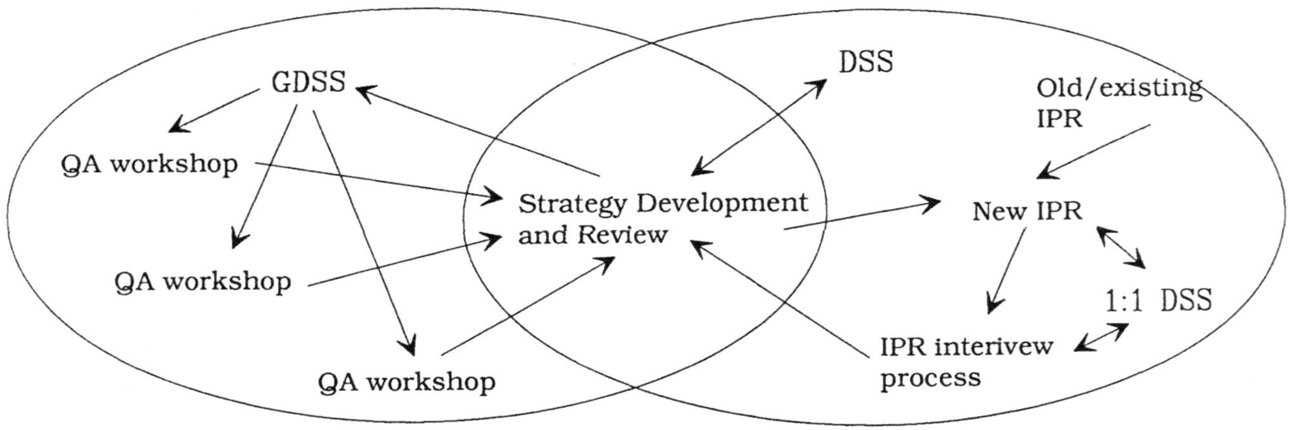

Figure 1 - The Relationship between the Strategy and IPR in relation to the GDSS and DSS

This next step of converting Quality Assurance tasks and other strategy related tasks into IPR responsibilities seemed a natural step to all participants. After all, the software and the SODA process had shown managers how their individual and departmental actions tied in consistently and coherently into a framework of organisational interests. The General Manager had been keen to develop and demonstrate the coherence of strategy as a basis for increasing the likelihood of implementation (a demand in line with the research of Pettigrew et al (1987) which identifies the significance of coherence of strategy on its organisational impact). In addition the General Manager chose to turn the "organizational memory" or "transitional object" (de Heus, 1988) created by the GDSS processes into a personal DSS which would allow him to keep track of the general progress of the strategy (the middle part of figure 1)(Ackermann et al 1992a).

3.2 Stage 2 - IPR Influences Strategy

The shift to using the strategy to guide IPR interviews was interrupted by the merger of two hospital Units. The General Manager became Director of Operations of the new composite Unit. As a result the strategy which had had a significant influence on the original Unit could no longer be adopted. The now Director of Operations however, having seen the benefit of having all the IPR objectives captured in a single model decided to continue to use the modelling method but to capture the data in a more traditional manner of one to one interviews. These IPR interviews conducted by the General Manager took place within a more open framework rather than being focused on quality and the individual managers were encouraged to raise issues facing their own department and the new Unit as a whole.

From these one-to-one IPR interviews with the individual managers the General Manager was able to identify a number of interconnected issues and responsibilities. Whilst the individual managers had brought to the interviews their own desired objectives some of these responsibilities were related to the previously agreed strategy, others derived from previous IPR interviews and agreements, but many others raised new issues. At the end of the interview the Director of Operations summarised the tasks related to the individual as well as ensuring some of the established agendas, for example a balanced skill mix was included within the objectives for the Unit. In addition the summary sought to demonstrate and acknowledge the link between individual responsibilities (by objectives, targets, and tasks) and the corporate objectives of the Unit or the broader based objectives that translated into concrete tasks for each manager.

Out of this IPR interview process came the modification of old IPR responsibilities and the overall strategy itself (right hand part of figure 1). Thus Quality Assurance workshops influenced the Unit strategy which in turn influenced the IPR agreements. The IPR process had been influenced by historical considerations through an acknowledgement of the existing IPR agreements - so "honouring history" in the development of strategy (Ackermann et al 1992b). The whole process was now locked together so that review at the individual level (one-to-one DSS), managerial awareness and monitoring (DSS), and group work (GDSS) occurred in a cyclical manner (expressed by the totality of figure 1).

3.3 Stage 3 - The IPR Decision Support System

From the IPR interviews the strategy model residing in COPE was extended so that the Operations Director could monitor and review progress as a whole and with each of the individual managers. In the first model the IPR objectives had related to quality issues, and the quality issues had related to the overall strategic objectives and organisational values of the Unit. In this second development the IPR responsibilities and individual hierarchies of activity covered all the areas of the Unit.

Figure 2 shows a typical DSS screen from COPE. The screen shows a number of IPR objectives surrounding a corporate objective which is linked in turn to an organisational goal. The concepts with a person's initials at the beginning, and in some instances agreed completion dates, are related to individual IPR data. Two IPR objectives for person "EP" are related to two corporate objectives, and the display shows that persons "WAT" and "RB" are dependent upon the completion of these objectives. The screen also shows that there are other interrelationships that might be acknowledged and brought onto the display as wished. Concepts numbered 86, 105 and 67 alongside the dashed arrows have an impact on two IPR objectives and one corporate objective respectively; and concepts 136, 156, 32 and 278 are "unseen" ramifications. It is thus possible to relate the "cascade" by recognising that actions can have more than one (beneficial) consequence and indeed to suggest that they should be designed in order to improve their contribution. For example, 202 *"WAT keep within budget"* has 12 other IPR objectives linked to it.

Because the software allows the user to give any concept a style distinguished by both colour and typeface, the screen portrays through tones and shapes the overall sense of the particular part of the model the user is focusing upon. In this case the corporate goals were in a larger, italicised, typeface and coloured white. Whereas IPR objectives were coloured red and set in a smaller bold typeface. In general the IPR objectives have target dates embedded in the statement. This allows the user to display all objectives to be achieved in, say, three months hence and review the state of progress on each. Similarly an analytical process, of set logic manipulation, allows the user to identify all the objectives of all the managers in one department, that are targeted for a particular date, and have a consequential impact on another department's activities. Many other similar analyses enable the user to identify in a simple manner matters of interest in relation to a review with a particular manager, or management team.

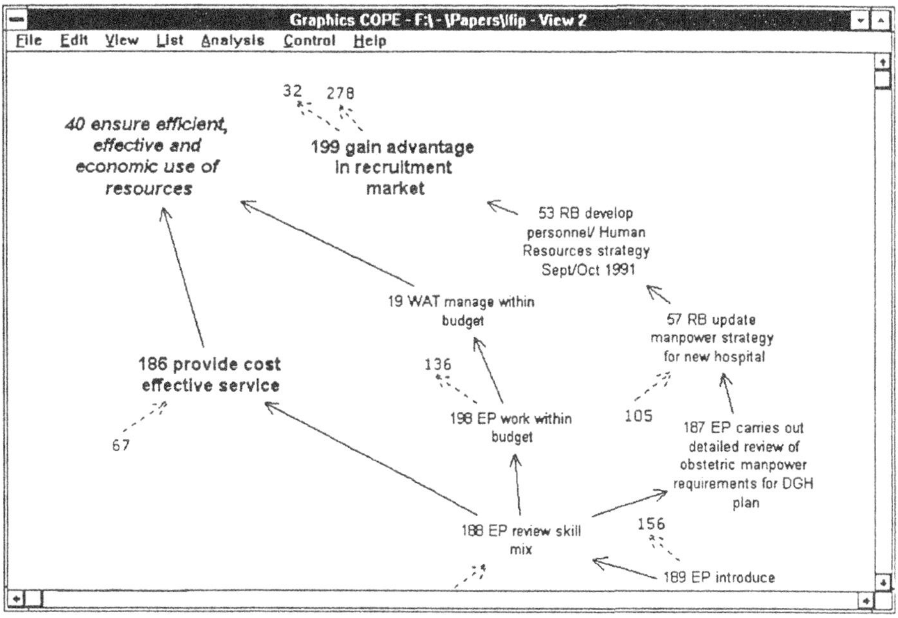

Figure 2 - A Sample IPR COPE screen

IPR objectives were also distinguished from other tasks which were of a lesser priority, or which might be added to reflect a take-up of new work during the IPR year. Statements could be added or edited during review meetings by simply "pointing and clicking" with the mouse and typing directly to the screen and cross linking to other parts by dragging the mouse. The statements on the screen are linked by arrows to show that one activity, task, or objective may help to achieve another.

If the system is to be regarded as a DSS then it should be helping with decision making (Ginzberg and Stohr, 1982; Emery, 1987) and should be used by the manager without continuous help from the designer or from a chauffeur. In this case all of the analysis and changes to the model, reported above, were activated by the Operations Director. Indeed the Director often suggested new analysis routines that he felt would help his decision making. The software enables a "power-user" to design rapidly new analysis procedures, including the design of new menus and windows, and supply these to the user within a working day.

4 Use of IPR for monitoring and control

For the most part, the Operations Director used the system as a DSS to monitor and chase progress. Ansoff and McDonnell (1990) coined the term "forward control" in which the monitoring emphasis shifts from a concern with identifying and correcting deviations or errors in past performance to one of assessing the difference between current achievement and the level of performance agreed for some future date. In this view, which matches closely with the spirit of the IPR system, management control is about action to support achievement of objectives. Within the context of hierarchy, the emphasis is on monitoring "performance against the arrow" rather than a simple focus on the activity itself. Managers are given encouragement to meet targets in relation to ensuring that activities achieve agreed ends rather than being completed as if they were an independent activity. Many strategies fail in changing the organisation because monitoring fails to focus on means *and* ends, but rather focuses only on means without context.

Within the Unit upon which this case is based, the Director of Operations has two computer based systems. The first system, which has been used for several years, sends out standard memos on IPR objectives as they approach the target date, reminding the responsible manager of the commitment. The decision support system discussed in this paper holds all the records of IPR objectives and their relationship with one another and the overall strategy. It sits on the Director of Operations desk and is set up to allow him to monitor progress at regular "checkpoint" meetings by way of a simple colour code which extends that discussed above.

The IPR objectives are initially coloured red, but they are then recategorized when the task is initiated and then again when significant progress has been established, and finally when completed. This four part categorization enables a picture of overall progress to be established on the computer screen - red changes to green when initiated, to purple when progress is reported, and to dark blue on completion. Thus a general dark blue hue to the display signifies encouraging progress in relation to the particular part of the hierarchy of interest to the review group. As well as graphical displays, quick listings of a particular manager's responsibilities at one of the "checkpoint" meetings clearly shows overall progress for the manager concerned. The use of colour, in this way, has added considerable power to analytical checks. When little progress has been made in relation to superordinate corporate objectives it often becomes clear that subordinate concepts are blocking - the display shows a dominant red or green hue indicating no starts or starts with no progress.

Monitoring the workload of individual managers or their departments has been a matter of considerable concern within the NHS. The pace of change has made incessant and stressful demands on managers, and so a senior manager is continually juggling and balancing the absolute and relative demands across staff. Thus the DSS is acting as a powerful way for checks of balance to made as new tasks are added and old tasks completed. Through the analysis of the colour categories discussed above, tasks can be transferred or re-prioritized in the light of the ramifications of changes on the organisation as a whole.

In these ways the "model-as-memory" provides some help in setting the agenda for IPR reviews and other meetings, both informal and formal.

5 Summary

The focus of this paper has been on the development and use of a DSS for agreeing and monitoring IPR responsibilities. The research collaboration with a general manager in the NHS resulted in more wide reaching outcomes where the aim to use a GDSS for the work of Quality Assurance teams became linked developing a DSS for IPR purposes. Gradually the team work evolved into a strategy review process which then acted as the central guiding framework for linking Quality to strategy to IPR. The DSS is installed on a Windows based PC on the desk of the now Director of Operations for an enlarged hospitals Unit. It used as an integral part of informal and formal meetings as well as being used to inform his own decision making. It has promoted strategic thinking, kept the general manager "in touch" with the purpose of the organisation through the continuing "fire" and improved communication of intentions.

Many of the mangers believe the system has helped develop their strategic thinking and enhance their own individual performance without feeling excessively controlled. In this instance the system has been used creatively to keep track of progress and to indicate where individual managers or departments may be overloaded. Clearly the reported success of the system reflects more on the capability of the manager who has developed it and uses it. The system itself may however be regarded as an important contributor to his managerial competence - which is, after all, the most reasonable expectation of a DSS.

The authors are continually monitoring the use of the system. The manager is making further demands of the software and other managers and administrative staff within the organisation are gradually being trained in the use of the system.

Acknowledgements: Our thanks are due to our collaborator in this work - Bert Telford, who is currently Director of Operations, Burton, Litchfield and Tamworth Hospitals Unit, SE Staffs Health Authority; and to ICL who provided support to some of the project.

References

Ackermann, F., Cropper, S. and Eden, C. (1992a) 'Moving between Groups and Individuals using a DSS', *Decision Systems* forthcoming

Ackermann, F., Bryson, J., Eden, C. and Finn, C. (1992b). 'Critical Incidents and Emergent Issues in the Management of Large-Scale change efforts' Paper presented to the Academy of Management conference, Las Vegas, August.

Ackermann, F. (1991). *COPE: a user's guide*. Glasgow, University of Strathclyde.

Ansoff, I. and McDonnell, E. (1990). *Implanting Strategic Management*, Prentice Hall, London.

De Heus, A. (1988) 'Planning as Learning', *Harvard Business Review*, April-March

Cropper, S., Telford, W. and Ackermann, F. (1992) 'Quality Assurance and Improvement: the Role of Strategy Making', *International Journal of Health Care Quality Assurance*, 5, 5-11

Cropper, S., Eden, C. and Ackermann, F. (1990). 'Keeping Sense of Accounts using Computer-Based Cognitive Maps', *Social Science Computer Review*, 8 345-366

Eden, C. (1989) 'Using cognitive mapping for Strategic Options Development and Analysis (SODA)' in J Rosenhead (Ed) *Rational Analysis for a Problematic World*, Wiley, Chichester.

Eden, C. and Cropper, S. (1992). Coherence and Balance in Strategies for the management of Public Services', *Public Money and Management*, 12 43-52

Eden, C. and Ackermann, F. (1992). 'Strategy Development and Implementation - the role of a Group Decision Support System' in S. Kinney, R. Bostrom and R. Watson (Eds) *Computer Augmented Teamwork: A Guided Tour*, Van Nostrand and Reinhold, New York

Emery, J.C. (1987) *Management Information Systems: The Critical Strategic Resource*, Oxford University Press, New York

Freyenfeld, W. A. (1984) *Decision Support Systems: An executive overview of interactive computer-assisted decision making in the UK.* NCC Publications, Manchester

Ginzberg, M.J. and Stohr, W.E. (1982) Decision Support Systems: issues and perspectives in M.J. Ginzberg, W. Reitman and E.A. Stohr (Eds), *Decision Support Systems*, North-Holland, Amsterdam 9-31

Institute of Health Services Management. Individual Performance Review in the NHS: a report by the IHSM for the NHS management executive. IHSM, Portland Place, London (1991).

Nelson, M.J. (1989). *Managing Health Service Professionals.* London:Chapman and Hall.

Pettigrew, A. (1977). "Strategy formulation as a political process", *International Studies in Management and Organization*, 7, 78-87.

Scott Morton, M. (1971). *Management Decision Systems: computer-based support for decision making.* Cambridge, Mass:Division of Research, Harvard University.

Sprague, R.H. and Watson, H.J. (1986) *Decision Support Systems: Putting Theory into Practice*, Prentice Hall, London

Turban, E. (1990) *Decision Support and Expert Systems: Management Support Systems* 2nd Edition, Macmillan, New York

Wigley, D. (1989). "Performance Review, Motivation and Organisational Culture", *Health Services Management*, 85, 252-255.

Decision Support in Public Administration (A-26)
P.W.G. Bots, H.G. Sol and R. Traunmüller (Editors)
Elsevier Science Publishers B.V. (North-Holland)

Decision Support Systems within the NHS: An Investigation into the Application of Case Mix Management Systems in the UK National Health Service.

Philip J. Baugh[a] & David M. Walters[b]

a Deparment of International Business, University of Central Lancashire, Marshall House, The Ringway, Preston, Lancashire PR1 2HE

b Department of Business Information Management, University of Central Lancashire, Lowthian House, The Ringway, Preston, Lancashire PR1 2HE

Abstract
In a previous paper we examined the impact of Decision Support Systems in the context of organisational change, looking at a Socio-Technical Systems approach to the NHS. As part of the study we examined briefly the role of Case Mix Management Systems (CMMS) in the control of hospital costs. This paper represents the first stage of a longitudinal study examining the development of CMMS in the UK context over a period of three years and sets the agenda for the issues to be investigated and monitored. In analysing the interfaces between management and clinicians we have adopted a Socio-Technical approach.

1. Introduction

In a paper presented at the IFIP conference on Decision Support Systems at Fontainbleau in July 1992 we examined the role of DSS in the British National Health Service (NHS)[1]. The paper gave an overview of the changes in the NHS in the UK as a result of the Government's White Paper of 1987[2]. In the analysis we used a Socio-Technical Systems approach to organisational change. As part of the study we examined briefly the role of Case Mix Management Systems (CMMS) in the control of hospital costs. This paper represents the first stage of a longitudinal study examining the development of CMMS in the UK context over the next three years and sets the agenda for the issues to be investigated and monitored.

Before developing the main theme of this paper it would be useful to recapitulate on the main issues raised in our previous paper to provide the context for the present discussion. We primarily highlighted two changes that had been introduced into the NHS:

a) the change from a command-administrative system to the internal market system and consequently,
b) the separation of the purchaser and provider functions, the former being in the main the Health Authorities, the latter the hospital and community care units.

To operate successfully in the new environment our 1992 paper suggested that the providers need comprehensive information systems to decide on a range of issues. Prior to the 'new' organisation, the information systems had been too data-oriented with an emphasis placed on basic patient details and limited information available for decision support purposes. There are, however, a number of key areas in which decisions will have to be made by provider units if the new NHS organisation is going to fulfil its mission. In support there will be a need for comprehensive decision support systems which have not been hitherto available. Decision support systems are being developed to aid in the following processes:

- Case Mix Management for Providers
- Patient Profile for Clinicians
- Hospital Information Support for a variety of hospital functions

All the above systems are at an early stage of development. However, some progress is now being made with Case Mix Management Systems at or just beyond the implementation phase. The purpose of CMMS is to provide support to the contracting process by enabling hospital managers to monitor and evaluate treatment outcomes, time involved and costs in delivering the treatment. This is done on the basis of case type. This will help in enabling providers to strike realistic contracts with the purchasing authorities.

The 1992 paper also considered the manner in which the changes were being brought about. The authors have adopted a Socio-Technical Systems approach in analysing these changes as they consider that this is the only way in which the introduction of IT into the NHS structure can be realistically explored. As was previously noted the NHS provides a variant on the Socio-Technical Systems approach in that 'management', rather than being a homogeneous group, consists of two distinct factions - the former administrators, now managers who have no clinical background or experience and the medical staff, primarily clinicians who, at best, have experience only as Clinical Directors managing other doctors. Each faction has separate agendas, interests, professional associations, beliefs and allegiances. This complicates the introduction of new systems into an area where rapid development of systems is required to serve the needs of the new operating environment.

2. The Concept of Case Mix

In order to analyse the issues concerning the development of CMMS, it is important to define the concept of the case mix carefully and set it in its proper context. We shall use the example of cardio-thoracic (heart-lung) surgery for illustrative purposes. In the past the NHS placed emphasis primarily upon specialties and specialty costs. Cardio-thoracic is an example of such a specialty which has a large number of different case types and procedures within it. In practice it has been found that, within such a specialty, costs have been difficult to estimate because of this variety. At one end of the spectrum there are case types which are complex and expensive surgery such as double heart valve replacement where the patient spends 24-48 hours in intensive care and 2-3 weeks in recuperation. At the other end of the spectrum are case types involving the straightforward and relatively cheap procedures of a bronchoscopy or a lung biopsy which may require only a matter of an overnight stay. If specialties consisted of only one case type then it would be relatively simple to estimate what the costs of the specialty would be but, since the case mix can vary appreciably over time, it is difficult to predict specialty costs with any degree of confidence.

This problem of specialty costs is not unique to the UK. The problem is one which hospitals and insurance companies in the US have been grappling with for some time. The issue is essentially one of attempting to define a level of costs where one can be reasonably assured that costs are stable without having to descend to the level of costing out every single procedure that could be involved in every case, i.e. to define cases which use similar amounts of resources and group them together. These are known as iso-resource groups. In the US such groups are called Diagnostically-Related Groups (DRGs). The DRG concept has been used in the UK context but it has been found that it does not provide the most appropriate basis for costing. This is essentially due to the fact that procedure costs in the UK differ markedly from those in the US resulting in the need for different groupings to be formed. These have been developed recently and are known as Health Related Groupers (HRGs). Case Mix Management Systems have been developed using HRGs to keep track of case types and their associated costs without the need of drilling down each time to the individual cases and their procedures.

3. The Use Of Decision Support Systems to Monitor and Control the Case Mix

The first step in the process of controlling costs is to be able to monitor the case mix and assess how it is changing over time. In most cases the evidence could be obtained from a case-based Management Information System with suitable report-writing facilities which highlighted the mix of cases in each specialty. This, however, is a very limited approach since CMMS can aid managers in ensuring that the case mix outcome and associated costs are be brought back into line with the intended projections during the contracting period. However, control of the case mix cannot be completely ensured by managers without clinicians spreading good medical practice which can help in cost control. Thus, in order to be effective, it is necessary for systems in place to meet the needs of the clinicians as well as the managers. In this case, Management Information Systems are insufficiently flexible since clinicians need to look at evidence in a number of ways right down to the level of the individual patient. There is a need for Decision Support Systems which in some way meet the twin needs of manager and clinician. Executive Information Systems may provide the type of solution required to satisfy both groups. In the use of technology, clinicians are similar to executives. They have in general little or no IT background with a degree of aloofness about their own use of IT. To persuade them to use IT similar tools are needed to those used by Executives i.e. Executive Information Systems which will enable them to drill down to the individual patient data level to provide the required output.

4. The Socio-Technical Systems Approach

In order to examine the issues more clearly, we need to look at the interface between the management and clinical elements in the Socio-Technical System. In our previous paper, this was simply represented as shown in the diagram below. This can be investigated in more detail since we wish to specify in more detail the exact relationship between managers and clinicians and how it impacts upon the requirements for the technology to be used.

THE SOCIO TECHNICAL SYSTEM
IN A CLINICAL CONTEXT

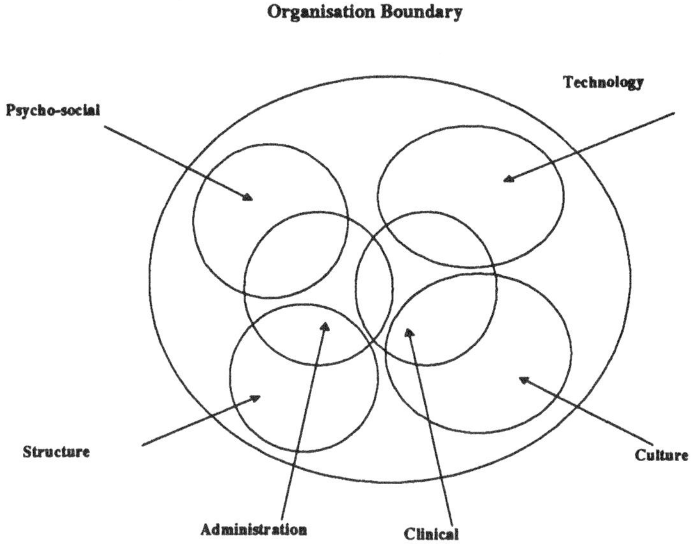

Diagram 1

In the NHS, the critical concern is with the overlapping areas of management (or administration), clinicians and the information technology employed in the NHS. The development of NHS information strategy in the past has placed great emphasis on the administrative component and has tended to neglect the clinical requirements for information and information systems. Whilst obviously concerned with the quality of care delivered to patients, NHS managers, particularly finance managers, are principally charged with controlling costs and ensuring that revenues accrue to the unit for which they are responsible. In so far as the systems have been patient-based in the past, they have been so only in the context of collecting data on patients and processing it for administrative purposes. The Patient Administration Systems (PAS), provides basic patient information of most use to the administrator or manager. Clinicians are primarily concerned with patient care and require the collection of data on patients and its use in the care process. There is a need for Patient Profile or Clinical Information Systems to provide such information but, in the UK context, the development of such systems is slow. There is a stark contrast between the use of systems by clinicians - it is doubtful whether more than 1 in 100 clinicians use an information system on a daily basis - compared with doctors in primary care where at least 60% use medical systems in their surgeries.

Information systems have served the needs of the administrative rather than the medical staff. Below we show how the development of CMMS, whilst serving the needs of managers with information for the contracting process also have to take into consideration the requirements of clinicians and the needs of patients if they are to be successful. Over the next three years we shall be monitoring the development of CMMS to ascertain whether they are successful in being effective decision-support systems.

5. Clinical Aspects

Firstly we shall examine the clinical aspects. Clinicians are concerned with examination and evaluation of the outcomes associated with the procedures which may be carried out on patients; these may be medical or surgical. Concerning the individual patient, the clinician wishes to know whether the procedures undertaken have had a successful outcome in ameliorating the patient condition. There is a need for monitoring the patient and evaluating the outcome. This can take place not only at the level of the individual patient but also at the level of the case type. For example, the surgeon may monitor a patient who has undergone a pneumonectomy (removal of lung) and then evaluate the outcome to assess what further treatment the patient may require. Information systems can play a vital role in this individually-based monitoring and evaluation process. Furthermore the clinicians either singly or as a group within a hospital, need to monitor all such cases of pneumonectomy and evaluate all procedures associated with this case type in order to ascertain their efficacy in the patient treatment process. In fact, over the past few years this has become a major issue in the NHS as there is a drive to ensure that good practice in clinical work is disseminated as widely as possible. This process is known as Medical Audit. Doctors therefore have an interest in a wide variety of information about casework not only at the patient level but also at the case type level. The diagram below illustrates the cycle of events.

FINANCE AND CLINICAL

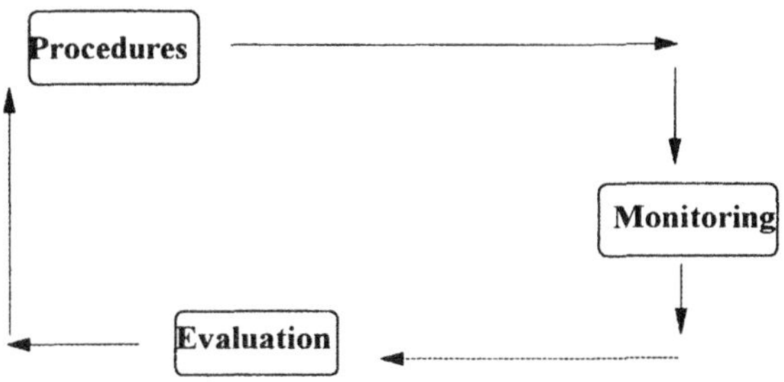

Diagram 2

This is the common input, transformation, output diagram which however in the case of the hospital information system is more complicated as illustrated by the diagram below. The input, transformation, output is different for the managers and clinicians. However there is an area of overlap in patient procedure and patient costs. The clinicians are mostly interested in patient procedures while the managers are mostly interested in patient costs. However the managers will not be able to generate the correct information for patient costs unless they have the data for patient procedures. They could thus be constrained by the clinicians willingness to accept and use the new information systems such as CMMS. If clinicians do not accept these systems then managers are going to find it much harder to generate the correct information to calculate costs.

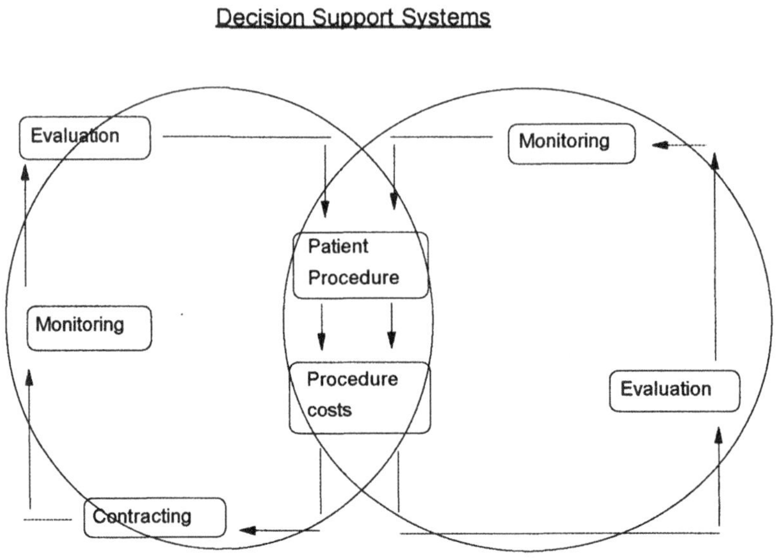

Diagram 3

In the past, the strict separation of clinical and managerial roles within the NHS has been unsatisfactory and has been the source of much tension. Unless clinicians have a managerial role, there is always a danger that the cost implications of clinical decisions will be ignored.

In an attempt to deal with this problem, the NHS has introduced in each hospital, a Clinical Directorate. Each specialty is led by a Clinical Director whose responsibility is both clinical and managerial in nature, an interface between the two, as in Diagram 4 below.

Since this has been a recent development , it is not yet possible to assess the extent to which its implementation can be judged successful. However, it provides a model which allows for the bringing together of clinical and managerial decision-making, and for ensuring consistency between them. This is crucial for the development of CMMS since it implies that an integrated clinical and managerial approach is the more appropriate form for system development.

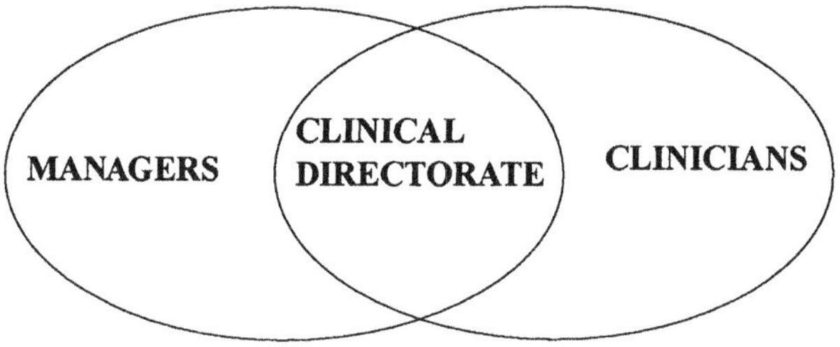

Diagram 4

6. Managerial Aspects

The National Health Service contracting process has been outlined in our previous paper. What follows is an elaboration of that process insofar as it impinges on the development of Case Mix Management Systems. It was noted that costing under the previous administrative system of the NHS was based upon average specialty costs-an inadequate basis for costing since specialty costs represent too broad a category. The contracting process involves hospital managers making contracts with purchasers concerning the number of cases which the hospital is willing to undertake. Taking the cardio-thoracic specialty, a hospital may contract to undertake numerous cases on a block contract basis e.g. 20 double heart valve replacements, 10 single heart valve replacements, 200 lung biopsies. Managers need to feel reasonably confident that the costs within a specialty are reasonably stable. If the structure of costs remained the same throughout a given period of time for each hospital unit, then it would be possible to base contracts on the specialty costs but in practice no one yet knows the stability of costs within any given specialty although some will be more predictable than others. Tracking the mix of cases on the basis of DRGs or HRGs will aid the contract manager in determining what cases the hospital should undertake for a purchaser and at what price. If the case mix is not stable or predictable, there is a danger that they may set prices below average costs, in which case they will incur losses or alternatively they may set prices well above costs which, in the NHS context is equally unacceptable since, in a politically sensitive area of a free healthcare system, hospitals cannot not be seen as making profits over and above the normal return they are required to make on their activities.

7. The Evidence

We have commenced by interviewing health service managers at two hospitals in the North West of England concerning the Decision Support Systems in use. Both hospitals are at the stage of piloting the development of CMMS. At this stage in the research it is too early to determine exactly how successful the systems have been in meeting their objectives. The preliminary evidence is that one is actively involving the clinicians in the use of CMMS and are using the clinicians to pilot the CMMS in the hospital. The other views the CMMS as the preserve of the managers and sees the involvement of clinicians at a later date as a matter for their information.

This appears to show two distinct philosophical approaches to the issue of clinician involvement. One of these approaches we believe to be sound, in that it is consistent with the Socio-Technical Systems approach we have outlined; the other which we believe will throw up problems for managers and clinicians in the control of costs .

The next stage of the research will involve follow-up questionnaires to and interviews with a larger number of hospital units in order to validate the results so far.

Hospital A

Hospital A has adopted an approach of clinician involvement at every stage of the process. This fits in with some of the recommendations as put forward by Coombs & Cooper[3] in their paper on the implementation of the NHS White Paper that:

> "clinicians should be directly involved in the decision on how diagnoses should be coded in the system, and at what level of aggregation the data should be reported."

Clinicians were involved in the procurement team which decided upon the technology to purchased. It was a requirement of the system that it had good clinical audit facilities and that it had good ward order communications so that basic data on patients could be entered by the clinicians directly. Clinicians are also actively involved in looking at the coding structure of the system to ensure accuracy. The system had to have good interfacing capabilities with the Patient Administration System (PAS) to ensure consistency of data and to obviate the need for entry of basic patient administration details which the PAS can already provide. Over a period of more than 6 months, the piloting has been initially amongst the clinicians to get them to see the benefits of keeping on-screen details of patient treatments. Acceptance is not wholly uniform. Some clinicians are very enthusiastic and are even willing to key-in the basic patient data; others leave this task to their secretaries. In order to meet all the requirements it was decided to purchase

ICL's proprietary CMMS in conjunction with its Executive Information System EIS-EPIC - primarily because of its good clinical support function.

Hospital B

The approach at Hospital B is entirely different. The assumption has been made that clinicians will not be interested in case mix as such and that this area is mainly the preserve of the manager. As a result the hospital has taken the decision to tackle the issue of information systems for managers and clinicians entirely separately. The result of this approach has been as follows: the clinicians have been supplied with a Clinical Information System (CIS) which will allow them to enter treatment details for each patient and carry out the monitoring and evaluation both at an individual and group level. The hospital has also purchased a Case Mix Management System and an EIS from SMS to support the contracting process. Whilst the CIS can act as a feeder system to the CMMS, the interface is not yet in place to allow for data transfer. Even when this has been done, there is a danger that the clinicians, seeing that the CMMS is not in their ownership, will not use the output from the CMMS in support of the Medical Audit process, rather they will use the CIS both to monitor and evaluate individual cases and case-types. Thus treatment will remain divorced from costs with a consequent lack of control over the latter.

8. Conclusion

This paper has stressed the need for measures relating clinical activity to the cost of that activity. This can be achieved via a CMMS. Without this a hospital will find it very difficult to produce reasoned charges for the treatment that it has performed, to the purchasers of that treatment.

Whereas previously, cost and price data would only have been of interest to the managers, it is also now of interest to, and will have an impact on clinicians. The basis of cost and price data is information on the treatment of patients. This is in the control of the clinicians. There is thus a real need to induce the clinicians to become involved in the use of new IT systems in the NHS. Without their co-operation implementation, of this will become very difficult. Luk and Boss[4] put the argument succinctly when referring to quality assurance:

> "Perhaps the most important barrier to implementing quality assurance programs is health professionals' expectations of autonomy... Simply put, quality assurance programs cannot be implemented without the co-operation and support of physicians, nurses, and other key actors in health institutions."

Whilst the approaches in terms of the technology would appear to be remarkably similar as far as the use of CMMS and EIS is concerned, this belies a completely different philosophical approach. At Hospital A, the CMMS purchased reflects clinician involvement; at Hospital B, a more corporate approach has been developed allowing for the use of a Clinical Information System and a CMMS which reflects manager needs. From our longitudinal study over the next three years we will be able to judge how successful CMMS are and what is the correct approach in relation to generating clinician involvement and commitment to their use.

9. REFERENCES

1. Baugh P. & Walters D.M. - Impact of DSS within the context of Organisational Change: An application of the Socio-Technical Approach to the NHS. IFIP Transactions. Decision Support Systems: Experiences and Expectations. Jelassi T. Klein M. R. Mayon-White W.M. (Eds). North Holland 1992.

2. Department of Health (1989). - Working for Patients. London, HMSO 1989.

3. Department of Health (1989) - Contracts for Health Service: Operating Contracts London HMSO 1989

4. Coombs R. & Cooper D. - Accounting for Patients?: Information Technology and the implementation of the NHS White Paper. ESRC (1990).

5 Griffiths R - Report of the NHS Management Inquiry. London DHSS 1983

6 IMG - Working for Patients. Framework for Information Systems, the Next Steps Department of Health 1990

7 Kast F. & Rosenzweig J. - Organisation & Management. McGraw Hill 1986

8. Luke R.D & Boss R.W. - Barriers Limiting the Implementation of Quality Assurance Programs". Health Services Journal, Vol. 16 No.3, 1981.

9. Willcocks LP & Mark A. - IT Systems Implementation: Research Findngs from the Public Sector. Journal Of Information Technology. June 1989.

Decision Support in Public Administration (A-26)
P.W.G. Bots, H.G. Sol and R. Traunmüller (Editors)
Elsevier Science Publishers B.V. (North-Holland)

Applications of Decision Support: The State of Minnesota Experience

Gary W. Dickson
Department of Information and Decision Science
Carlson School of Management, University of Minnesota
E-mail: dickson@umnacvx.cis.umn.edu (Internet)

Abstract

The State of Minnesota (USA) is a very active user of decision support systems (DSS) and group decision support systems (GDSS) technology. This paper reviews several applications of DSS and GDSS within the Department of Human Services (DHS) and Department of Finance (DoF) within the government of the State of Minnesota. In particular, the following systems are illustrated and evaluated: (1) An automated JAD application for the design of a Social Services Information System [GDSS/DHS], (2) A Children's Social Services Information System [DSS/DHS], (3) A Budget Information System [DSS/DoF], and (4) a Revenue Forecasting System [DSS/DoF]. In addition to describing the purpose and nature of each system, the paper discusses the benefits of each application and focuses on lesson that have been learned in developing and using these applications.

1. INTRODUCTION

Public sector organizations in the United States are growing ever larger and more complex. Government at all levels is being asked to provide more services for more individuals and to do so with continually constrained resources. In this environment, information technology is being called upon to assist not only in the provision of services, but in aiding the management process itself.

Two areas of the application of information/decision technology being applied to management problems within the State of Minnesota (USA) are decision support systems (DSS) and group decision support systems (GDSS). The purpose of this paper is to illustrate these applications in four specific instances, two each in the departments of Human Services and Finance. In addition to describing the applications, the paper will focus on benefits and lessons learned in the applications.

2. THE STATE OF MINNESOTA AND ITS GOVERNANCE

The State of Minnesota is located in what is referred to in the United States as the "upper midwest." The state is centered on the 45th parallel and borders Canada on the north. It is the 12th largest of the states in area and, with more than 4 million residents, ranks 21st in population.

Governmental units in the state include the state government itself, subunits called counties, and city governments. Within the State of Minnesota, many services are provided at the county level. There are 87 counties in the state which is a very large number by standards of other states. Key governmental positions include the governor, the legislators (a state senator and state legislator from each district), county commissioners, and city officials. The total staff of governmental units in the State of Minnesota numbers in excess of 120,000.

The largest single unit of government in the state is the state government itself. Approximately 55,000 people work for the State of Minnesota (not including the 15,00 staff of the seven state universities), most within the various departments making up the government, e.g., the Department of Administration, the Department of Revenue (taxation), the Department of Human Services, the Department of Transportation, the Department of Finance (state accounting, budgeting, and financial management), the Department of Employee Relations.

Information technology is widely applied to assist operating the state government and in its management. For example, within the Department of Administration there is the InterTechnolgies Group. This group runs a very large (several IBM MVS systems) data center which, for example, support systems such as the statewide accounting system, the payroll system, the medical payments claims and reimbursement systems, and the like. In addition, the InterTechnolgies Group provides support for advanced technologies and manages the state data communication network.

Many state agencies (e.g., the Department of Human Services, the Department of Revenue) have their own information systems staffs and many have their own minicomputer systems at the departmental level (e.g., an IBM AS/400 at the Department of Human Services, an IBM RS/6000 at the Department of Finance). Just to indicate the size and complexity of the state use of computing, no less than four major (mainframe) database management systems (DBMS) are supported (due primarily to the fact that large applications systems used in different state agencies were transferred from other states and are based on different DBMS software).

In addition to applying information technology to large scale transaction processing systems, the State of Minnesota has moved to more advanced concepts such as DSS and GDSS. The next section of this paper will illustrate this fact with four examples.

3. DSS AND GDSS APPLICATIONS

The authors of this paper have been associated with four excellent applications of decision support and group decision support in two agencies within the State of Minnesota. Two applications come from the Department of Human Services (DHS) and two from the Department of Finance (DoF) One of the DHS applications involves group decision support and was the basis for a subsequent DSS application. Because of this relationship, we will begin our presentation with an example of the state's use of GDSS. In each of the four presentations to follow, we will begin with a statement of the problem to which DSS or GDSS was applied, follow with a description of the application itself, and complete the discussion with brief highlights of lessons learned.

3.1 A GDSS Supported JAD for a Social Services Information System

In this example, GDSS technology was used to support a complex management process, namely that of determining the requirements for an information system supporting a number of user groups, each potentially having different needs. The traditional approach would have been to conduct a systems analysis and then, with user involvement, agree on the requirements for the system. Historically the traditional approach has been time consuming, expensive, and frequently failed to meet user needs.

In this case an alternative approach, based upon GDSS was employed to attempt to more efficiently produce a superior product. Although the alternative process involves having access to GDSS software and personnel familiar with its application, it will be seen that the GDSS (and alternative requirements determination process) was highly effective in this example.

3.1.1 The Problem

The Assistant Commissioner within the Department of Human Services responsible for financial management and information systems had been frustrated for several years in attempting to build an information system to support the management of the delivery of social services. Social services cover areas such as: chemical dependency, mental health, developmental disabilities, and services for children. In particular, he was frustrated by the problem of the definition of basic data needed to support the management of the delivery of social services and the special needs presented by various subgroups (e.g., developmental disabilities vs. mental health).

For more than a year, this commissioner had attempted to get the various groups to agree upon the data definitions needed to support a departmental social services information systems and to define the functions the system would perform. He had not achieved this objective and turned to his Director of Information Systems for assistance.

The IS director had been thinking of applying a new and different information systems requirements approach and recommended this approach to the commissioner as a potential solution to the problem. The approach in mind was to support a Joint Applications Design (JAD) process with GDSS technology. In addition, it would be an opportunity to test the approach for its more general applicability. In particular, the two individuals wanted to see if a GDSS supported JAD could do the following things: (1) adequately determine the requirements for a new information system, (2) solve the data definition problem posed by several different communities of users, (3) define common and unique system functionality for the users, and (4) do these things in a timely and efficient manner.

3.1.2 The GDSS

It was decided to use the GDSS available at the University of Minnesota called the SAMM (Software Aided Meeting Management) system. In addition, the JAD process would be aided by personnel from the university's well known management information systems group. Working with the university personnel, three two-day meetings were planned with social services subunits: children's, developmental disabilities, and mental health. Approximately eight persons from each group took part in each meeting. In addition, each meeting was attended by about four people from the administrative area of the social services unit. Thus there were three sessions involving different users, but a common core of administrators.

The GRIP process developed by the University of Minnesota personnel was used in these sessions (See [1] for additional detail on this process). Each of the three groups began by brainstorming their "critical success factors." The GDSS was then used to prioritize these factors. Then the GDSS was used to eliminate any factors that were not related to the information systems project.

Next, the GDSS technology was used to develop "main menu" items that would be used in a social services information system (differing, of course, by which group was using the system). This activity took the first day. The second day was devoted to doing two things with the GDSS. One was to further refine the detail of the main menu functions. The second, and very important, was to define and describe the data that would be required to support the detailed functions. This process was repeated for each of the three groups. Thus, over about a two week period involving six days of meetings, the JAD was completed. In this amount of fairly intense activity, much more was accomplished than had been able to get done in the previous year of activities by more conventional approaches.

Overall, the project was evaluated as being very successful. All of the objectives were met. In the first place, the JAD process worked. Not only was it the case that requirements were stated, they were more complete and better agreed to than by traditional approaches. In the second place, the data definition problem was solved. Somewhat surprisingly, a core set of data was defined that met approximately 85% of the needs of the three user groups. The remaining data needs unique to only one user group were defined and determined to be such that they could be easily supplied. Finally, a common set of functions was identified and unique functions related to a particular user (e.g., developmental disabilities) were determined.

Moreover, the process was completed in two weeks and there was a common exposure to the results on the part of the disparate groups of users. Thus, the development and implementation of the system was anticipated to be made easier by this experience. In this instance, the use of a GDSS system was judged to have significantly aided the solution of a difficult problem, namely the efficient determination of the requirements of an information system which would support several sets of users having somewhat differing needs. The use of the GDSS was so successful in this instance that the decision was shortly made to develop a first prototype of the actual social services information system based upon the children's area of application.

3.1.3 Lessons Learned

In this example, the lessons learned were quite positive. The use of a GDSS supported JAD process for determining information requirements worked exceedingly well. So well, in fact, that the university group who had the GDSS and developed the modified JAD process have done a number of other such systems requirements determination exercises. This application has become a major one for the GDSS system.

3.2 A DSS To Support Children's Social Services

As an outgrowth of the JAD process, management at the Department of Human Services decided to implement a Social Services Information System (SSIS). Rather than adopt the traditional approach of implementing a total system for all functional areas (e.g., developmental disabilities, mental health, etc,) it was decided to take a prototyping and piloting approach (See [2] for a complete description of the process and its underlying rationale). In this instance, a prototype for one functional area would be developed and then a full-blown pilot test would be conducted based on the data from a few counties. Following the pilot, the system would be spread out to all 87 counties. Finally, additional functionality would be added to accommodate the other functional areas.

3.2.1 The Problem

Personnel working at the state level managing the delivery of social services to the residents of the State of Minnesota were frequently frustrated by their limited ability to supply information to various stakeholders as to the status or the effectiveness of the social services systems. For example, a legislator might call a program manager with a question such as, "What percentage of native americans living in my district are receiving chemical dependency treatment in comparison to those in the state as a whole?" The program manager would not have the data at hand to answer such a question and would undertake a special study to attempt to answer the question in the best possible manner. This might take several weeks to get a "good" answer or be in the form of a wild guess if the answer had to be produced in a short timeframe.

Another question might involve budget planning. The governors office might want to know the cost implications of making a change in a mental health eligibility policy. Again, there existed no easy way to respond to the request and a one of a kind special study had to be conducted. Frequently in such instances a request would have to be made to all 87 counties to request the data to respond to the question. Obviously much time was involved on the part of county workers and each new question would generate a new request. There were complaints from county staff about the time they were spending trying to respond to requests at the state level. Additionally, the parties requesting the information in the first place were complaining about the time taken to get a response. Parenthetically, it could be noted that there would have been even more complaints had those making information requests known of the inaccuracy in the information they were receiving.

In addition to the DSS itself, there was great interest in this case in its construction. The notion of building a DSS using prototyping and piloting rather than a traditional building approach was a focus for the information systems group within the Department of Human Services. The building of the SSIS was to serve as a test of the prototyping method of systems development.

3.2.2 The DSS

One major output of the SSIS JAD process described in Section 3.1.2 was the form the SSIS would take. It was learned in the JAD process that the system would be fed by data collected at the county level. The SSIS database needed to be updated only monthly. Thus a system architecture was established such that the IBM AS/400 computers located in the 87 counties would upload SSIS data monthly to an IBM AS/400 located in the state. Program managers would access a DSS running on that machine from their individual workstations.

The Children's SSIS prototype went through nine versions over about the period of a month and a half. Version 1 was a very simple user driven method of selecting logical queries off the database. By version 9, the prototype had been enhanced considerably in terms of its sophistication as well as its ease of use. All the prototyping was done using a forth generation language on an IBM personal computer. The prototyping language was selected such that it runs on IBM systems from personal computers to minicomputers (the AS/400) to mainframe computers.

The Children's SSIS has two levels of operation. At the first (pre-DSS) level, the system can be used to create ad hoc reports. There is a feature in the system that can add an ad hoc report to a standard menu for quick access without restating the logical query. Thus demands on the system such as represented by the first example in Section 3.2.1 can be addressed by this level of operation. A query could be put into the system to generate the number of native americans receiving chemical dependency treatment in a selected geographic region .

This result could then be input to the DSS module to compare to other standards such as by the state as a whole or by selected geographic regions. In addition, "what if" questions could be answered by the system such as the impact of a cost increase in a particular type of treatment or service. It is important to note that the data types and classification schemes for the

SSIS were determined in the JAD process described earlier. This definition materially aided the rapid development of the prototype.

Data for the prototype came from one county (not the largest one, but one of the larger). Approximately 5000 data elements were used in the prototype in order to avoid responding with null cases when users involved in the prototyping process input test queries. This practice was useful, but had some limitations as well.

One difficulty working with users in building the Children's SSIS DSS was that logical queries took a long time (frequently several minutes) to create a response. For many of these users, this was the first time that they had ever sat in front of a personal computer this long without getting any response. The problem was that, even though the PC was fast (a "383" machine) and the database quite small, complex logical queries take a long time to complete in a forth generation language. Had the system been running on the AS/400, this problem would not have occurred. Nevertheless, the lack of response time substantially bothered the users of the prototype DSS even though the situation was explained to them.

Another problem encountered in building the DSS was that there was, in this case, no user champion. The system was sponsored by the information systems division as a test of the prototyping process in building a DSS. Unfortunately, this condition made it difficult to get the time on the part of the users to become involved in the prototyping process (even though only a couple of hours per week were needed).

After the prototype DSS was completed, the highest level social services managers were impressed with what the system could do. In addition, the information systems managers were quite pleased with the DSS prototyping process, even though this was a first attempt and it was agreed that the process could be improved upon in subsequent cases.

In order to take the next step, the pilot of a Children's SSIS, it was necessary to seek a modest amount of additional funds (say U.S. $50,000). Unfortunately, this level of funding was not forthcoming given the fact that the state was, at the time, facing a substantial budget shortfall. Thus, the DSS prototype worked and did what it was supposed to (functionally), but did not have enough support in the user community to carry forward to find internal funding to continue the project into the pilot stage.

3.2.3 Lessons Learned

On the positive side, we learned that an infrequently updated database system fed by a transactions processing system is a very good application for a query and DSS application. We also learned that a prototyping development works given the use of a powerful forth generation language to support it.

We also learned that what others have pointed out--it really helps to have a powerful champion from the user community to support the implementation of the installation. In our case, we were successful in passing the test of using prototyping to develop a DSS. We failed the test of getting the prototype moved onto the pilot stage of operation. Of course, our situation would have been improved on the implementation side had we not faced the serious funding problems at the state level.

3.3 The Buget Information System DSS

The decision support system used in the Minnesota Department of Finance to support the legislative bugeting process is more along the lines of a classical DSS than the first two examples. This decision support system focuses on "what if" types of analysis.

Funding for the operation of the state and for special programs comes from the legislature. The legislature typically meets from January through early June. Most of the final budget decisions are made into law in the last few days of the legislature, but analysis leading up to budget decisions and last minute changes in funding due to political give and take make for many instances of hectic demands for quick analysis of very significant and complex situations.

There are several users of the budget information system DSS. Included are Executive Budget Officers that are analysts working in the Department of Finance, Analysts and staff working in the many agencies within the state government, and legislative staff. All of these parties have access to the budget information system DSS.

3.3.1 The Problem

There exists a vast multitude of situations requiring fiscal analysis associated with potential fiscal and policy decision making within a state as large as Minnesota. There are obviously too many to generate an exaustive list, but a few examples will serve to illustrate some of the situations that can occur.

Recently, the Minnesota Department of Employee Relations (DOER) has been considering a change in the way in which its funds the large amount of training it provides to state personnel (and, in fact, to parties outside the state government). Currently, the department has a training budget as part of its overall budget established by the state. Consideration is underway to charge training participants on a fee basis for classes received. The objective of an analytical exercise is to reduce the overall part of the department's training budget received from the state to 50% and to recover the other costs from training fees. The analysis supporting how to accomplish this (in terms of fee structure, numbers of hours for charging fees, etc.) is supported by the DSS in the buget information system (BIS).

Another, more typical type of analysis, might involve what would happen if a particular bill were to be passed in terms of fund balances (there is the general fund and then there are a number of "special" funds associated with more limited issues, e.g., the enviornment) and cash flows. What makes the situation so difficult during the legislative session is that parties and individuals are constantly making proposals and changes as part of the political process. Thus there is a constant need for "what if" questions to be examined, often with the requirement of very quick response. Other example of using this DSS would involve exploring the issue of inflation, salary increases, and changes in employee benefit structures.

Finally, like the SSIS, the budget information system also has a good deal of ad hoc query capability that supports analysis and decision making, but is not of the "what if" type of application. Breaking out reports by gender, employee classification, and tracking legislation are examples of this type of functionality within the budget information system.

Overall, the problem addressed by the BIS is determining (on a very rapid response basis) the impact of pending fiscal and policy decisions under consideration by the legislature. The various stakeholders involved in the process (especially the legislators and their staffs and the analysts in the Minnesota DoF) needed some way of efficiently generating "views" of the consequences of various actions. The BIS was developed to meet this need, and for the most part, is a DSS in the classical sense.

3.3.2 The DSS

The BIS is a very large and technically complex system. It consists of four modules: Biennial Buget System, Higher Education Financing, School Financing, and Fiscal Note Tracking. It is not a transactional system. It is based upon query and update plus analysis. The systems represents the budget process itself. It is open-ended for reporting and for changing process and procedures. In particular, it is designed for quick response.

When the system was first designed and built in the late 1980s, it was based upon flexibilty and rapid response to change. Originally, the system, built in a well known relational database management language and using SQL (Structured Query Language), was run on a mainframe computer (service provided by the InterTechnolgies group). As operational costs (computer charges) escalated, the system was transferred to a state-of-the-art midrange computer (the IBM RISC/6000) in the early 1990s.

The system is managed and operated by a small staff located in the Department of Finance. The RS/6000 system is connected to the mainframe computer system by an SNA network. The network is used to connect users located in other office buildings in the capitol city of St. Paul. Excutive Buget Officers located in the Department of Finance access the system through an Ethernet-based local area network.

Work is constantly underway to make the BIS DSS more responsive to user needs. In particular, ease of use, is a driving force and work on the BIS is frequently associated with making it easier to use on the part of legislative staff and other remote users.

3.3.3 Lessons Learned

The lessons learned from the BIS at the State of Minnesota are mostly associated with issues related to the DSS rather than the DSS itself. Perhaps the most pressing issue regarding the BIS is its reliability and availability. During the legislative session, it is critical that the system be up and running to support analyses required on a very quick response basis. Moreover, the system response time must be acceptable.

Availability and response time are potential problems because of technological factors. The system availability is threatened by the fact that there is only one RS/6000 computer system and, should it go down, the system itself is down. Response time is affected by the use of the SNA network and is, at present, slow enough in some periods of high use to cause concern on the part of the users.

Both technical issues are being addressed. A dual RS/6000 system is in the planning stages. Additionally, potential solutions are being examined related to the network slowness affecting system response time.

A second issue is associated with the very small staff supporting the BIS hardware and software system. There is only one manager, one software and one hardware system specialist, and one person available on a user "help line." Turnover (and even vacations) on the part of any of this small staff makes the system vulnerable to problems of availability.

Thus, the main lesson learned with regard to the BIS DSS is that, because of its high visibility and critical nature, more effort has to be expended to protect against the system being down or unavailable to users. Extra resources must be expended to ensure that the hardware and software is up and running at virtually all times. External consultants have argued the case to management that it is necessary to spend extra money on hardware to protect against system failure. Similarly, the case for backup personnel (expensive and hard to get when dealing with a new technology like the RS/6000) has been made.

3.4 The Revenue Forecasting System

As this is being written, there is a budget crisis of unparalleled magnitude in the United States in the State of California. That state is facing a budget shortfall of $11 billion. Because of the magnitude of the crisis, dramatic steps have to be taken. Arguments over the nature of the exact nature of these steps such as major cost reductions, significant tax increases, or combinations have the state legislature and the governor unable to take action. Because of this deadlock, the state is paying employees and creditors in "script" rather than money. Recently, major banks have indicated that they no longer will accept the script. Other symptoms of the magnitude of the problem are, for example, large numbers of tenured faculty at the state's universities are going to be terminated (over 100 at San Diego State University, for example, and that is only one of more than 20 such institutions).

One (among many) reasons that this problem has occurred in California is that there was a failure to accurately forecast the state's income in terms of tax revenue. This same problem has faced the State of Minnesota, although because of the size of the latter state, to a much less dramatic level.

3. 4.1 The Problem

Years ago, fiscal crises would occur in Minnesota in times of economic slowdown. One reason for this happening is the failure to accurately forecast state revenues. One reaction to this series of happenings was to create a state "budget reserve" of half a billion dollars. In essence, this reserve protected against poor economic times. It also protected against poor revenue forecasting.

One step in solving the forecasting problem was to create a decision support system to assist in making improved revenue forecasts. Whereas the Budget Information System operates on the cost side of state operations, the Revenue Forecasting System addresses the income side of the equation.

3.4.2 The DSS

As with the Budget Information System DSS, the Revenue Forecasting system is a DSS in the classical sense. "What if" type of analysis is supported. There are a variety of sources of revenue within the State of Minnesota. Taxes are the major source of revenue. Income taxes on individuals and corporations are the major source of revenue with the revenue generated from a 6.5% sales tax representing the second largest source. There are also taxes on transfers of assets such a real property. Another source of revenue comes from fees, especially from licenses. The state derives revenue from licenses on drivers, automobiles, boats, snowmobiles, boats, and marriages to list the best known.

Obviously all of the revenue amounts are related to the level of economic activity in the state (and in the nation as a whole). The revenue is also very sensitive to the tax and fee structures. For example a small change in the income or sales tax rate will have a large impact on the amount of revenue raised.

The Revenue Forecasting System is a decision support system that allows testing of all sorts of assumptions regarding the generation or revenue for the State of Minnesota. This DSS runs on large scale personal computers. The reader can probably imagine the types of use to which this DSS is put, but two rather non-obvious examples will illustrate how it has recently been put to use.

The first example involves the forecasting of revenue generated from capital gains taxes associated with the sale of assets such as real property and stock. The United States has been experiencing a period of economic difficulty since the late 1980s. During this time, tax revenue to the state has dropped dramatically due to the general economic decline and its direct impact on producing reduced tax revenue. One area of particular concern was that of revenue from capital gains.

During poor economic times, individuals and business have less money to spend on acquiring assets such as property or stock. The problem was to attempt to adequately anticipate how the capital gains tax would be reduced because of less activity in sales of assets. The Revenue Forecasting DSS was useful in modelling this situation and helped the State of

Minnesota head off an even worse budget deficit because of reduced revenue in this area.

A second example involves forecasting the revenue from increased tax on cigarettes. The problem in this case is to be able to model the effect of situations such as the following. First, there is the impact that an increased tax rate would have on producing revenue. The increase is obvious if the level of purchase remains constant. The problem is that an increased tax on cigarettes may lessen the total demand for cigarettes because of the increase in the cost. An even more difficult situation involves the smokers who may travel to border states to buy cigarettes at a lower cost. Again, due to this factor the total demand for cigarettes will drop and the expected level of revenue will not be realized.

3.4.3. Lessons Learned

The lessons learned in this case are quite obvious and are consistent with what others have observed. First, the DSS must have the capability of including the appropriate independent variables associated with the problem. This is a completeness issue. The Revenue Forecasting System meets this requirement.

The second lesson is that it is not the model (DSS) that makes the difference, it is the cleverness of its user. In our first example given, the easy part is to input the tax rates, and the level of capital gains activity. The art is in being able to anticipate the effect of a slowdown in economic activity so that the latter level is accurate. The DSS will accurately calculate the revenue from its input, but it is the human user who must pick the correct values for the input variables. In our second example, the ability to forecast the relationship between the demand for cigarettes and their cost (how many people reduce or give up smoking, or go to South Dakota to buy cigarettes) is the difficult.

Thus, the major message is one that is well known:

a DSS is only as good as its user.

4. BENEFITS

In these examples, we have seen three instances of very successful GDSS or DSS use. In the one instance that does not meet the success criterion, one could say that it was the implementation that failed rather than the DSS itself (the state budget crisis certainly did not help matters either in this instance). Among the benefits of using decision support that we note are:

1. The DSS (or GDSS) process has helped people make better decision whether they be in designing an information system or in making better forecasts of revenue available to the state.

2. In the case of the GDSS, there was definitely a better consensus (buy-in) on the part of several user groups than had been the case before the group decision process was employed.

3. The DSS systems used by the state offer significant improvements in the flexibility over previous systems.

4. The use of advanced technologies (such as forth generation languages and database software) used in these systems makes them much more evolvable (able to be changed) than previous systems.

5. CONCLUSION

In conclusion, we would like to again emphasize that our experience has been very positive regarding the use of DSS and GDSS technology within the State of Minnesota. We also would like to note as a sort of "lesson learned" from the lessons learned that it is activity associated with the use of DSS and GDSS that often affects their success.

Note that the GDSS was used in a well tested JAD process and its success was very much associated with how it was used rather than the use itself. In the DSS for social services, emphasis was placed on how it was built and on the use of prototyping. The inability to complete this project had to do with lacking a user champion and other factors of a behavioral nature rather than a technical nature. The Budget Information System DSS was very much affected by system availability and performance which in turn were related to technical and staffing issues. And, finally, the Revenue Forecasting System was dependent on the artistry of its user as much as the nature of the system itself.

6. REFERENCES

1 L. Wanninger and G. W. Dickson. "GRIP: Group Requirement Identification Process: The Integration of GDSS Technology into the Systems Development Life Cycle," *Proceedings of the Twenty-Fifth International Conference on Systems Sciences*, Kauai, HI, 1992.

2 L. Wanninger, and G. W. Dickson. "GRIP-P-P-E-R: The Use of Group Technology and Prototyping in Systems Development," *Proceedings of the International Federation of Information Societies Working Group 8.2*, Minneapolis, Mn, June, 1992.

PART II

SYSTEMS DESIGN AND IMPLEMENTATION

Decision Support in Public Administration (A-26)
P.W.G. Bots, H.G. Sol and R. Traunmüller (Editors)
Elsevier Science Publishers B.V. (North-Holland)

Decision Support for Financial Management in Local Government

Michel R. Klein
HEC School of Management
78350 Jouy - en - Josas
E-mail KLEINM at HEC11.Bitnet
FAX 33 1 39565742

abstract: After recalling some earlier results on the use of the financial analysis and planning DSS "Siad - Mairie" used in french towns this paper describes the user-interface and main functions of the four integrated DSSs which constitutes "SIAD Mairie". These DSSs support the tasks of financial analysis and planning, project financial management, debt management and monthly cash management. The use of the DSS by the town financial manager and outside analysts is described. The paper then outlines future research directions on impact of the system on planning practice and the difficulties faced when trying to increase the use of the system.

1. Introduction.

This paper describes (1) the set of Decision Support Systems which have been used to support financial reporting and planning in french municipalities, and (2) the use of the system to help computing financial consequences of scenarios considered by the town council.

We have in a previous paper (Klein 1986) described the main functions of the system and the standard steps in municipal financial planning. The present system is in fact the result of the integration of four DSSs :

- a DSS for financial analysis and planning,
- a DSS for project management,
- a DSS for cash management,
- a DSS for debt management.

The primary purpose of the DSS is to facilitate reporting on financial situations and to perform financial planning in order to estimate future financial needs. The DSS for financial management component is a recent update (1992).
We have in another paper (Klein 1991) described the new trends in french town financial planning and the result of a survey on the use of the system in 40

french towns. With respect to the tasks which are supported by the system the survey has shown that they are the following (the % represents the number of times this task was cited as one being currently supported by the system:

- computing the financial needs resulting from projects and maintenance work (80%),
- simulation of financing to forecast the evolution of debt and the servicing requirements (80%),
- simulation of fiscal policy (50%),
- computation of self financing capacity (50%),
- annual budget preparation (50%),
- variance analysis (actual - budget value) and management control (30%).

The main goal of this paper is therefore to describe briefly the user interface of the system and the extended possibilities introduced by the relations between the financial reporting and planning DSS, the Debt Management DSS and the monthly cash management system. The future developments will also be sketched out.

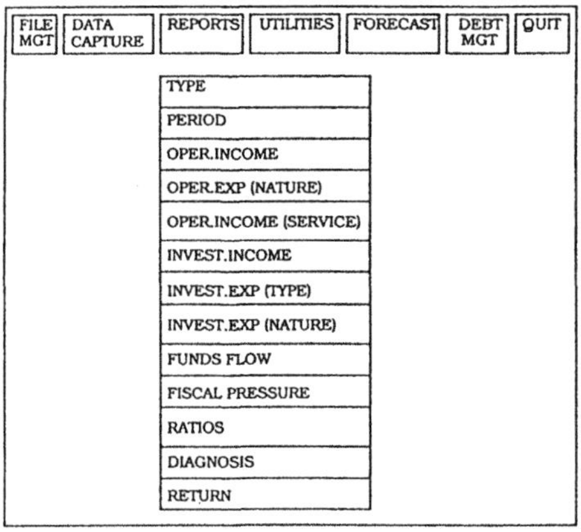

Fig. 1. Main menu of financial analysis and planning with report sub-menu

2. Description of the application

The functions of the application comprising the four integrated DSSs are best described by the system opening menu shown on fig. 1.They are as follows :

- file management,
- data capture,
- computing and display of reports and expert diagnosis,
- definition of ad hoc reports and graphics,
- simulation of financial strategies,
- cash management,
- debt management.

These four DSSs have been implemented using the knowledge based DSS development environment Optrans Expert (SIG, 1989).

2.1 Financial analysis and planning DSS

The financial analysis and planning DSS and project management DSS takes care of the five first functions described above.
The file management function enables the financial manager to create, delete, rename... the data file concerning a town finance.
The data capture function is used to enter and modify the historical data.The data used by the DSS is of two kinds . Firstly data relating to the town itself secondly data emanating from the Interior Ministry concerning national averages and statistics (see fig. 2). These data are from the french accounting plan called M12.

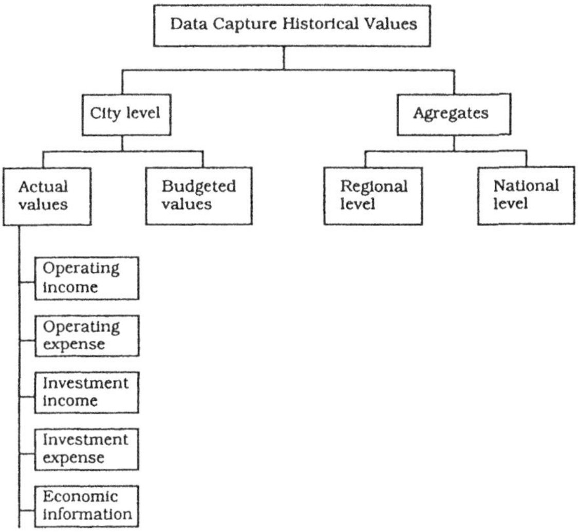

Fig. 2. Structure of historical datastored in the system

In France the cities above 10,000 inhabitants are required to follow this accounting plan M12, the structure of which is worked out by a special commission from the Interior Ministry and specialists from the French Accounting Association. The data is broken down between several groups of variables :

- operating income (31),
- operating expenses (sorted by nature 15),
- operating expense (sorted by service 24),
- investment income (13),
- investment expense (sorted by nature 21),
- economic information (sorted by service 19),
- national regional statistics (16).

We have shown in parentheses the number of variables in each category. These variables are the ones which have been found to be at the right level of agregation to use by the user group of towns financial managers.

The computing and the display of report function is used to compute a series of standard reports and diagnosis. The list of these reports is given on fig. 1. They are the following :

- operating income,
- operating expense broken down by nature,
- operating expense broken down by type of service,
- investment income,
- investment expense broken down by type of investments,
- investment expense broken down by type of service,
- fund flow statement,
- measure of tax burden,
- ratios,
- diagnosis.

All these reports (except the diagnosis report) are numerical tables which can be computed for their actual value, their budgeted value or the variance .They can also be computed in % of the the total or in % of variation from one fiscal year to the other.

The user can change the values of the variables presented in the reports using the options, he can also change the time period considered using the period entry.

The diagnosis is a text which describes the evaluation of the financial data of the town. This diagnosis uses several criteria such as activity level, investment, revenues, debt etc... and was briefly described in Klein (1991). This diagnosis uses the financial knowledge base of the system. This knowledge base is still at the experimental stage.

The "UTILITIES" function allows the user to define his own report or select any graphical presentation for variables used in the system. The reports are made of lines and columns , with variable names as lines and time periods as columns. Titles can be added to the report.

The simulation function is used to let the financial manager define scenarios. These scenarios correspond to various alternatives considered by the mayor and the city council.
The menu of this option is shown in fig. 3, with the sub menu of the operating expense option open. The fig. 3 shows the main options which represent groups of variables on which the user can act.

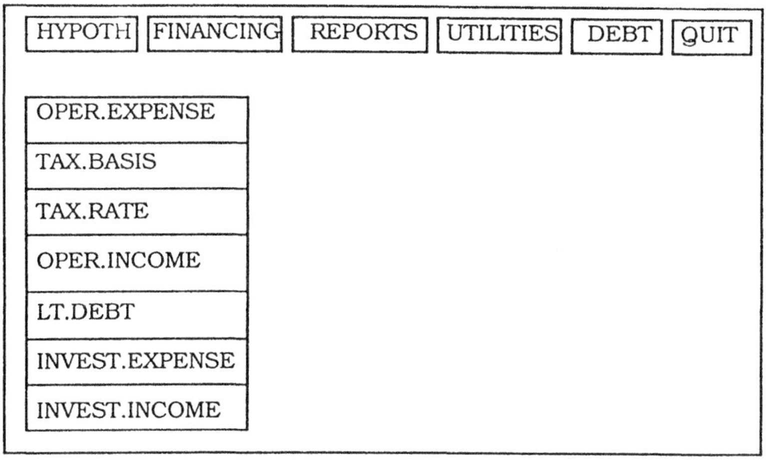

Fig. 3. Forecast menu, with hypothesis sub-menu

These groups are the following :

- operating expense,
- tax basis,
- tax rate,
- operating income,
- cumulative Long Term Debt,
- investment expense,
- investment income.

The system automaticaly provides estimates for future values which extrapolates the trend for some variables, which are computed for others and so in this way it is possible to request the printing of reports in particular the fund flow and ratios reports. The fund flows show the need or excess cash position , the ratios reports shows a serie of criteria to evaluate a scenario from the financial point of view. The finance option allows the user to enter a financing policy : amount of loan, type of loan, interest rate, duration, etc...
The expert option still at the experimental stage allows the user to obtain a diagnosis of the scenario using the expert module . In this way a scenario is evaluatedso as to be coherent with the historical diagnosis.

The investment option allows the user to enter an investment as an aggregate amount or as a portfolio of projects.

The investment as an aggregate amount is used for studies when no specific important investment whose impact needs to be evaluated.
This agregate option is used to ascertain wether if a level of investment over the planning horizon is compatible with the self- financing capacity of the town and its long term debt (LTD) evolution.
The portfolio of investment projects is used (usually in parallel with the agregate option) to study the impact of each specific investment project.
With this option (the DSS for project management) the user will be able to define for each new project: its name, the amount of investment needed, its type (building, refurbishing, depreciation or not...). For each period over the horizon the associated operating expenses :

- salary,
- exterior services,
- etc...

(This break down of expenses being coherent with the break down used in the operating expense report).

For each period over the horizon the associate operating income :

- project revenues,
- financing from local and central government specific to the project.

2.2 the DSS for debt management

In France many projects will be partialy financed by public money coming from the department the region or the state. The Debt management function is used to solve a particular problem may be specific to the french environment.
The option allows the financial manager to enter the list of all outstanding loans for the town with their caracteristics and compute an agregate repayment schedule over the planning horizon. This schedule is computed in term of agregate capital repayment schedule and agregate interest on a yearly or monthly basis. The yearly schedule is used for the financial planning DSS, the monthly schedule is used for the cash management DSS.
The debt management subsystem or DSS is a key element in the planning process due to the complexity of calculation implied, the number of loans and the type of loans.

With respect to the number of loans in France it is of the order of 50 loans for a town of 25,000 and over a hundred different loans for a town of 100,000 inhabitants . An important town such as Lyons has about 400 loans !.
This large number of loans was in the past due to the practice of associating a loan with each project of any significant size.
The second reason for the importance of the Debt Management subsystem or DSS is that although the french law requires a town to approve a balanced budget this is only true for the following year's budget.

It is often true that certain abuses of "in fine" loans has been observed (loans for which the capital reimbursment is made in one lumpsum at the end of the loan). In this kind of loan the capital reinbursment is made in one shot at the time of the capital final repayment installement.

Since towns still are not required to draw up a real balance sheet (a situation due to change in 1996) it is very important to compute the loan repayment schedule beyond the horizon of the one year budget and if possible on a 3 to 5 years horizon. Also, town councils guarantee banks loans to companies. These companies are usualy mixed private-public companies in which the town council is a participant. As a consequence a complete appraisal of the risk exposure for a town must included all the loans where the town acts as a guarantor.

The DSS for debt management is used to:

- enter modify, add, delete the loans which create the portfolio of debts of a town,
- compute and print as tables or present as graphics globaly or loan by loan annualy or monthly the loan repayments schedules,
- create and save filters. These filters are used to work on subsets of the loans according to the banks or the beneficiary or any combination of them.

The loans which can be taken into account are loans with:

- fixed or variable interest rate,
- with or without differed payment of capital and/or interest,
- with constant annuity or constant depreciation.

Given the amount of data to manage and their structure the DSS for debt management uses the Optrans DBMS.

2.3 the DSS for cash management

French towns do not have much flexibility to manage their cash. Given the fact that the money they manage is public money, they are only allowed to make deposit of their excess cash at the "Trésorerie". The Trésorerie is a service of the Financial Ministry .The excess cash receiving an interest at the rate of 2%.

However, a Cash Management Support System is very important since the city is receiving the income from taxes from the government on the basis of last year income. With updates during the year. Similarly the "Dotation Globale de fonctionnement (DGF)" is provided by the central government by twelves. By the month of March the town financial manager still does not know the exact amount he will receive per month for the current year. With respect to the expenses most are known.(salary expenses, interest and capital of present debt...). However the financial manager must recompute its monthly cash position many times according to:

- new investments or maintenance work decided,
- subsidies received,
- changes in the operating expenses,
- changes in the policy for paying suppliers,
- etc...

The DSS for cash management is then used frequently to recompute the monthy cash needs or excess. The cash manager usualy negotiate lines of credit with banks and will use these lines according to the needs. These financing in their turns create changes in the interest expenses and have to be taken into account.

This system requires the exact computation of the monthly global capital and interest repayment on loans. Given the large number of loans (see § 2.2) and the complexity of the financial computation needed this can only be done using a computer.

2.4 Integration between the DSSs.

The integration is carried out on two levels :

- one being the functional and interface level
- the other being the transfer of data from each DSS to the others whenever needed.

The first type of integration is presented on fig. 1 which shows the pull down menus with key words to select the subsystem (specialised DSS) needed.

The second type of integration is shown by fig. 6. The project management DSS provides input to the Planning DSS for the operating expenses , the non fiscal income and the investment variables. The Debt Management DSS provides input to the Planning DSS and the Cash Management DSS. The inputs being the interest and capital repayment schedule. It should be pointed out that presently the four DSSs are used on the same workstation (typically a PS with a 386 processor and a 80 MBytes hard disk). The most resource demanding DSS being the Debt management DSS. Due to the recent availability of a LAN version for Optrans (for Netware) it is now possible to consider a distributed version of the application with , if needed , DSSs located on different workstations. In particular the DSS for project management could be located in the technical services of the town and provide information to the financial planning DSS located in the financial services through the file server of the LAN.

3. Use of the application by the financial manager

The possibilities of uses of the DSS by the financial manager are best explained by fig. 6. At a given time the system stores :

- the present hypothesis for the operating income and operating expense of the city,
- the present list of loans with their parameters and current hypotheses for indexes evolution if the interest rate is index linked,
- the present portfolio of projects, whose size justifies their individual treatment.

It is then possible to compute global evaluation criteria such as :

- tax burden on the population and companies,
- debt level of the town.

At the present time the level of service supply is not explicitely measured in the model. Except that the level of change in each of the 15 classical services to the population are measure in term of operating expenses or investment expenses (Klein 1991). If a new investment is envisaged, the financial manager will add this investment into the portfolio of investment with the associated operating income and operating expenses.

The use of the Funds Flow option will then provide immediatly the new need or excess cash for the town over the planning horizon.
In case of excess cash (not a very frequent situation) it is then possible to consider decreasing the fiscal burden on inhabitants or companies (evolution which is heavy with political consequences).
The choice of spreading the tax burden between companies, freehold property owners, freehold land owners, land owner, and inhabitants is highly political.
In case where cash is needed (a more frequent situations it is then possible to :

- increase the tax burden ,
- take a new loan,
- reschedule the investment,
- sell some asset.

These possibilities can be directly tested by:

- playing on the four taxes rates (see fig. 4),
- entering a new debt at the debt management subsystem level (see fig. 5),
- redefining the project specifications at the portfolio of projects level.

A very frequent situation which towns all have to face nowadays is a change in the tax basis due to the bad economic conditions. The tax on companies is based on investment level and wages expense.
The consequences of the economic conditions on the financial situation of the town can be calculated instantly by just changing the hypothesis on the evolution of the "Professional Tax base".

The system has achieved a fairly large distribution (it is probably the most widely used financial planning system in french towns) since about 40 towns are using it, the author (and many users) consider that the system is far from being used to the extent it should be.

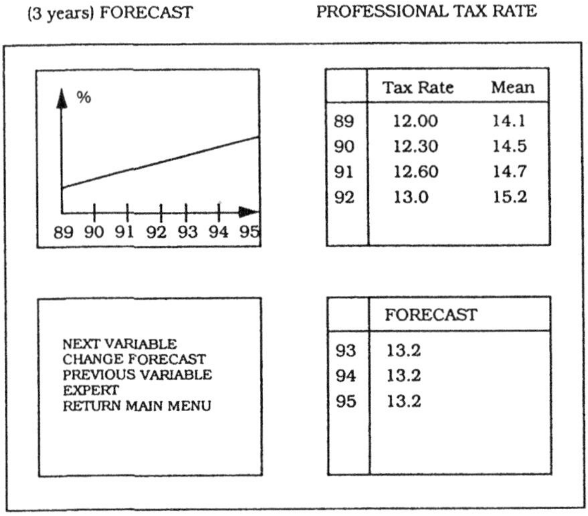

Fig. 4. Assisted hypothesis entry for tax rate

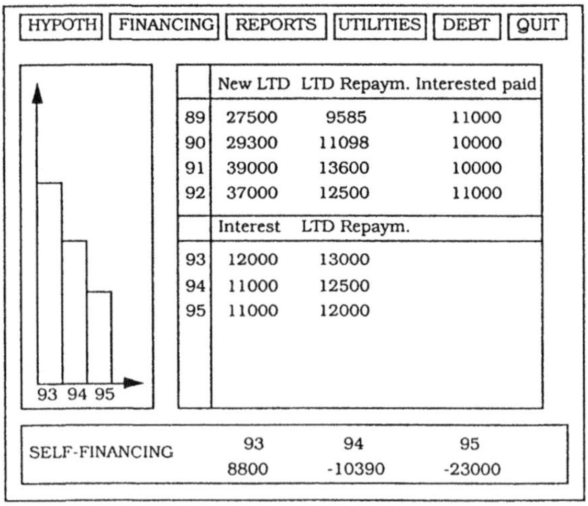

Fig. 5. Evolution of present stock of debt (the future debt repayment scheduled is transfered from the debt mgt subsystem)

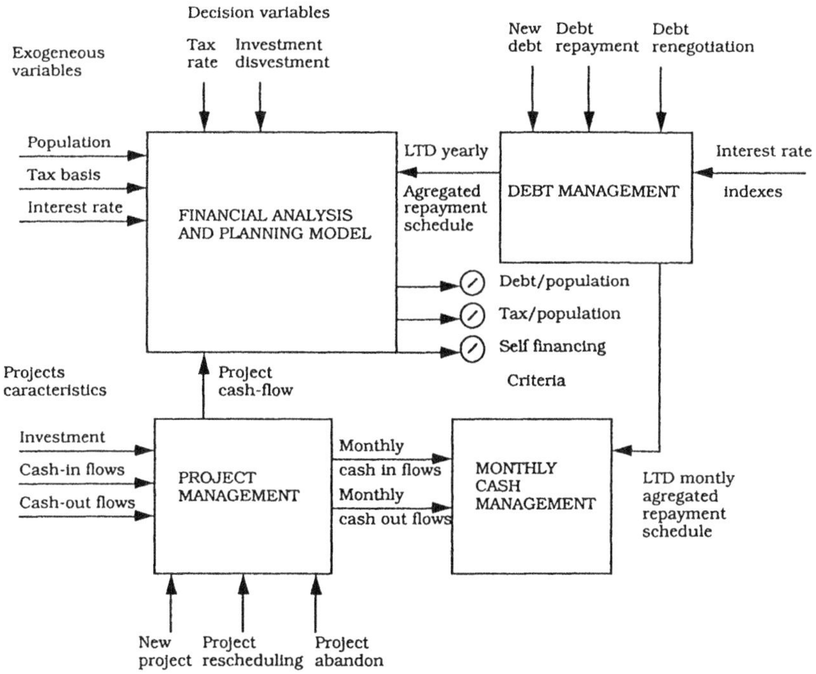

Fig. 6. The DSS models and their relationship

We believe this is due to the fact that the present users are exclusively the proffesionnals (the town financial manager). The mayor and town clerk are not using the system and the town financial managers do not seem to be motivated to present the system to the mayor .The problems encountered when one wishes to improve the use of the system seems to be related with the following dificulties:

- how to motivate within a bureaucracy (the problem of incentives),
- how to make members of the the elected council aware of the importance of financial planning ,
- how to embeded methodological support within the DSS tool,
- how to improve the quality of data (mainly project data).

For example it seems to be difficult for the financial services to obtain data on the projects(investment amount , cash-inflows and outflows, etc...) which they need from the technical services.
The training required to learn how to use the financial analysis and planning DSS and to know the financial models is covered in a two days seminar. The training required to use the Debt Management DSS is about half a day, a further half day being used to help the financial manager to start the data capture.

4. Use of the system by outside financial analysts.

It must be pointed out that even if the system is still mainly used by financial managers of french towns, it is more and more used to make the financial analysis of towns by bankers and outside financial consultants.This is due to a recent evolution which has seen several French towns in financial difficulties. As a consequence a more rigourous evaluation of risk of loans being tied up is now considered a requirement by most banks financing towns.

5. Future research directions.

The system is presently being used by about 40 french towns which have created a user-group. Given the size of this user group a very interesting research direction which is now feasible is to study :

- the impact of the system on the financial planning procedures of the towns using it,
- the critical success factors in having the system used by municipalities.

One of the problems is that the Director of Finance ("Directeur Administratif et Financier" or DAF in French) simply does not have the time to explore all the possibilities of the system. The elected town representative are not as yet using the system themselves but some attempts by the Directors of Finance to use system during meetings of the City Council have been observed. It is clear that the elected representatives in the town council especially the Mayor and the assistant financial Director should be interested since it helps them to understand and compute the various costs of their policies. Since french law only requires the establishment of a yearly balanced budget the incentive to make long range financial scenarios is not yet very strong.

So up to now the elected towns representatives have not yet fully explored the greater advantages steming from a better knowledge of such systems. A survey of elected representatives and financial Directors, using a questionnaire, to ascertain the perceived advantages and drawbacks of such systems should be very rewarding.

The introduction of such DSS is a relatively important change in the traditional financial management of towns. The management of this change is also quite difficult. Methodologies for introducing change described in Bouldin (1989) or Klein, Methlie (1990) have been used . The introduction of such a system is made more difficult due to the fact that many town financial managers claim to be overworked. A further difficulty is due to the fact that the mayors and his town councilors are often unaware of the advantages to be gained by using such software tools for the implementation of their policies and to generate financial savings.

An other research direction will be to study the impact of a new version of the developement environment allowing a better separation between decision models and user interface definition. This should lead to a better readability of the models and improve model comprehension by users. This research will imply transfering the system to the environment described in Klein (1992,1993).

6. Acknowledgments.

We would like to thank professor Victor Hargreaves for his comments on stylistics, professor Pieter Bots for some pertinent remarks .
A communication on the subject of this paper was made during the IFIP TC8/WG 8.5 meeting on Computer Supported Cooperative Work and Public Administration held at the University of Linz , Austria on February 25-27 1992. Comments made during this meeting were helpful in improving this paper.

Bibliography

Barbara M. Bouldin, Agent of Change, *Managing the Introduction of Automated Tools.,* Prentice Hall , 1989.

Joseph Carles, François Gendron, François Labie, Serge Regourd , Les Collectivités Territoriales et leur Financement, *Revue Banque* , 1990.

Michel Klein and Thierry Villedieu, A Knowledge based DSS for Financial Planning, in *Engineering Costs and Production Economics,* 12 (1987) p212-227 , Elsevier Science Publishers.

Michel R. Klein, Dominique Roux, Thierry Villedieu, Decision Support for Municipality Financial Planning in France , in *Governmental and Municipal Information Systems II,* R. Traunmüller (Editor), Elsevier Science Publisher (North Holland) 1991.

Michel R. Klein, Leif Methlie, *Expert Systems: A Decision Support Approach,* Addison Wesley (1990)

Michel Klein, Roland Traunmüller, Architecture and User Interface of Knowledge Based DSS, in *proceedings of the 26 Hawai International Conference on System Science,* Maui Island 5-8 january 1993. Ralph Sprague Jay Nunamaker (eds) , IEEE Computer Society Press vol 3 pp 108-118. (1993)

Michel Klein, Cyrille Danes, Design of a Second Generation Knowledge Based Decision Support System, Communication at the 2nd ISDSS Conference: Exploring the Next Generation of Decision Support, FAW , University of Ulm 22-25 June 1992.

Optrans Expert, *User Manual,* version 2.35. SIG (ed) 4 bis rue de la Liberation 78350 Jouy en Josas, France.

Decision Support in Public Administration (A-26)
P.W.G. Bots, H.G. Sol and R. Traunmüller (Editors)
Elsevier Science Publishers B.V. (North-Holland)

BAUX – A KB DSS for municipalities supporting legal decisions on building permits

Alfred Schramm

Abteilung für Rechtsinformatik, Karl-Franzens-Universität Graz,
Schubertstraße 6, A-8010 Graz, Austria

Abstract

The methods and techniques reported in this paper for the construction of KB Legal DSS go far beyond the immediate use made of them for the developement of the specific system BAUX. Indeed, BAUX is but an example for a more general approach towards supporting public administrations at "inferring" correct legal decisions. After a general statement of the problem of how to support officials at their duty to administer the law, especially to make legal decisions, the practical needs of such support are confronted with some theoretical problems encountering them. In order to overcome these problems, the strategy is proposed not to try to make computers think but to make them *look like* thinking. Next, some details of the project BAUX are presented as well as some features of its design. Outlines of an example session should help to realize how BAUX presents itself in real use.

Keyword Codes: I.2.1; I.2.4; I.2.7
Keywords: Artificial Intelligence, Applications and Expert Systems; Knowledge Representation; Problem Solving

1. The problem situation: (statute) administrative law and the duties of civil servants

By virtue of Article 18 of the Austrian Constitution (B-VG), any official action of the administration (resp. of its members) must be grounded on, and accord with, valid legal (usually statutory) rules. This presupposes, of course, that a civil servant must *know* the law in order to know whether, and if then how, to take action in accordance with his legal duties. But *to know the law* is a pretty complicated matter to which we shall attend, among other things, in Section 2. Suffice to keep in mind that there is a peculiar *Problem of Knowledge* to be dealt with.

The federalist organization of Austria adds some more complications which may be sketched here only as far as necessary for clarifying the problem situation. Austria is a federal state consisting of nine member provinces (Bundesländer). Accordingly, there exist legislative bodies on both federal and province levels. Administrative authorities are active at federal, province, and municipal (communal) levels. This leads in some cases to a peculiar mixture of authorities of differing levels, administering law of, again, differing levels.

Building law and its administration is a case in point. The building laws (Bauordnungen) as such are statutes at the provincial level (for instance, the Styrian Building Statute; Steiermärkische Bauordnung [Stmk BauO]). The law of administrative procedures (Verwaltungsverfahrensgesetze [VVG]) is federal law. And the administration of the building laws is in the first instance within the sphere of communal or municipal authorities.

In the province of Styria, to stay with our example, there are 544 communities and municipalities of different size (ranging from tiny, with 300, to comparatively large, with 270 000 inhabitants), each of them with their own mayor and local authority. The executive body of a small community may consist of only a few persons, none of them with a background of law education at a university level. But their duty is to make legal decisions which, at times, may be very difficult even for lawyers.

Our problem, in a nutshell, is then the following: *Civil servants at local authorities (possibly without much training in law) are obliged to make legal decisions, vic. to administer the provincial building laws under observance of the federal law of administrative procedures.* ***Can we help them to do their job more savely, quickly, and efficiently?***

2. Practical needs and theoretical issues

Let us consider now the practical needs of such an official who administers the building law, and, at the same time, let us theorize about what lies behind his dealings.

Standard situations are that an official decides on some brought in application, or that he considers whether, and if then how, to take proper legal measures in respone to some matters of fact having been made known to the authority. Typical output of the authority are decrees which are addressed at some individual and which contain a statement of some order and/or permission as well as a statement of the reasons for the respective order and/or permission plus an information about the procedures for eventual remedy. – *How can the official arrive at such output (a decree) from such input (an application or some matters of fact)?*

2.1 Logic

A standard answer (at least in most statute law environments) is that this works by "judicial subsumtion" which, schematically, looks like this:

Premise 1 (General Legal Norm):
Any individual ***x*** *showing qualification* ***Q ought*** *to meet legal consequence* ***C***

Premise 2 (Individual Matter of Fact):
Individual ***a*** *shows qualification* ***Q***

Conclusion (Individual Norm):
Individual ***a ought*** *to meet legal consequence* ***C***

This looks pretty "logical" and has been formalized along the following lines: read the *alethic* □-operator ("necessary") as *deontic* ("obligatory") and use the formalism of some suitable modal calculus, then you have:

P1:	$\forall x(Qx \rightarrow \Box Cx)$
P2:	Qa
C:	$\Box Ca$

Unfortunately, this is all to no avail (notwithstanding the hard labour from G.H. von Wright to Alchourrón and Bulygin). A Logic is, basically, a theory of correct consequence relations, i.e. of such relations which necessarily never obtain between agreed upon premises and unacceptable conclusions[1]. But no deontic consequence relation has been produced that far which is both rich enough to produce all obviously valid normative inferences and, at the same time, avoids all of the well known deontic paradoxes (like Jørgensen's Dilemma). In other words: to date, there doesn't exist any acceptable logic of norms which could be written down in the suitable format of a calculus.

But if we cannot *write down* the rules of some logic, then we cannot *implement* it either! Thus, there is no way of "logic programming" inferences of normative statements.

Nevertheless, our civil servant at the local authority *does* quite obviously draw normative inferences. If we want to help him with his duty, then, may be, we can *simulate* normative inferencing. Why bother that the computer can *really* draw normative conclusions! (We can't make it anyway.) Make, instead, the computer *look like he did* on the surface, and nobody will care about *what's underneath*.

There is no doubt that such a brutally pragmatic (behavioristic?) approach will raise violent protests among some AI purists. But theirs is a different problem than mine. It's none of my business to *make the computer think*. My business is to construct a machine such that, from acquaintance with the user interface, *the civil servant is tempted to think that the computer thinks*.

2.2 Reasoning

But even *if* we could implement deductive reasoning of normative statements, this would be only one minor step on our way towards solving our general problem, which was: How can we help an official to arrive from his knowledge of some general legal rules and of some matters of fact at a legal decision? Certainly, he does it by *some* process of reasoning. But it is also certain, that this process of reasoning is *non-deductive*. Only *after* the necessary reasoning has been done, the whole structure consisting of general norm, matters of fact and concluding individual norm can be presented in the nice form of a (deductive) judicial subsumtion.

The reasoning process has something to do with the old problem of what comes first: hen or egg. Some factual matter is "relevant" depending on whether there is an according legal rule at issue, and a legal rule is at issue depending on whether there exist according relevant factual matters. In other words, our official will consider some factual matter as relevant only if he remembers the "right rule". But which one of the rules that he knows can he consider as the "right one" if he doesn't first consider the factual matters?

---

1 This formulation is a bit vague in order to embrace all kinds of intensional logics. For extensional logics take "true" and "false" instead of "agreed upon" and "unacceptable".

There is no purely logical or generally algorithmic method for solving such problems within reasonably many steps. But judicial practice has developed heuristic procedures, mainly in the form of rules about "which questions to ask first", and these heuristic rules have much in common with so-called eliminative induction. One can often tell a good lawyer from a bad one, simply by observing how he systematically narrows down the range of hypotheses about possibly "fitting" rules of law through asking for matters of fact and eliminating those rules for which the given constellation of facts constitutes no .case in point.

Like above, we can argue that as there is no good algorithm for this kind of reasoning we cannot implement a general reasoning procedure for finding fitting rules of law, given a constellation of facts. But we can mimic the good lawyer and have the computer "ask right questions in right order". If it does, nobody need complain about that there is no reasoning process hidden behind the computer's surface behaviour.

2.3 Natural language

But even after achieving this, there is the language problem left. What, if we have the computer ask questions like whether there is "imminent danger" or whether some work "affords merely minor changes of the site"? Every competent speaker of a natural language believes to understand such questions. However, what he usually understands is their *everyday* meaning, but not their *legal* meaning. The legal meaning of such terms as "imminent danger" [Gefahr in Verzug] or "minor changes" [geringfügige Änderungen] has been specified by rulings of the high courts and do not fully coincide with the everyday meanings of the same terms.

In principle we could have the computer communicate (pose questions) under presupposition of everyday meanings. But this would be an ardous task both for developers and users, because then we would have to let the computer ask as many everyday language questions as are necessary to make sure whether, for instance, legal language imminent danger obtains or not.

It is better, to compromize on this and require *some* understanding of legal language on the side of the user. (After all, he is a civil servant.) As further help, we provide an easy to use dictionary of legal terms.

3. The project: team, tools, and methods

Such were the presuppositions for the BAUX project, and the goal was to build a system which systematically inquires all and only the relevant facts through posing questions to the user in a near to everyday language, finds out the relevant legal rules, tells the user whether and if so which legal measures to take, and produces, if appropriate, legally and formally correct decrees.

The team consisted of a project leader (Alfred Schramm), a systems engineer in charge of designing system details and the user interface (Heribert Moik), a knowledge engineer for the legal knowledge base (Stefan Soukup), a knowledge engineer for the decrees knowledge base (Stephan Moeller, later Johann Potakowskyj), a lawyer as general legal domain expert (Peter Pavich) and a lawyer and civil servant as practical domain expert (Robert Schober).

As tools we employed the expert shell Nexpert Object which suited well our purposes because of its hybrid rule/object nature.

There is an example from the rule network:

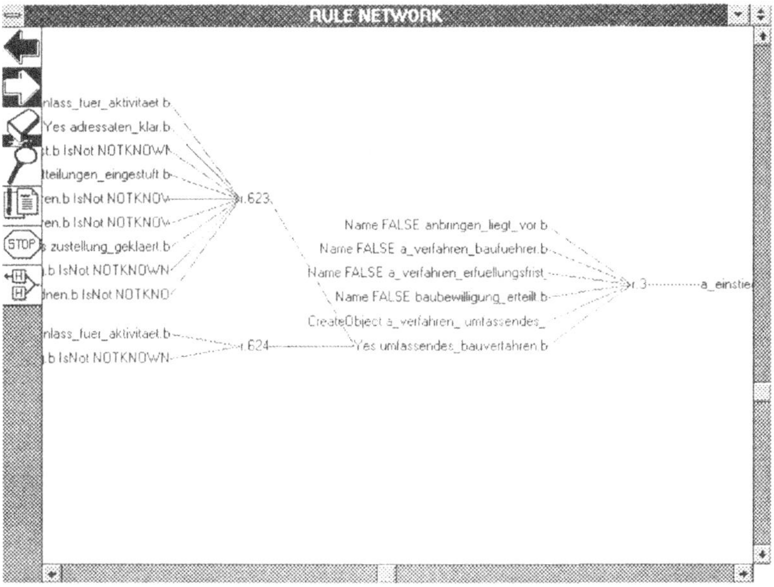

... and there is one from the object network.

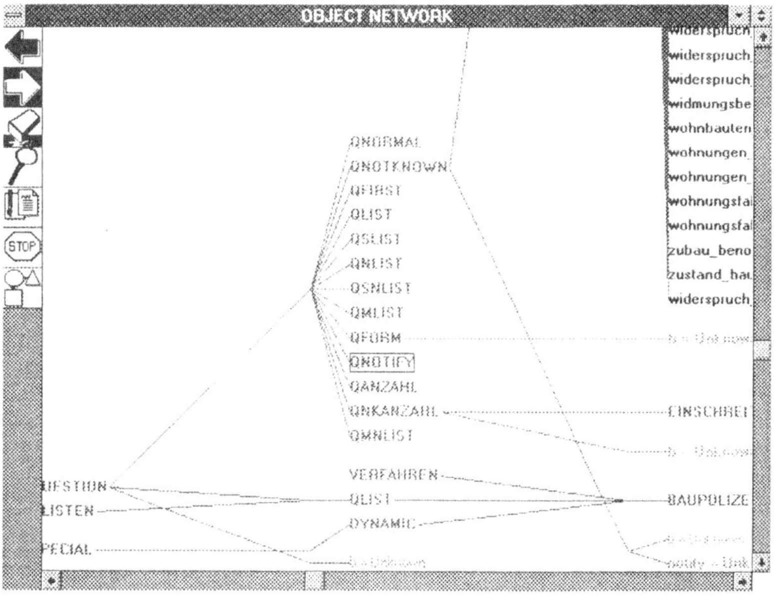

The user interface was designed under strict obedience to MS Windows standards and programmed in C. It consists of a *dialog window*, where questions are posed by the system and *answer buttons or answer menues* offered to the user, and a *protocol window*, where the user's answers and the system's conclusions are recorded. The *legal language help* (implemented with the Windows help tool and its hyper abilities) pops up sensitive to the context of the respective question to be answered.

Development procedures for suitably chosen "chunks of law" consisted of a pre-structuring of the laws in quasi logical form by the legal domain expert, a first implementation by the knowledge engineer, and a joint adaptation session; similarly the procedures for the implementation of the decrees.

The project started in September 1991 and was finished (one month late) in January 1993.

We expect the system to be well maintainable, at least we have taken according measures already at the system design phase. The test period showed that a not too complicated bug in the knowledge base usually would need half an hour for repair.

4. An example session

BAUX.ICO

From the Windows Program Manager doubleclick the BAUX icon ...
... and, when the BAUX opening screen shows up, choose the intended legal procedure:

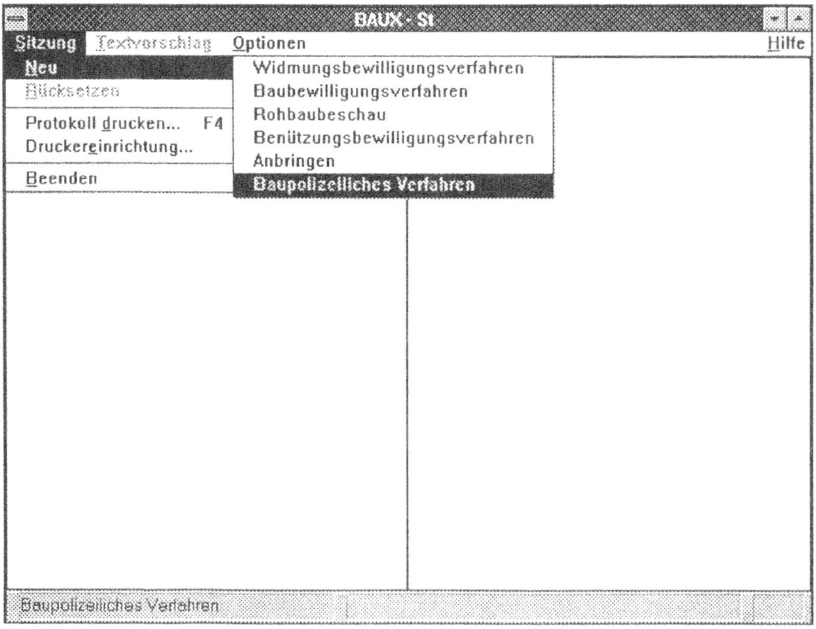

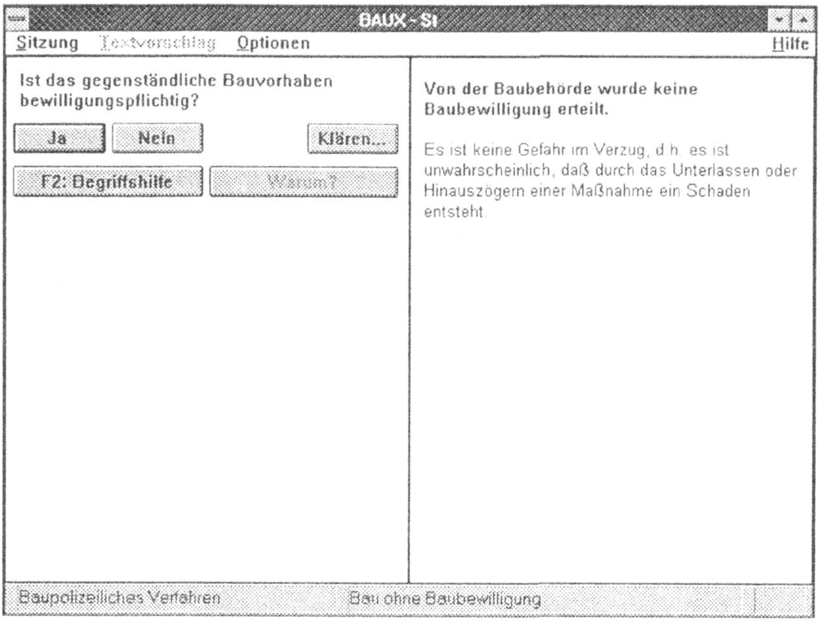

You may answer 'Yes', 'No' or have the question investigated. Context sensitive user help...

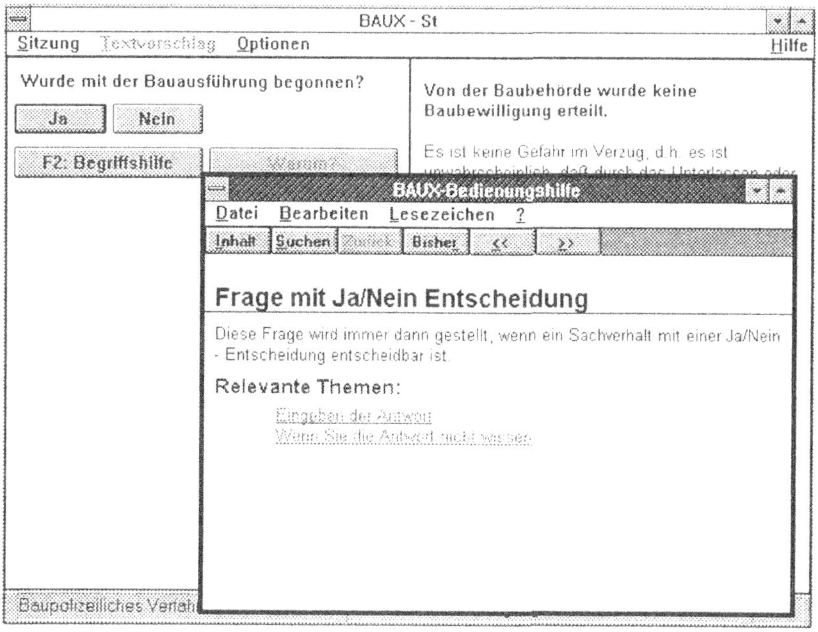

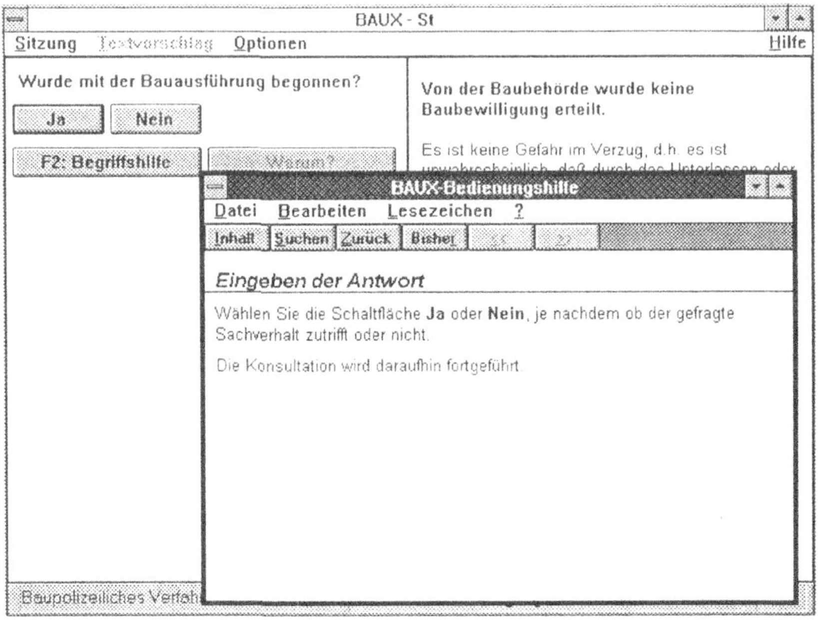

... tells you how to handle windows and buttons. First legal inferences drawn by the system...

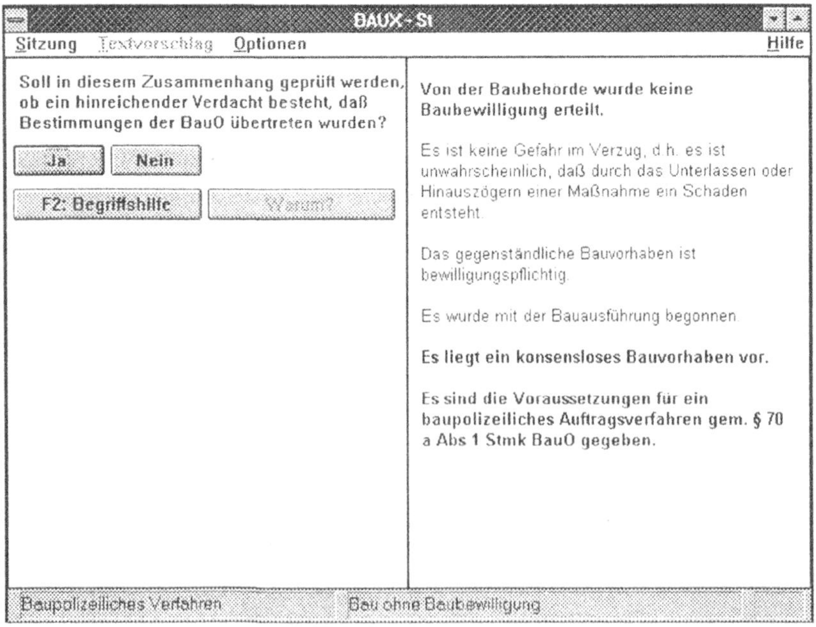

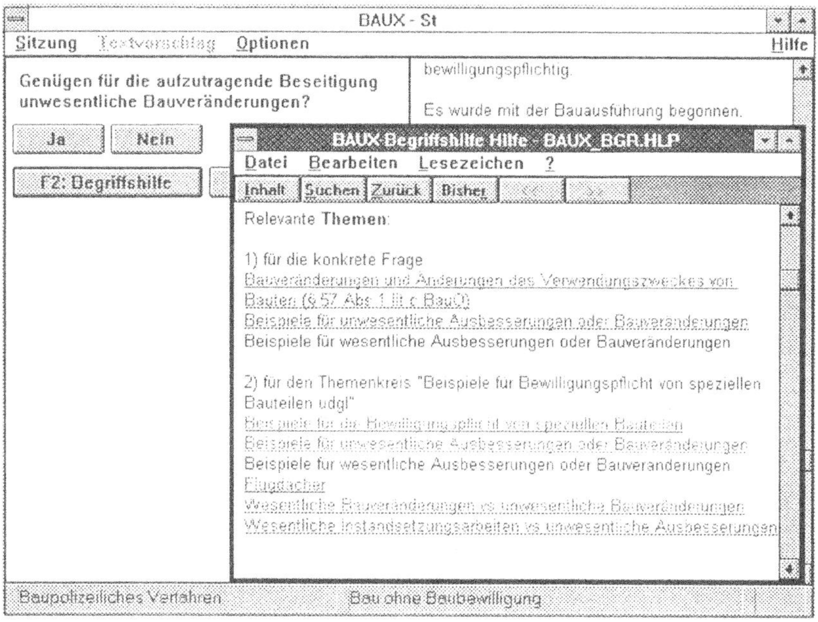

Kontext sensitive legal dictionary explains the meaning of the relevant terms of the questioı

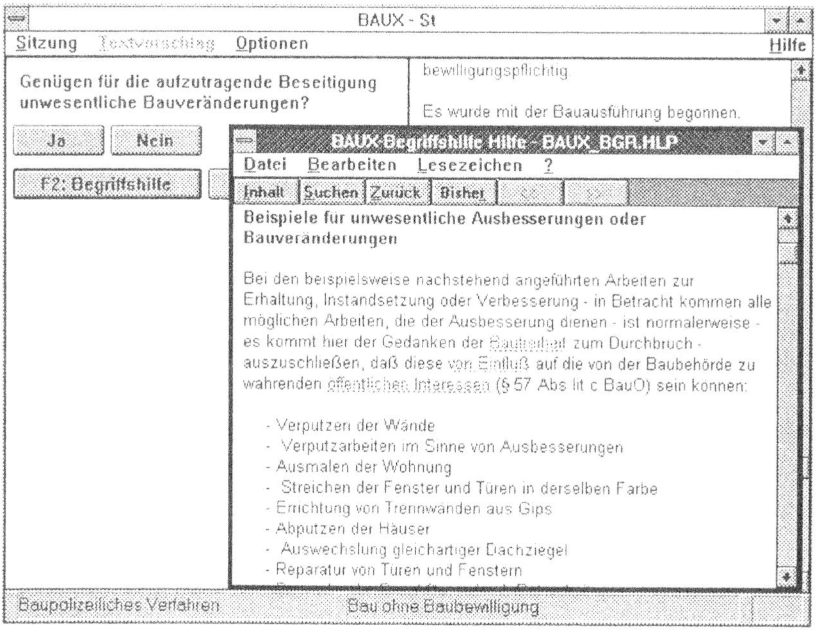

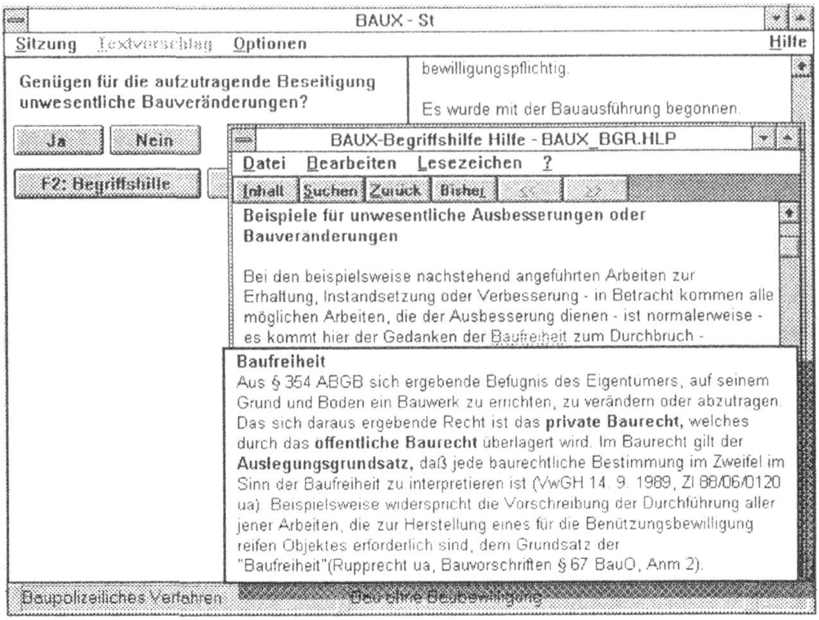

Session finished; notification of legal measures to take

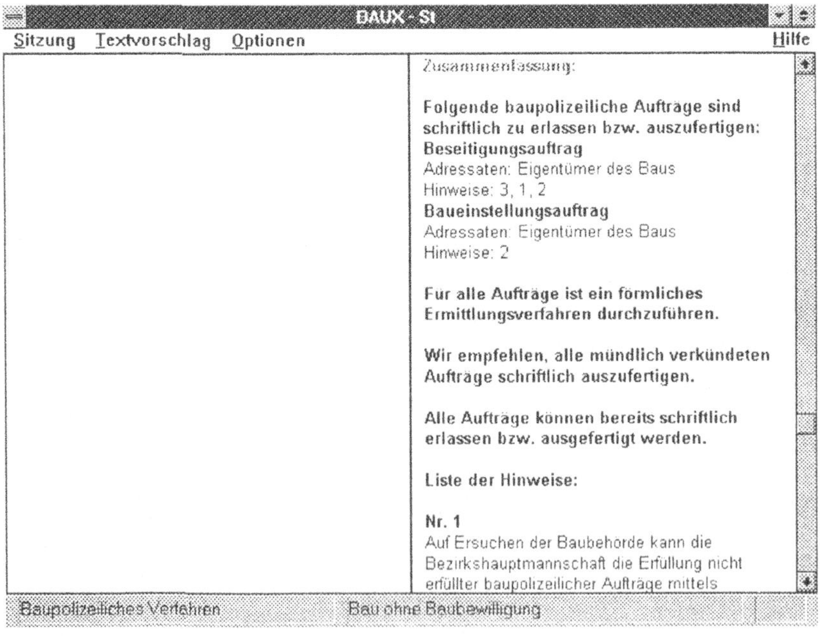

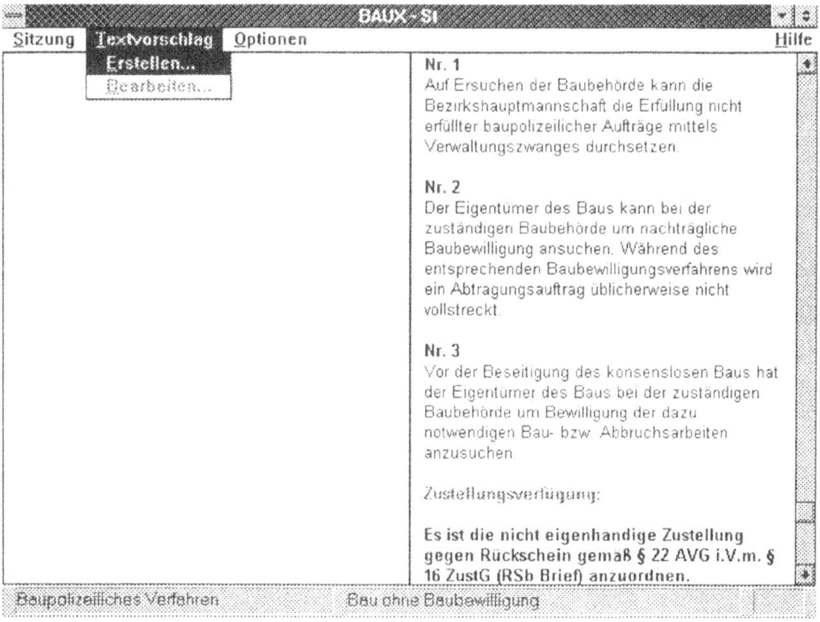

Next ask for producing an decree ...

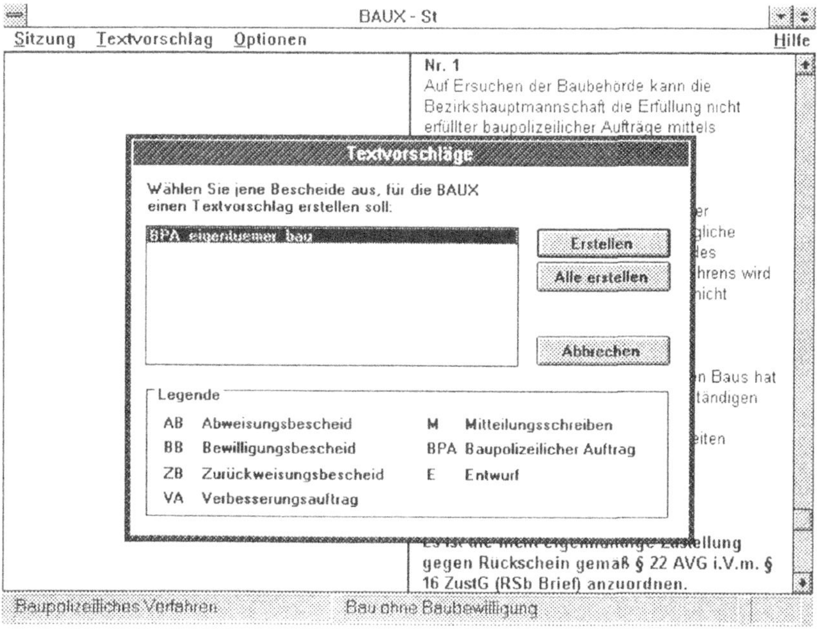

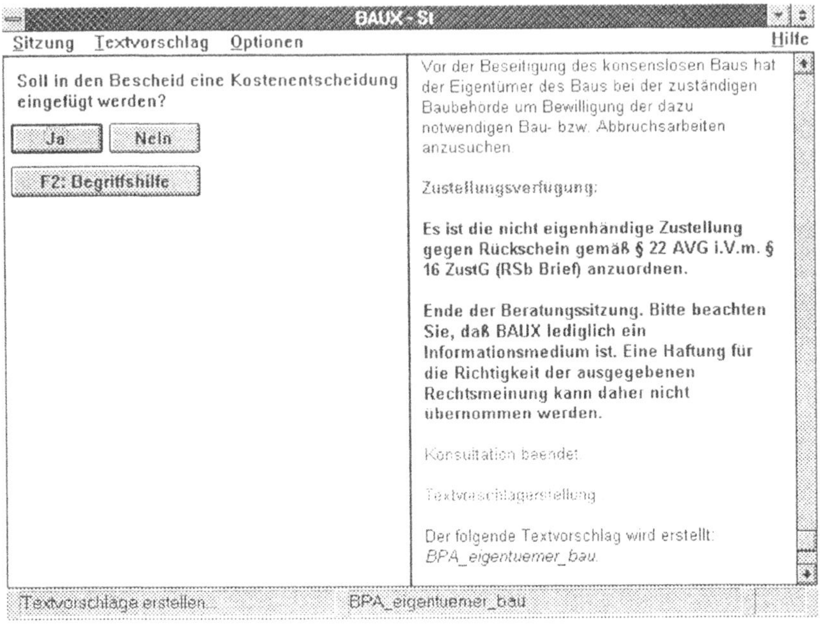

... and after some more questions ...the decree is loaded in the text editor

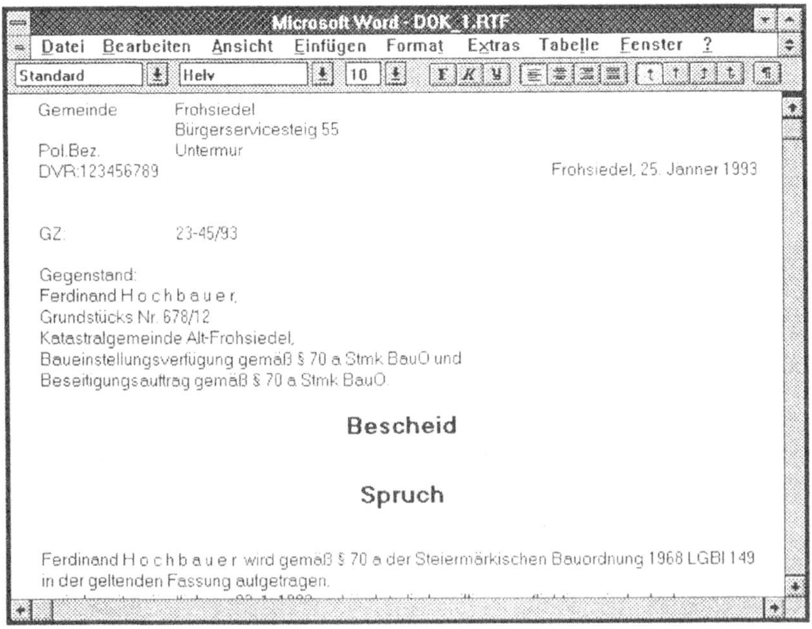

Decision Support in Public Administration (A-26)
P.W.G. Bots, H.G. Sol and R. Traunmüller (Editors)
Elsevier Science Publishers B.V. (North-Holland)
1993 IFIP.

Work-Time Measurement System (WTMS): The Front-End Tool for Redesigning the Work Process

Binh Q. Nguyen

The U.S. Army Institute for Research in Management Information, Communications, and Computer Sciences (AIRMICS), 115 O'Keefe Building, Georgia Institute of Technology, Atlanta, Georgia 30332-0800. Note: On 1 October 1992, the name AIRMICS was changed to Software Technology Branch, Army Research Laboratory.

"Out of all the time we know, today is the hardest to judge. There's so much before our eyes it blocks our sight; and the details move so fast we cannot see any of them fairly; and the noise they make confuses."

The Gift of the Unicorn—Percival Hunt

Abstract

Trying to understand the current work process in detail was the prelude to change for improvement. Since April 1990, AIRMICS has been using an internally developed work-time measurement system (WTMS Tool) to increase efficiency and to utilize the work force more effectively. Efficiency was realized by using more advanced computing technologies to improve or to automate certain work activities. Effective utilization was achieved by tracking and ensuring that the work force was spending time doing the correct tasks in the correct priority.

The WTMS Tool described in this paper is an automated system successfully implemented at AIRMICS for providing the management with critical information on how work time is distributed among assigned tasks and what activities are associated in doing a specific task. Work-time data are collected from the work force by using a windows-based computer application. Data are statistically calculated at non-working hours, and the results are electronically mailed to management and interested members during the night on a monthly basis.

Organizational cooperation and leadership were the two critical factors that led to successful implementation of the WTMS Tool at AIRMICS. Cooperation was secured because measured data were not used for evaluating the quality of work or setting performance standards. Another factor was that management used the information to improve the organization, its people's skills, and the work process.

1. INTRODUCTION

1.1. AIRMICS Identification

AIRMICS is a subordinate element of the United States Army Information Systems Engineering Command (USAISEC) based in Fort Huachuca, Arizona. The USAISEC exists to provide the U.S. Army with vital engineering and acquisition services supporting the Information Mission Areas: telecommunications, automation, visual information, record management, publications and printing.

AIRMICS is a research organization that exists to investigate advanced technologies that can be inserted into Army information systems within the next three to five years. Technology areas being investigated at AIRMICS include: Decision Support, Distributed Systems, Software Engineering, Communications and Networks, Very Large Databases, and Management of Information. Serving AIRMICS are engineers and scientists, the civilian and active-duty members of the U.S. Total Army Team. We conduct, sponsor, and administer exploratory and applied research programs in cooperation with other government agencies, industries, universities, and industry-university cooperative research centers.

The Work-Time Measurement System, also known as the WTMS Tool, is one of AIRMICS' recent accomplishments in the Decision Support area. Because the tool is assisting members of AIRMICS in better managing work and time, AIRMICS would like to share the experience. The reasons and approaches in developing the tool, descriptions of the tool and its uses for gathering data and generating information, examples of how the information supports AIRMICS' decisions on redesigning its work process, and the lessons AIRMICS learned from using the tool are described in this paper.

1.2. Background

Since 1989 international and national trends and events have affected the U.S. Army tremendously. While the world is looking forward to enjoying the new era of peace and prosperity, the end of the Cold War and the American public's demand for peace dividends have caused the U.S. Army to undergo a major restructuring although its mission remains the same [1].

Consequently, AIRMICS, as well as other U.S. Army organizations, faces the most challenging time in its history. While its mission will be the same, its resources will not. To do more mission-essential tasks with less resources, AIRMICS had to cut its overhead drastically. AIRMICS has reduced 75% of its administrative and clerical support personnel, and it might be losing one management level.

Having anticipated the changes to the organizational structure and its members, AIRMICS found innovative ways to cope with its highly uncertain future. In February 1990, we decided that we had to redesign our work process; however, before we could do anything, we had to understand the detailed information about how our projects and tasks were done and how work time was distributed among them. We needed to know where our time was spent doing our work and what activities were required in doing it. Detailed understanding of the current work process was our prelude to change.

Meanwhile successful projects of redesigning/reengineering work processes had been reported, and the Department of Defense (DoD) had just begun a major program to reorganize its information systems. The use of modern information technology to eliminate outdated workload was one of the main factors that led to successful reengineering work processes of some major U.S. Corporations [2, 3, 4]. The reengineering and transferring of an old software application running in a large computer to a smaller computer resulted in a change of the work process with significant increase in efficiency and cost saving at an U.S. Army installation [5, 6]. Applications of Strassman's method of Return on Management to the reengineering of DoD's functional processes were also expected to save system cost tremendously [7, 8].

Measuring work-time spent on current activities of an existing process was perhaps the easiest technical step but most critical step to do in a business process redesign [9]. Accordingly we decided to do the easiest step while other steps were the topics of our research and development projects. In addition to the effort of developing the WTMS Tool and in a joint effort with other researchers, we have sponsored and conducted a research project to model business processes using object-based methodology. The first result of this effort was presented at a technical conference [10].

1.3. The Goal

AIRMICS' goal for this effort was simple: To be able to get detailed information on work-time distribution accurately, conveniently, and quickly. We needed to know how much time was spent on each task, what activities were involved in doing a specific task, and how much time was spent on each activity, organizationally and individually.

AIRMICS' goal was neither to set time-and-motion standards for any of our activities nor to use the computerized information system to ubiquitously monitor its members' work activities because AIRMICS is not a capital-intensive labor organization. AIRMICS is part of the intellectual capital of the U.S. Army.

1.4. The Objective

AIRMICS' objective was to develop a computer-aided work-time measurement system for our staff to systematically decompose their work process into a set of associated activities and to record the time spent on doing each. The system had to meet our goal and to be easy to enter and to retrieve data, so that it would not consume large amounts of valuable time and effort of our staff.

2. THE WTMS DEVELOPMENT DECISION

The decision process involved us in making several intermediate decisions before selecting the final alternative that best suited our goal, objective, and our existing computer network. The process also helped us in assessing ourselves before deciding whether we had to develop the tool by ourselves or acquire it from a third party and then adapt ourselves to it.

2.1. Assessing the Situation

At that time AIRMICS had a list of projects and tasks grouped under our major research areas and a list of activities that we assumed would be required to do the work. We had very little idea on how much time our professionals spent on doing specific activities. We also had a network of Sun workstations that enabled all of us to transparently share our electronic data and information. The network was set up to take advantages of the Sun's Network File Server (NFS) technology. What we needed was a work-time measurement tool that could exploit the *SunView* window environment, electronic mail, and file sharing capabilities of our network.

2.2. Estimating Consequences

AIRMICS leadership understood its members might have a negative perception about, or perhaps resistance to, collecting detailed work-time data. Resistance could arise if its members perceived that AIRMICS would behave like a manufacturing plant in which the management would constantly be looking over their shoulders and requiring them to spend more time and effort doing the extra work of entering the data.

Our director explained to all members the goal and the challenge AIRMICS had to face to preclude the negative perception. We devised an easy-to-use work-time measurement tool that took less than five minutes of use per day to minimize the effort involved in collecting data.

2.3. Developing and Evaluating Alternatives

To meet its goal, AIRMICS had to automate the process of keeping track of activities and reporting work-time distributions and to reject all methods requiring manual computation of data. Rejected approaches included the use of a notebook to log daily activities and interviewing members. Although the use of the notebook met the accuracy specified in our goal, it failed to meet the convenience and the quickness. Had we taken this approach, we would have spent much more amounts of time than we ever wanted to compute the statistical results, even if we were augmented with an electronic calculator. While the approach of interviewing members gave us the convenience and the quickness, it failed to deliver us the accuracy of the information. With this approach, we would have had the convenience of not keeping a log book and still getting the information any time we needed it; however, the information would have been very inaccurate because it would have been only the best recollection of our members.

Having rejected all manual methods, we then still had to determine whether we had to develop the tool by ourselves or acquire it from a third party then adapt ourselves to it. A quick library search revealed only one electronic work-time measurement method using an electronic spreadsheet [11]. Although it could greatly reduce calculation time and could be adapted to suit our needs, the use of the spreadsheet would still consume more time and effort to input data than we were willing to sacrifice. Furthermore, the sharability and integratability of work-time data using the spreadsheet were questionable.

2.4. Selecting the Alternative

We had no other alternative but to develop the tool ourselves because we found no existing tools that could meet our goal. Moreover, by doing it ourselves, we had the opportunity to generate further ideas for improving our productivity and for future research projects in the decision support area.

3. IMPLEMENTING THE DECISION

3.1. Developing the Philosophy

To ensure the success of developing and using the tool, AIRMICS leadership specified and believed in the following:

- *Centralized Projects and Tasks Distribution.* AIRMICS leadership had to reserve the right to manage and control each project done at AIRMICS. Non-management members were to focus on a management-prepared list, which specified current projects and their associated activities to be done at AIRMICS.

• *Decentralized Control of Work.* AIRMICS members were empowered to do their work by freely selecting whichever activities were necessary to accomplish their assignments.

• *Flexibility.* Because of dynamically changing requirements, the organization had to be flexible, so did the WTMS Tool. When AIRMICS did different tasks or projects, the only thing related to the tool that had to be changed was the task list—not the tool.

• *Information Availability.* Measured work-time information had to be available and accessible to all members—not just management—whenever they needed it.

3.2 Developing the WTMS Tool

Having assured that members would cooperate in using the tool for logging their daily activities, AIRMICS management decided to develop and implement an electronic logbook. We started an internal project called *Timesheet* to develop a work-time measurement system consisting of two main components: a recorder and a reporter.

3.2.1. The Work-Time Recorder

The Work-Time Recorder is a *SunView* window-based computer program written in the C programming language running within the *SunView* environment. Using software buttons and three-level pop-up walking menus, the recorder program provides the user with a graphical user interface (GUI) for entering and retrieving work-time data stored on disk files with dates and activities used as the references. The first level of the menus contains major technical areas; the second, tasks or projects; the third level, work codes or activities. All menu items are taken from a management-prepared, centrally controlled task list. Whenever the task list is edited, the contents of the menus are dynamically changed accordingly.

The names and physical locations of data files are completely transparent to the user; that is, an average user does not know their names or locations. The user is completely free from the task of managing data files. The program also provides the user with a nicely formatted weekly worksheet using documentation tools available in our computer system. Hence, the work-time recorder is better known as the Weekly Timesheet (WKTS) Program at AIRMICS.

The WKTS Program is so easy to use that not one of our members had to spend more than five minutes to learn it. Furthermore, the program even includes an on-line, electronic user-manual page, but our members never need to read it. The user-friendly feature of the WKTS Program really helped our members to quickly learn the tool and has helped to ensure that all activities and time are accurately reported. End-user productivity is tied directly to functionality and ease of learning and use [12].

3.2.2. The Work-Time Reporter

The Work-Time Reporter is a non-interactive computer program written in the C programming language running within Sun Operating System environment. The program is designed to convert work-time data into work-time distribution information by performing some basic statistical calculations that include the absolute time and percentage of time that an individual, a team, or the whole organization spent on doing each task or project and each activity.

The Work-Time Reporter also prepares data files in the format that can be loaded into the Oracle Relational Data Base Management System (RDBMS) to provide more flexibility in analysis about work activities and work time. The Structured Query Language (SQL) can be used to retrieve more specific information from the database. Statistical values not calculated and information not reported by the Work-Time Reporter can be obtained by querying the RDBMS.

4. METHODOLOGY

4.1. Gathering Work-Time Data

Our professionals use the WKTS Program to log their time spent on doing daily work activities. The program is usually left running in the form of an iconized application placed at the corner of the screen to serve as a reminder and a convenient means readily available to enter work-time data. With a single click of a mouse button, the iconized application reappears on the screen as a fully interactive application ready to accept input data.

Entering work-time data on a single task requires the user to spend about 30 seconds performing a three-step sequence. First, the user presses the mouse button to invoke the task-and-activity menus; second, selects an appropriate task and an associated activity; last, uses the keyboard to enter the time spent on doing the activity.

Printing weekly work-time worksheet on a laser printer is simple. The user simply moves the mouse cursor to the software button labeled print and clicks the left mouse button without being concerned with the technical details of how the worksheet is prepared and printed.

4.2. Generating Work-Time Information

We obtain our monthly work-time distribution information very easily by setting the Work-Time Reporter to generate the information at the first hour of the first day of each month using the *crontab* utility available in the Unix-based system. The *crontab* utility is a very convenient way to generate periodic work-time information without human intervention. When the information is accumulated, it is electronically mailed to management and interested members during the night. Upon arriving at work, the information is already available for reviewing in their electronic-mail boxes.

5. APPLICATIONS OF THE RESULTS

We began collecting data in April of 1990. Monthly reviews of the current work process and its environment have been conducted since that time. We have incorporated our work-time distribution information into our decision processes to improve our organization and work processes throughout the period.

5.1. Supporting Decision Makers

• *Planning for the Inevitable Change.* One of the most useful applications of our work-time information was that we heavily relied on it in preparing a transition plan for our organization as it was being transferred into a different headquarters. While the on-going restructuring was taking place, we were much better prepared to accept the changes because we knew where we were and what we could do. Measuring work time was our prelude to change.

• *Increasing Efficiency and Effectiveness.* The work-time information provided us with more concrete evidence on exactly what we did, how much we did, and how much we could do. Measured work-time information could be used as the basis for requesting staff increases, but more importantly, it helped us prioritize our efforts, improve on efficiency, delete unnecessary work, and thus increase our effectiveness without adding personnel resources.

• *Correcting Deficiencies in the Work Process.* After having analyzed the work–time information and talked with members who had reported the information, we were able to discover which activities could be automated or improved by the use of a computer hardware or software. Activities that were automated were things we had done periodically such as sending out messages reminding members to prepare weekly or monthly reports. Activities that were improved by the use of a more functional software or a faster computer were mostly document preparation and information distribution.

• *Cutting Meeting Time.* The work–time distribution information helped us realize more concretely how large a portion of our time had been spent in meetings. To reduce meeting time, we started using Group Decision Support System (GDSS) tools [13] to conduct some of our meetings. We have seen a dramatic improvement in productivity using these tools.

• *Controlling Work.* To effective employ our professional work force, we needed to ensure that our engineers and scientists were working on the correct tasks in the correct priority. We also wanted to monitor the amount of efforts they spent on administrative and clerical tasks, which had been previously done by support personnel. The work–time information was used to identify these tasks and prioritize efforts to reduce the time spent on them. In Sassone's words [14], we needed to maximize "intellectual specialization" of our professional work force.

5.2. Supporting the Non–Management Workers

• *Tracking Work Time.* The work–time distribution information helped staff members better control their own time and focus on their performance objectives, for they understood where their efforts and time had been spent in doing work.

• *Estimating Completion Time.* Members who tracked their time carefully gave management more accurate completion dates for their currently assigned tasks and better estimated person–hours needed for future tasks. Better estimates were essential for managing technical projects, monitoring contractor performance, and preparing or evaluating technical proposals.

6. LESSONS LEARNED

• *Facts vs. Perception.* Measured data were the facts. These facts changed our perceptions. Activities we enjoyed doing, we had thought we did not spend enough time on them; conversely, things we disliked, we had thought we spent too much time on it. For example, our leave time (vacation, sick, holiday, administrative leaves) represented a relatively larger percentage of our work time than we had previously thought.

• *General vs. Specific Information.* General information about the distribution of work time sufficiently met our needs. Our monthly reports, automatically generated by the Work–Time Reporter, provided us with adequate information about what we had done and how we had spent our time. Although we could get more specific information by querying the relational database, we found it unnecessary.

• *Centralized vs. Decentralized Control of Activities.* AIRMICS' philosophy enabled members to work more creatively. Some projects and tasks were technically similar, but their associated activities were different from each other. This difference indicated the autonomy that AIRMICS members enjoyed in doing their tasks.

• *Planned vs. Unplanned Tasks.* The organization's stability was reflected on the percentages of time spent on planned and unplanned work. When the organization was in stable condition, more planned work was done; otherwise, when requirements were constantly changing and sometimes conflicting with each other, time spent on doing unplanned work represented a large percentage of the total time.

• *Graphical User Interface (GUI) vs. Non-GUI Application.* The response time of a user command determined the applicability of a GUI. Time spent waiting for the computer to finish its work was a waste of productive time. That was the reason the work-time reporter was designed to run non-interactively, so that we were able to run it in the background or during non-working hours. On the other hand, the decision to incorporate GUI in the work-time collector was a successful decision, for the GUI provided the user with a convenient method for entering, saving, retrieving work-time data.

7. CONCLUSION

Organizational cooperation and leadership were the two critical factors that led to the successful implementation of the Work-Time Measurement System at AIRMICS. The first factor was the management's decision not to use the information to evaluate members' performance encouraged members cooperation by providing accurate data. Another factor was that management used the information to improve the organization, its people's skills, and the work process.

The WTMS Tool has been an effective decision support tool satisfying our organizational goals, objectives, and needs. The AIRMICS leadership has incorporated the work-time distribution information into its decision making processes to find a better way to do our business. The WTMS Tool has also become our convenient, indispensable tool to track our work process and to generate critical information for making more facts-based decisions to cope with new challenges and uncertainties in the future.

8. REFERENCES

[1] Gordon R. Sullivan, U.S. Army General, "How the Army Sees a New World: We're Smaller and Non-Nuclear, but Defense Is Still Our Mission," *The Washington Post,* 23 February 1992, p. C3.

[2] Michael Hammond, "Reengineering Work: Don't Automate, Obliterate," *Harvard Business Review,"* July-August 1990, pp. 104-113.

[3] Peter Krass, "Building a Better Mousetrap: What Role to MIS Executives Play in Business Reengineering Projects?" *Information Week,* 25 March 1991, pp. 24-28.

[4] Wayne Eckerson, "Process Redesign Increases Return on Net Investment," *Network World,* 22 April 1991, pp. 1-2.

[5] Hobbs, Nealon, Wassmuth, "Ada Transition Research Project," *Report Number ASQB-GI-91-005,* U.S. Army Institute for Research in Management Information, Communications, and Computer Sciences, 115 O'Keefe Bldg., GIT, Atlanta, Georgia, December 1990.

[6] Peter Sassone, "Economic Justification," *Report Number ASQB-GM-92-008,* U.S. Army Institute for Research in Management Information, Communications, and Computer Sciences, 115 O'Keefe Bldg., GIT, Atlanta, Georgia, December 1991.

[7] Ulric Weil, "DOD Must Master Basics Before Strassmann's CIM," *Government Computer News,* 16 September 1991, p. 56.

[8] Gary Anthes, "Pentagon Wields IS Strategic Weapon," *Computerworld*, 8 June 1992, pp. 1-2.

[9] Louis Fried, "A Blue Print for Change," *Computer World*, 2 December 91, pp. 91-95.

[10] McCracken, Shilling, Gale, Anton, "Object-Based Requirements Modeling for Process Continuity," *Proceedings 26th Annual Hawaii International Conference on System Sciences*, Editors, Jay Nunamaker and Ralph Sprague, 6-8 January 1993.

[11] Lisa Day-Copeland, "Using Excel Spreadsheet Software to Design and Conduct a Work," *Industrial Engineering*, January 1990, pp. 47-50.

[12] Gerlach, Kuo, and Feng-Yang, "Understanding Human- Computer Interaction for Information Systems Design," *MIS Quarterly*, December 1991, V. 15.

[13] Cathy Beise and Michael Evans, "Bringing the Meeting to the Group: Groupware on a Portable Wireless LAN," *Proceedings GroupWare '92*, David Coleman, Editor, Morgan Kaufmann Publishers, San Mateo, California, August 1992, pp. 503-510.

[14] Peter Sassone, "Office Productivity: the Impact of Staffing, Intellectual Specialization and Technology," *Project Number M-23-604*, School of Economics, The Ivan Allen College of Management, Policy and International Affairs, The Georgia Institute of Technology, November 1991.

Acknowledgments

Everyone at Software Technology Branch of the U.S. Army Research Laboratory, formerly known as AIRMICS, helped me complete this paper. I sincerely thank Mr. John Mitchell, the former AIRMICS Director, for providing me the information on the managerial use of the results; Dr. John Gowens, my mentor, for supporting and encouraging me; and my colleagues for providing the work-time data.

Disclaimer

Although the research was done as an in-house project, ideas expressed in this paper are not to be construed as an official Army position unless so designated by other authorized documents. The names of some products and their manufacturers are mentioned in this paper, but neither the use of the products nor their manufacturers are implicitly or explicitly endorsed by the author or the government.

Decision Support in Public Administration (A-26)
P.W.G. Bots, H.G. Sol and R. Traunmüller (Editors)
Elsevier Science Publishers B.V. (North-Holland)

Toward the implementation and use of 'electronic' files in public administration

M. Vintar

School of Public Administration, University of Ljubljana, Kardeljeva ploščad 5, 61000 Ljubljana, Slovenia

Abstract

In an effort to improve the efficiency and reduce the costs of public administration on the local and state level, the area of handling written materials and records within administrative processes plays a very important role. The purpose of this paper is to present the results and experiences of a five year project carried out in Slovenia in this field. The main aim of this project was to introduce the information technologies to the area, to analyze the impact of the IT on the organization of administrative processes in public administration and to explore new technical and organizational solutions. Special attention has been paid to the filing systems and questions of introducing of the so called 'electronic files' in the work of public organizations.

1. INTRODUCTION

Practically all procedures in public administration are based on written materials, documents. The majority of records, that flow through information systems in public administration today, can be categorized as different kinds of applications, official letters, contracts, budgets, memos, minutes, personnel records, publications, etc.

Written materials are the reflection of all administrative activities in every public organization. They are constantly changing their nature as well as media on which they are written, transported and archived. Besides paper documents we have to recognize new media, like electronic records, optical disks, floppy disks, microfilms, video tapes, etc. Therefore filing systems, that were organized and maintained for tracking paper documents within governmental bodies and local authorities in the past, can not meet the requests of today.

In order to illustrate the complexity of the area and its importance within the public sector we will state some results from the survey carried out in Slovenia on local administration level:

- Authorities in public administration have to handle over 5 million of administrative files (or about 20 million of documents) every year (Slovenia is relatively small country with only about two million inhabitants) on the local level only.

- 10 - 15 percent of working force in public administration are directly employed in clerical jobs involved with activities of classification, registration and transportation of paper documents, keeping records and files, archives, etc.

- About 20-30 percent of the whole office working time is spent for handling, writing, searching, etc. of written documents.

- The transportation of administrative files in paper form is the most time-consuming activity within the processing cycle of a file and can be accounted for up to 90 percent of the whole time (12) spent for the processing of the file.

A great deal of communications among different parties within public organizations and outside world i.e. with citizens, are still based on written form and paper medium, even though the new communication technologies like electronic mail, telefax, telex, etc. are well under way. The administrative procedures within which written materials are processed, can be divided into some characteristic phases like input, output, classification, processing, etc.

All phases are strongly influenced by new information technologies, like electronic communications, filing systems, text processing systems, scanners, optical disks, etc. The processes of implementing new IT in different segments of public administration in Slovenia were left to the incentives and skillfulness of local authorities and different governmental bodies themselves.

The area of handling written materials was not under prime concern at all in our public administration, so at the beginning of our project in 1987 the situation in this field was far from being satisfactory. Therefore the whole project was divided into three phases :

1. Phase :

The analysis of the existent situation in different types of public organizations at the local and state levels and development of an efficient, cheap and reliable solution to support the activities of handling written materials.

2. Phase :

The evaluation of the impacts of IT based solutions on the existent organizational paradigm, efficiency of public administration and social or other changes.

3. Phase :

The design and specification of steps for future development, activities on organizational, legal and technical level through which would be gradually introduced the concepts of 'electronic files' in the every day work of public servants.

The first two phases of the project have been completed and we are at the beginning of phase three. Since we will describe our approach, solutions and examine the results of our work carried out so far.

2. ANALYSIS AND DEFINITION OF THE 'OBJECT OF DISCOURSE'

The majority of all activities in the public administration are accompanied by documents which can contain textual, numeric or graphic information. Documents with textual and/or numeric information prevail in majority of governmental organizations. However in some agencies graphic information i.e. blueprints, drawings, photos, etc. represent vital part of the IS. Nowadays the term "document" has to be understood in the broadest sense, i.e. it can be a paper, a diskette, a cassette, a magnetic tape, a microfilm, an optical disc, etc. We can say that written documents represent a mirror image of all administrative activities. Systematic handling of written documents is an important part and an instrument of efficient management and control of all public systems.

Activities comprising the processes of handling written documents can be therefore decomposed in the following distinct phases:

- **input-output**
- **classification**
- **registration**
- **processing**
- **internal transport**
- **documents retrieval**
- **archival**

In the past these activities were normally supported by the classical organizational form which is shown in figure 1.

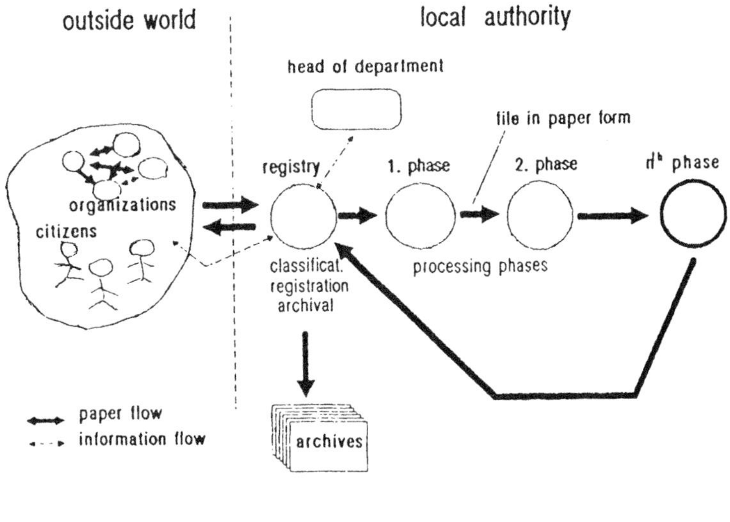

Figure 1 : The classical organizational model

Classical organizational model has been based on the assumption that paper document is a basic communication medium. Administrative files have started their live cycle at registry and then proceeded from phase to phase being physically transported from one public servant to another. This organizational model contributed to the following weak points :

- very slow motion of files from phase to phase due to transportation delays, up to 90 % time spent on transport,

- no control and managerial information for the management of the organizational units and departments. Namely once on a way nobody knew exactly where the file was until it came back to the registry,

- strict sequential order of activities has been imposed even though that was unnecessary from the processing point of view,

- retrieval of documents and files was very slow, possibility of losses of documents and files at somebodies desk was quite likely.

Especially sequential order of activities, which was imposed because of the nature of files in paper form, was most common cause for delays. A delay which occur at some processing phase, produced so called 'chain effect' i.e. delays at all succeeding phases.

3. IMPLEMENTATION OF PC-BASED SOLUTIONS

According to our surveys carried out in 1987, about 98 % of all written materials at that time entered and left organization in the classical way, which means by classical mail. Although new 'electronic ' media and communication technologies were well under way, we concluded that paper has to stay as a primary medium for communication between different parties inside public organizations and outside.

That fact influenced farther development of computer based solution in many ways. With this decision were all more radical organizational reforms in this field ruled out and we were forced to take it into account by designing technical solutions. After the analysis phase carried out in 1987 and in the beginning of 1988 (9),(10), we concluded that we needed a solution with the following characteristics :

- it has to be suitable for PC's, either stand alone or in LAN's environments,

- it has to support the activities of registry and all other departments in public administration and has to integrate the following activities :

    - registration of all documents and files (regardless of media or form),
    - writing of documents,
    - registration and storing of documents written by text processors,
    - retrieval of documents/files regardless of media (paper or

in 'electronic' form),
- tracking of documents and files through all processing phases from registration to archiving,
- supervision and control of individuals and organizational units focusing on their efficiency and punctuality at solving administrative files,
- planning and reporting.

The general and most important decision regarding the new computer based solution was that documents , regardless of their origin can stay in their original form and media, i.e. documents which enter public authority in paper form can stay and flow through succeeding processing phases in paper form and on the other hand, documents which are created in 'electronic' form can stay and be processed in that form. Selection of data base management system (DBMS) and development tools was one of the first steps within the development phase. The selection criteria were as follows:

- the ability of DBMS to handle large data bases of prevailing textual information at reasonable speed on the pre-defined hardware,
- reliability and recovery procedures,
- price/performance ratio,
- availability of development tools around the DBMS for design and programming of the applications,
- maintenance costs.

After surveying and testing some of the standard software packages and tools available on the PC market (especially dBASE and ORACLE), we concluded that none of the products was able to fulfill all the necessary conditions. Particularly performance and ability to handle efficiently relatively large textual data bases on the PC hardware were the weakest points of the products tested. Since we decided to build our own solution in accordance to the thoroughly defined specifications. The solution had to fulfill, among many other, also the following requests :

- to handle a great number of files and documents with mostly unformatted textual information (the number of documents which enter some ministries could exceed 100.000 per year),

- to enable the search for documents by unlimited number of keywords (descriptors),

- to provide reliable backup and recovery of great data bases which can grow very quickly at bigger public organizations.

We had to develop our own data base management system suited for handling mostly unformatted textual information. Programming language C has been chosen as a basic working tool. We had to develop some interfaces to standard text processors in order to be able to store all documents written by standard text processors directly in our own data base.
We started to implement this solution in 1989. At the end of the year 1991 the number of installations exceeded one hundred. About 85 percent of local authorities, 75 percent of ministries and many other public organizations decided to implement this

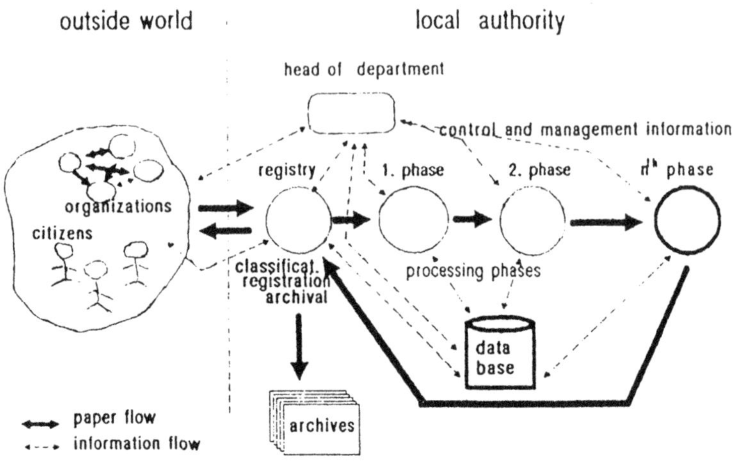

Figure 2 : The organizational model based on the first generation of the computer based filing systems

solution. As we can see from the figure 2, the implementation of the application left the organizational model basically unchanged.

4. EVALUATION OF THE RESULTS AND EXPERIENCES

After two years of extensive use of the described solution we decided to start the evaluation of the results and experiences in order to :

1. improve the existent solution,
2. suggest changes in organizational forms and working procedures if necessary,
3. prepare steps and directions for future development toward the implementation of the concept of 'electronic' files in public administration.

In order to get the opinion of the users and their views of the necessary further steps we prepared and sent out a special questionnaire. A one day conference for the users and the experts in the field has been organized and a sample of five users has been selected for thorough survey and examination. We will try to summarize our findings in the following points :

- common opinion among the users was that flow of information has been improved considerably, which contributed to the improved efficiency and increased productivity,

- searching of files and documents has become a trivial business,
- heads of organizational units and departments have a much better insight into the state of files and important administrative cases,
- with status and statistical data about files and activities carried out on them, the system provides valuable control and managerial information and serves also as a decision support and control tool,
- response times and overall quality of service for the citizens improved considerably.

Nevertheless many shortcomings of the past remained virtually unchanged, for example :

- although the system provided a platform for new, better organizational pattern for processing administrative files, no great changes happened,
- the throughput of organizational units didn't change in a considerable way,
- the problem of transporting physical files (in paper form) from one processing phase to another remained unsolved,
- the transport times of files remained unchanged.

We concluded that next 'generation' of filing systems will have to solve the question of the role of paper as a basic processing medium more radically and make deliberate and decisive step towards the implementation of the 'electronic files' in the administrative practice.

5. FUTURE DEVELOPMENT

First 'generation' of office automation systems was relatively easy to implement, because it has been possible to fit them in the existent organizational models and working procedures in public administration. However next 'generation' solutions will request deep changes in organizational, technological and even legal procedures if we want to make a real step forward. There is a very strong technological push from new hardware and software solutions and new storage media, but on the other hand, public administration is to complex structure and to big area to allow experiments with unproven solutions (2),(5),(7).

The expectation, that electronic media will soon replace paper as a main communication means is not very realistic (4),(8),(10). The recent surveys in the public administration in many countries revealed that the amount of paper documents increases steadily despite of all new media end technologies penetrating this area. Offices are the environment where the processing of a variety of very different media becomes reality. All researchers agree that with the automation and informatization of public administration the role and importance of filing systems increases and changes (1),(3),(4),(6),(11). Filing systems will have to change radically to cope with this situation.

In order to make the concept of the 'electronic file' reality in public administration, we have to transform filing systems to the integrated multi-media documental information systems (IMDIS). They will have to be able to handle pictorial, numerical and textual information in a very efficient way and enable to integrate variety of technologies, input-output devices, storage media and communication systems.

There are many vendors of software packages on the market today who promise to solve all or nearly all of the above mentioned requests. However to our opinion we have to thoroughly examine and analyze at least three groups of questions, which have to be solved or answered, before we could start to implement the newest solutions on the frontal basis in the public administration. These groups of questions are:

- transition to new organizational paradigm of office procedures in public administration,

- reliability and suitability of new technologies and storage media in the long run,

- 'paper-less office' a myth or reality.

5.1. Transition to new organizational paradigm of office procedures in public administration,

Implementation of new IT in the offices of public administration in the past left the organizational structures and models practically unchanged. That has been possible due to the fact that a vast majority of documents remained in paper form and that partial activities have been automated instead of integral processes. However next generation of office automation solutions in public administration can't be implemented successfully without global changes in organizational paradigm. We will try to point out only a few of necessary changes on the organizational level :

- With new IT the inter-organizational information systems are becoming reality. We will have to redefine organizational structures, duties and borders to make progress in the direction of inter-organizational IS.

- Strict sequential processing of administrative files, which was necessary in the past because of the physical nature of paper based files will have to be redefined.

- There will have to be less taylorism and less strict labor division.

- Mostly centralized functions of registry offices will have to be decentralized.

All mentioned changes will bring about many other changes in the personnel structure, necessary skills, etc. As shown in figure 3 organizational paradigm of the office will have to be redesigned completely.

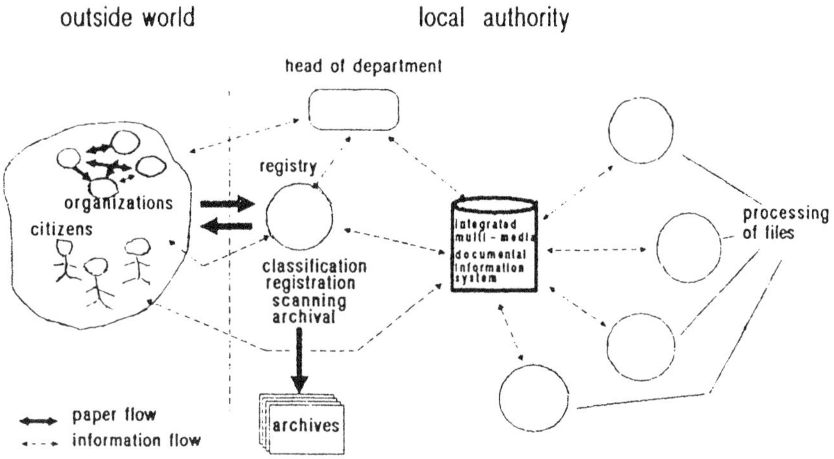

Figure 3 : The organizational model based on the concept of use of the 'electronic' files

5.2 Reliability and suitability of new technologies and storage media in the long run

The number of technical and technological solutions which are entering the area of interest increases every day. New technologies are becoming available for all processing phases of administrative files. But the implementation of these new solutions has been carried out in a very inconsistent manner without the necessary organizational, legal and operational adaptations and without an integral conceptual platform. We can summarize the evaluation of the influence of the new technologies and media in the field of handling written materials in public administration in the following points :

- the new technologies are not ripe yet for their frontal implementation in the big organizational systems like governmental organizations and agencies,

- the new media (i.e. optical disks) are complementary rather than a replacement for the old ones (i.e. paper),

- the lack of standards and partiality are the main attributes of the existent new technologies.

5.3 'Paper-less office' a myth or reality

The heterogeneity of documents regarding form, format, content, image, etc. is the main problem which is not easy to overcome especially when we are dealing with correspondence documents and other most frequent groups of documents in public administration. From purely technological point of view we have at least three possibilities for processing the input flow of paper documents :

- classification, registration and further handling in classical form, i.e. original paper form,

- classification, registration and reading of the document content with OCR (optical character reading) and storing in 'electronic file' on the computer media,

- classification, registration and scanning of the document image in a 'electronic file' and storing on the computer media.

Technical solutions for the second and the third option are available but in practice they aren't yet extensively used because of several limitations connected with these new technologies. Electronic documents as a replacement for paper ones are in many dimensions unexplored and unpredictable. We do not know how to handle them through a long period of time i.e. decades or even centuries. Many documents, especially those in governmental agencies play a great role in different legal procedures and have historical or cultural meaning. It will be necessary to analyze thoroughly all these and many other questions before we can make a great step into an era of electronic office.

6. CONCLUSIONS

We have tried to present our own experiences by implementing office automation in public administration in Slovenia and especially automating filing systems as a central point of all office activities. The implementation of new computer technologies and media is on the way very rapidly but organizationally, legally and even psychologically there are the majority of public organizations unprepared to carry out this step.

Even though several sophisticated solutions for filing and storing documents, based on new technologies and media can be found on the market today, a close look reveals, that these are partial solutions for organizations with a relatively small number of documents flowing through their organizational units.

However what is good for small and medium size business companies is not necessarily good for public administration where we have to take into account many historical, organizational and legal issues before we start with 'revolution'. We are in an urgent need of a new strategy in this field.

7. REFERENCES

1 P. Abele et al., PROMPT - Postlauf und Registratur in oeffentlichen Verwaltungen - Moeglichkeiten partizipativer Technikentwicklung, Forschungsgruppe Verwaltungsautomation, Gh Kassel - Universitaet, 1991.

2 L. Beyer et al., Registratur und Postlauf in oeffentlichen Verwaltungen, Werkstattbericht Nr. 42, Fallstudien, Forschungsgruppe Verwaltungsautomation, Gh Kassel-Universitaet, 1988.

3 L. Beyer et al., Registratur und Postlauf in oeffentlichen Verwaltungen, Werkstattbericht Nr. 80, Fallstudien, Forschungsgruppe Verwaltungsautomation, Gh Kassel-Universitaet, 1990.

4 L. Beyer, H. Bielefeld-Hart, K. Grimmer, Die Zukunft der Schriftgutwervaltung als technikgestuetzte qualifizirte Assistenz, Deutsche Verwaltungspraxis, Year 42, Nr. 9, 1991.

5 H. Bielefeld- Hart, K. Grimmer, Qualifizierte Asistenz oder Autarke Sachbearbeitung, Beitraege zu einem Workshop, Forschungsgruppe Verwaltungsautomation Gesamthochschule Kassel - Universitaet, 1990.

6 C.C. Dolecheck, Electronic Filing, Journal of Systems Management, Nr. 2, 1986, pp. 34-39.

7 C.A. Ellis, N. Naffah, Design of office Information Systems, Springer-Verlag, Berlin, 1987.

8 R. Traunmueller, Kanzleiinformationsysteme, ADV Tagung, ADV - Handelsgesellschaft, Wien, 1990

9 M. Vintar, Upravljanje s pisnimi gradivi in nove informacijske tehnologije, Zveza ekonomistov Slovenije - V. posvetovanje sekcije za raziskovanje informacijskih sistemov, Izlake, 1992, pp. 1-6 (in slovenian)

10 M. Vintar, Organization and handling of written materials in business and public administration under new information technologies, Proceedings of the International Conference on Organization and Information Systems, Bled, 1992

11 M. Vintar, The new information technologies as a means of handling of written materials in business and public administration, Meeting of the International Association of Information and Documentation in Public Administration, Vienna, 1992

12 H. Voglmayr, Application of PC-Networks in Public Administration, Annual Conference of the International Association of Schools and Institutes of Administration, Vienna, July 1992

Decision Support in Public Administration (A-26)
P.W.G. Bots, H.G. Sol and R. Traunmüller (Editors)
Elsevier Science Publishers B.V. (North-Holland)

Decision Support System in an administrative context : The case of the reinsertion of Long-Term Unemployed in France

Jean-Charles Pomerol, Michel Futtersack and Jean-Marc Labat
LAFORIA-IBP, Université Paris VI, 4 place Jussieu, 75252 Paris cedex 05, France

Abstract :

The French Employment Ministry has established different kinds of actions and aids to deal with the problems of reinsertion for the long-term unemployed. This paper describes a Decision Support System, which has been designed to help decision makers in the task of programming the actions intended for the long-term unemployed. This system includes an expert system, which proposes a multicriteria evaluation providing the users with advice to choose an appropriate policy. Moreover the paper examines the reasons why the system, though it may bring real help, has been abandoned by the organization.

Keywords : Interactive Decision Support System, Multicriteria Analysis, Knowledge Based Systems

1. INTRODUCTION

The problem of unemployment in France is very serious from both social and political points of view : three million unemployed people (10% of the work force) and among them, almost one million people unemployed for more than one year, who are called LTU —Long-Term Unemployed—. For these people, there is a high risk of social exclusion. So the French Government decided on special actions for them. During the eighties, a lot of difficulties have appeared regarding the management of these actions :

1) National planning is bound to fail. There probably do not exist general solutions to the unemployment problem and a great deal of local information must be taken into account.

2) It is well known that in France professional training is not sufficient. Once more, general actions have not succeeded. Decentralized negotiations between the different people involved are necessary to cope with professional training improvement.

3) The relationship between training and employment is difficult to establish because it is almost impossible to forecast future needs in terms of qualifications.

4) Throughout this period, the ministry have launch many actions to fight unemployment. These actions are not very different from each other. It is generally difficult to choose between these actions and to share between them.
5) To take into account the local information, in the framework of the decentralization laws, the ministry wished that the distribution of the total budget should be devolved to the same local level (regional or departmental).

For all these reasons, in 1989, the French Government decided to reduce the numbers of actions from 9 to 5 and to transfer the decisions at a local level. To help the decision makers in charge of the programming of the measures intended for the LTU, a decision support system (DSS), named MUPALU (an acronym for MUlticriteria PlAnner for Long-period Unemployed), has been designed. Several imperatives were essential regarding the conception of the DSS. Firstly it was necessary to provide the decision makers with a synthetic vision of all the relevant data about employment at a regional level. To dispose of a comprehensive view of the information is, itself, a form of support. Secondly, it is important to filter this information. We have designed an expert system which performs the reasoning relative to this information. The expert system scans the various data relative to employment and to the previous actions carried out for LTU and it synthesizes these data according to certain indicators which are used by experts. Each of the possible actions is then evaluated by a multicriteria module. The aggregation is made according to the Borda method (Pomerol and Barba-Romero, 1993), but with the particularity that the weights depend on the indicators provided by the expert system. Based on this multicriteria evaluation, a distribution of the actions is proposed by the system. This policy will finally constitute a basis of reflection for making the final decision.
As such, the MUPALU system is a true DSS (see e.g. Sprague and Carlson, 1982), which is not intended to replace the decision maker but to provide him, by means of visual display, with a global view of the main parameters likely to guide him towards the choice of a decision (Jelassi, 1990, Levine et Pomerol, 1989, Klein and Methlie, 1990). At each stage, the decision maker can either bypass the system and make the evaluation by himself or perform a sensitivity analysis around the recommendations of the system. Endowed with this usual " What if ? " capability (Keen, 1987), MUPALU may be used as a learning system in order to improve the thinking of the decision maker and to widen his/her search for a adapted policy.

2. PROBLEM STATEMENT

2.1. Definition of the problem

To understand exactly the problem, let us firstly define the three administrative levels. The highest is composed of the decision makers belonging to minister's cabinet. We will call this level (where essentially two persons are involved in our system) the ministry administration. The second level is the regional level and the

third the "departmental" level, each region being composed of departments. The total amount of money voted to struggle against unemployment, is distributed at the ministry level to the regions. The desire of the ministry administration should be that the distribution between the actions should be made at the regional level.
This distribution must respect two constraints : the total amount, given by the ministry administration, cannot be modified and the number of people concerned with certain action, is fixed by the ministry. Furthermore, the regional decisions must be transmitted to the ministry administration.

Among the LTU, there are people more socially vulnerable called "Target-publics". The categories of target-publics are : very long-term LTU (unemployed for more than 3 years), more than 50 years old, isolated women, people who get the RMI (Minimum Income for Insertion), disabled people.

Table 1
Description of the 5 actions

Action 1 : CRE, Contrat Retour à l'Emploi	Action 2 : AIF, Action Insertion et Formation
Direct access to employment	Social help for reintegration by training
Companies are helped financially	Individual needs are taken into account
100 000 possible actions by year	240 000 possible actions by year
cost = $ 3000 per person	cost = $ 2500 per person
Only for LTU > 26 years old and RMI	Only for LTU with priority to the RMI
Action 3 : SMAN ,Stage de Mise A Niveau	Action 4 : SRP, Stage de Reclassement professionel
A training session prepares the salaried employee to take an already existing job	Allows the unemployed to adapt themselves to emerging technologies
30 000 possible actions by year	40 000 possible actions by year
cost = $ 4 000 per person	cost = $ 2 000 per person
Not reserved for the LTU, but LTU % must be > 25%	Not reserved for the LTU (preventive action)
Action 5 : FNE/FI, Fonds National pour l'Emploi/Femmes Isolées	
Reintegration of single women	
Several steps : results, general knowledge session, professional training	
10 000 possible actions by year	
cost = $ 3 500 per woman	
Single women with children and with a low income	

The five possible actions are CRE (Contract for Return to Employment), AIF (Action for Insertion and Training) , SMAN (Session to Adapt the Level of Skill) , SRP (Professional Training Session) , FNE/FI (Single women). Each action has a target public. We present the main characteristics of each action in table 1.

2.2. Characteristics of the available information

To make the decisions in this domain, it is necessary to cope with various qualitative and quantitative data. Unfortunately, quantitative data about unemployment are often too detailed and not always reliable. In particular, it is possible to observe some incoherences between the statistical data from different sources. Moreover, some qualitative (or even quantitative) data concerning the companies are not easily available via data bases (e.g. recruitment trends, required qualifications). Another problem arises from the non-standardization of data and of the nomenclatures concerning the jobs. Thus, there exist, in France, three different nomenclatures used to describe jobs and there is no easy method of bridging them.

2.3. The needs

As there is a large amount of existing information, it is not useful to produce new data, the problem is rather to allow the best processing of the scattered data. Thus, the system should be an intelligent information filter (Simon, 1977) to result in a manageable set of data. One way to get this result is to handle the statistical data by means of composite, more or less comprehensive, ratios easily understable by the users. From these ratios, calculated by the system, it is possible to reason about the actions to perform. This reasoning being partly qualitative, we have adopted an expert system approach.

Our problem emerges in the head of a member of the ministry cabinet, he defines it as an aid to help the regional administration to "cleverly" distribute the budget between the possible actions. Startly from this rather imprecise commitment, we began with a knowledge analysis of the task. Thinking in term of aid naturally leads to the idea of building a DSS. Hence, the ministry administration asked our laboratory to design and develop a DSS to help the regional decision makers to distribute the global budget between the five possible actions. The knowledge acquisition was made at two levels : on the one hand, with the ministry administration and, on the other hand, with the regional decision makers, who more or less volunteered to participate in the developing of MUPALU. With the ministry administration, we have designed the architecture of MUPALU and the main functionalities according to their objectives. This part of the work lasted about 3 months ; in fact we met the ministry people only six times, and we have had some difficulty in bringing these people together.

The ministry administration also chose four regions to acquire the expertise. These regions presented different characteristics (industrial or rural region, widely computerized region (databases) or not, decisions makers favouring or not the using of spreadsheet,...). With the local decision makers, the process was divided into two steps. Firstly, we analysed the information necessary for making the decision and which is easily available. The second step was the acquisition of the expertise to distribute the budget. We visited three regions twice, and the last one about six times. In this last region, we met not only the decision maker but also the field workers (departmental level) in charge of the management of the actions. With the decision makers, we drew up the precise list of information we had to put in the diagnosis module (see next section).

3. THE MAIN FUNCTIONALITIES AND THE ARCHITECTURE OF MUPALU

MUPALU includes three main components: the diagnosis system, the programming system and the distribution system (see Fig. 2).

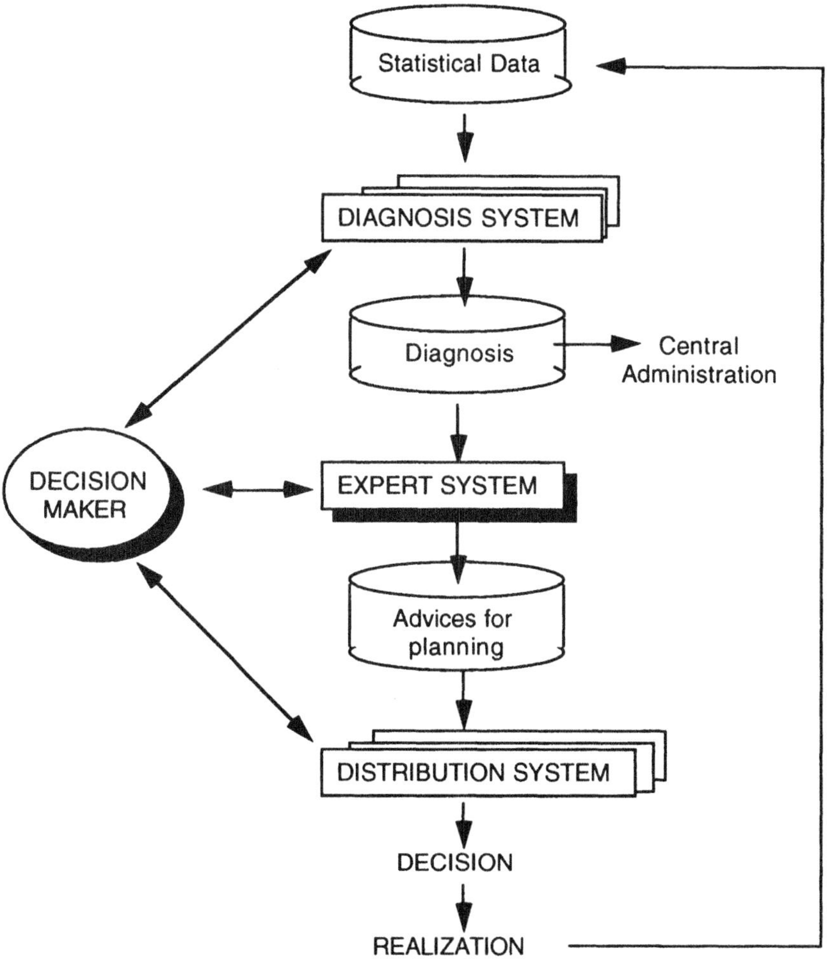

Figure 2 : The general architecture

Each subsystem corresponds to a stage in the process of planning the distribution among the five possible actions. At the first stage, the information concerning employment in the region is gathered and displayed on a spreadsheet. The aim of the second stage is to propose a policy for the distribution of the financial resources. The third stage is the interactive definition of the final distribution. The diagnosis system and the affectation system use the functionalities of a spreadsheet, whereas the expert system uses a shell, named SNARK (Laurière, 1988), based on first order logic.

3.1. The diagnosis module

The first purpose of the diagnosis module is to collect the information and to make it easily available for the decision maker. This module exploits two major sources of information : the statistical data provided by various social institutions to describe the employment situation ; it also involves qualitative information interpreting local knowledge transmitted by the regional ministry staff to the central ministry administration.

The diagnosis system displays the information in the form of two types of spreadsheet tables. The first tables are used for data acquisition. The information is extracted from a data base and fed to the decision maker. The other tables synthesize the collected data to summarize and display a comprehensive view of the situation in the region by using different kind of ratios.

At this stage, there was a real need by the administration to deal with data that was neither recorded nor examined, at least according to the perception of the ministry administration. To make decisions, the main information is the relative evolution of the different categories of LTU. The best idea, at this stage, would probably have been to use a graphical display, but one of the constraints was to use ordinary PCs and software available in local offices. We therefore decided that the spreadsheet solution was better to allow a sufficiently interactive presentation of the results (see figure 3 and 4).

Employment situation	S
Jobs supply	M
LTU according to their age and to their duration of unemployment	C
% of target-publics among LTU	P
Results of the last year	R
Initial data (Region, Department, Year)	
Acquisition of the data at the regional level	
Acquisition of the data at the departmental level	
Acquisition of the data relative to the results	
To QUIT the diagnosis system	Q

Figure 3 : The main menu of the diagnosis module

In fact, the spreadsheet (MULTIPLAN in this case) was already being used by the people involved and the synthetic tables we have designed may be regarded as containing the main parameters relevant to an overall appreciation of the LTU situation.

Annual Statistics		N		N / N-1		N-1 / N-2		N-2 / N-3	
		Dépt	Rég	Dépt	Rég	Dépt	Rég	Dép	Rég
%of unemployed									
LTU / Jobs supply (%)									
LTU	CLD								
	1-2 years								
	2-3 years								
	+3 years								
RMI									

Figure 4 : A table synthesising the situation of LTU and its evolution over 3 years

3.2. The knowledge based module

Whereas, on the one hand, the sheets (figure 3 and 4) would probably be sufficient to make a decision regarding the distribution of the various aid, one of the concerns of the ministry administration was the lack of homogeneity in local decisions and also the lack of reactivity, the usual trend being to reproduce with a uniform shift the past distribution. On the other hand, nobody has the expertise to define a "model" for the distribution policy. The ministry experts have a good idea of the efficiency of the aids according to the type of LTU, but the decision must include the local data about the local possibilities for training, because one of the difficulties is that some types of aid may be difficult to implement locally. So in order to keep a large possibility for change in the possible decision model and to cope with qualitative and local data, we have suggested the development of an expert system.

The knowledge base is divided into six main sub-modules. The first sub-module performs a quantitative analysis on the data provided by the diagnosis module or introduced by the decision maker (for example some specific local data). This analysis results in the **evaluation of synthetic** indicators (Giffard, 1989). These indicators measure the evolution of the parameters or compare the values of the regional and departmental parameters.

The second sub-module is concerned with the qualitative data, introduced by the decision maker, regarding his/her knowledge about employment in the region and the effectiveness of the already launched actions. Our objective was to define a minimal set of indicators involving a sufficient number of variables describing the employment market and training offers. At this point, it was necessary to prove the usefulness of a reasoning system for the distribution of aid because the local agents where not convinced of the possibility of processing their local information.

The third sub-module produces some conclusions, which are displayed under the form of a conclusive warning relative to the employment in the studied region. For example, the indicator "unqualified situation" appears with a warning value if the employment of unqualified people decreases and the local training offer seems to be unable to propose an adequate formation.

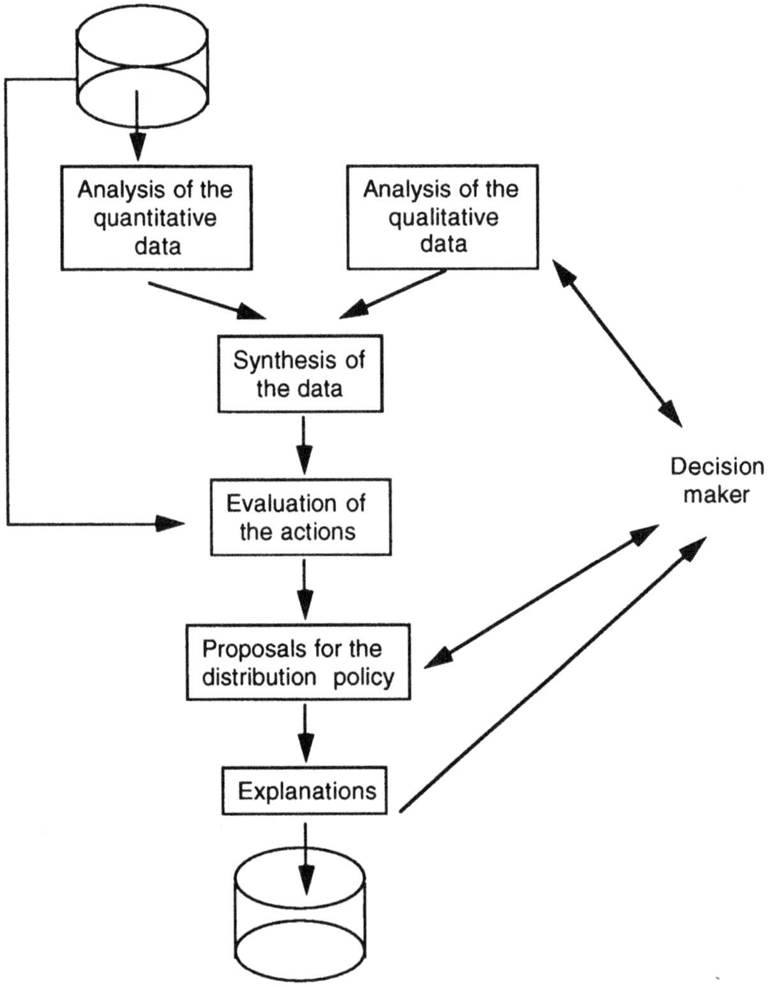

Figure 5 : The sub-modules of the expert system

In the fourth sub-module, the expert system contains some rules, which are used for the multicriteria analysis, as we will see below. The result of the multicriteria analysis is an aggregated priority factor which enables the actions to be ordered. A high priority means that it is recommended to increase the financial volume of the action in question.

The fifth sub-module is intended to provide some proposals for the distribution policy. These recommendations take into account the evolution from the year N to the year N+1. Moreover it should be noted that among the five actions, two (CRE and AIF) are greater than the others : the number of possible actions is about 10 times more than for the others (see table 1), so that it is not possible to increase simultaneously the two actions CRE and AIF. Following these considerations and some other rules, the expert system produces its recommendations in the form <increase I decrease> <slightly I strongly > the aids <name> .

One of the advantages of the expert systems is their ability to justify their reasoning. The last module is the explanations module. It relies on rules structuring by "knowledge sources". To each "knowledge sources" some explanation rules are tied (see table 6), which explain the reason for the final recommendation. Thus, the end-user can understand the value of the reasoning.

Table 6 :
An explanation rule (? denotes the variables)

```
IF    ?x is an action
      priority of ?x is ?p
      ?p >= 4
      the evolution proposed is "to increase slightly"
      ?x was increased the year ?n+1
      the increase of ?x was ?y
      ?y >= 10
      Quality of relations with ANPE are ?q
      ?q >= good
      physical % of ?x the year ?n is ?z
      ?z >= 90
THEN
      Print :    "The priority of ?x is ?p because :
                        * relation with ANPE are good
                        * physical % of ?x during the year ?n is very good
                 However, we only propose a slight increase because there was
                 already an increase of ?y % last year"
```

3.3. Multicriteria analysis

From a decision making point of view, one of the main feature of our system is that it has adopted a multicriteria representation. The expert system methodology has often been criticized for blending in an inconsistent way facts and decision parameters (see Keeney, 1988 and 1992, White, 1990). From our point of view, the decision parameters must be clearly connected to the decision maker's utility. In this case, it seems illusory to reduce the decision maker's utility to a single comprehensive criterion. This is the reason why we have chosen to isolate five criteria against which the possible actions are evaluated. Moreover, the evaluations are explained to the users in such a way that they can appreciate their relevance and understand the priority attributed to each action.

The quantitative criteria concern the already observed impacts of the action during the preceeding year. The qualitative criteria take into account the effectiveness of the vocational training program and the availability of support from the administration. The aggregation of the criteria follows the Borda method. Let M(i, j) the rank of the measure i for the criterion j of weight Pj, the priority factor Ni attributed to the action i is computed using the formula :

$$Ni = \sum_{j} M(i,j) * Pj$$

The aggregation of the criteria by a weighted sum of the ranks is often criticized because the weights are fixed, once and for all. For example, it is impossible to express the fact that criterion Cl is three times greater than criterion C2, if the value of criterion Cl is large and of equal importance when the same value is small. In our system, the weights of the criteria are computed according to the context, by means of production rules within the ES. For example, the criterion "Impact of a measure on LTU" will be of greater importance, the greater the number of LTU and the more unfavourable the overall economic situation in the related region. Briefly, the weights depend on the context and on the qualitative knowledge involved in the expert system.

3.4. The distribution module

One concern of the ministry administration was the difficulty in introducing a new technology such as expert system in a context where people are rather "computerization reluctant". To avoid an immediate rejection, it was thought that the best thing to do was to offer the possibility of bypassing the expert system and to insist on the "what if" capabilities. Once more, the best way to offer easy "what if" capabilities is to use a spreadsheet. For this reason, we have decided to present the distribution suggested by the expert sytem on a "distribution" sheet using the same spreadsheet as previously.

The decision maker must take into account both the distribution policy, proposed in the preceeding phase and the external constraints (thresholds imposed by the ministry administration, mainly concerning the percentage of variation compared with the previous year and with respect to the amount of available money). The distribution proposed by the system is displayed by the spreadsheet (see Fig. 7), which enables the user to simulate various hypotheses before fixing the final distribution of the money. The column PERSONS contains the number of LTU which are concerned by each measure. In the column FINANCIAL is displayed the cost of the actions. In the right-hand column the expert system's recommendations are recalled.

DPT : YEAR :

	Persons		% of variation	Financial	Recall of the distribution proposed by the expert system
	N+1	N+2		N+2	
CRE					
AIF					
FNE					
SMAN					
SRP					
TOTAL					

Figure 7 : Interface of the distribution module

4. INTEGRATION AND IMPLEMENTATION OF MUPALU

4.1. Emergence and identification of the problem

The idea of developing MUPALU comes from the ministry administration. Among the people in charge of the unemployment problem at the ministry level, it was thought that the various aid was routinely distributed and that people at a local level did not have a say in aportioning various aid. This thinking was not supported by any study, it was just a feeling and, as we shall emphasize, no analysis of the task of local agents was ever carried out. While developing the system, we have discovered that the management of actions is much more important for the local decision makers (departemental level) than the distribution choice and that it is regarded as their real job. Actually, when one has decided to attribute one aid package, it is important to be able to implement it, i.e. to find an ad hoc training team and a company with which to organize the training. Another point of interest, in this job, is the negotiation with local companies to create new aided jobs. In these two situations, when the people involved agree to work together, they will adapt their project to one of the aid packages, regardless of the theoretical purpose of the ministry administration. During the acquisition process we also realized that the possibility to change the repartition of the budget among the various actions was weak and that the power balance between the different people involved largely determines this distribution. So MUPALU addresses only a small part of the task of the regional and departemental agents, spefically the part that they regard as rather theoretical because it is useless to decide to increase one type of aid if you are, downstream, unable to implement it. In a nutshell, the question appeared not to be crucial in the preoccupation of the local agents and to have been defined by the ministry administration with perhaps a hidden control motive. Actually, we cannot exclude that one of the reasons of the ministry administration was to dispose of a tool to follow what is made in the regions and departments.

4.2. Organizational constraints

4.2.1 Computerization and integration constraints

Being defined at the ministry level , the project and its diffusion was under the responsibility of the small computer cell of the ministry administration, and this team never manifested a real enthusiasm for the system. One of the reasons was probably that they thought that, owing to the low level of acceptance of the computerization by the ministery agents, the popularization of the spreadsheets would be a more urgent and sufficient task than developing a new system. The second reason was the ignorance of new technologies (both about Knowledge Based System and Decision Support System). The third reason was that they did not perceive the difficulty in getting the data. This point deserves a few words. To make an efficient system, it is necessary to gather a lot of data about the unemployment situation. Up to now, these data have neither been centralized nor normalized. This is the reason why we have tried to reduce, as far as possible, the number of relevant data. Even with this small number of data, the burden is on the user who has to introduce them. Introducing the data has no immediate interest for local agents who are very reluctant to do this job which can be viewed as time consuming and generating no advantage.

4.2.2. Administrative constraints

Among the five actions described in section 2, two (AIF and CRE) are much greater (in volume) than the others. These two actions are managed by two different administrative subdivisions of the ministry administration. The CRE is managed by the National Agency For Employment (ANPE) and the AIF by the Regional Direction of Work and Employment (DRTE). These two services are of course somewhat jealous of their prerogatives (this depends on the region), so it is difficult to modify significantly the distribution between these two actions. Hence, to avoid any problem, the local decision maker is incited to make only marginal changes.

4.3. Realization

We did not meet any real problems during the knowledge acquisition of the system. The local agents we encountered were always very cooperative in explaining their jobs and the way they proceed. We have tested the system in one "department" and it has given reasonable results. Without doubt, it provides a valuable tool for recording the data and reasoning on the distribution of aid. After this testing, MUPALU was delivered to the computer cell who never tried to introduce the system into the regions confirming that they have never shown any interest for its development. Now MUPALU may be regarded as abandoned.

4.4. Analysis of the failure

We think that the failure of the implementation could have been predicted for at least four reasons : inappropriate determination of the task to be performed (central definition of a system destined for local agents), no simultaneous computer integration of the system leading to an automatic acquisition of the data, changes in the administrative executives and computer ignorance of the people having to implement the developments. We have already explained that no previous analysis of the job of the local agents was made and that the task addressed by the system was very narrow regarding the whole concern of the agents. The second point is that, like many administrative systems (see Pomerol and Retour, 1990) MUPALU requires hand-entering of the data. This is not acceptable for the agents except if they get an immediate and large gain from this effort. This was not the case here, because the gain arising from recording and comparing the data over several years is not immediate (long term learning) and is probably greater at the ministry level than at the local one. This leads to the third reason. This system was conceived by ministry administrative people in charge of unemployment aid policy. These high level executives felt the need for a tool for watching the evolution and the impacts of the actions. To do this job, they need to know and consolidate local data and then to verify the usefulness of the aid. Clearly from their own points of view, MUPALU might be regarded as a necessary step in this direction allowing a ministry vision and perhaps, although it was never said, the possibility of re-introducing central directives. Of course, the threat was probably recognized at the local level which diminished the chances of the system being used. The last point, i.e. the lack of manager involvment, is often recognized as a failure reason in the DSS literature (e.g. Keen and Scott Morton, 1978). In our case, we faced a rather general situation. The system was needed by the administration executives (mainly one person, say Mr. Andrew). Mr. Andrew obtained the resources and imposed the supervision of the development to the head of the computer cell (say Mr. Bernard). But Mr. Bernard was never interested in the project so he had no commitment to its success. Mr. Bernard never believed in the ability of local agents to use what he regarded as a technique too sophisticated. When Mr. Andrew was called to another higher job, the system was not yet complete. So that by the time the system was finally finished, it had lost its champion and Mr. Bernard was now in charge of introducing the system. It is not surprising that Mr. Bernard did not make much effort to launch seriously the system.

5. CONCLUSION AND PERSPECTIVES

As a conclusion, let us summarize what appear as the main drawbacks for the introduction of this kind of system to the administration.

1. A very cautious analysis of the task to be performed by the system has to be made. And this task must be analysed from the point of view of the aid-users (local in our case) not from an idealized, more or less far-sighted, definition of the task.

2. An administrative hierarchical level n should resist the temptation to impose a computer system at a level n-1 to facilitate its n level task. There is no reason why the n-1 level should appreciate a system which appears to be designed for the n level purpose, even if the system is equally useful at the n-1 level. In such a case, the lower level will remain very suspicious.

3. In an administrative setting, acquiring and introducing the data is often a burden which should be avoided by automatic acquisition from an adequate database. This connection to databases is a prerequisite to the realisation of "Intelligent" Decision Support Systems.

4. The administration should maintain the "champion" in charge of the development up to the operational introduction of the system. Furthermore the administrative executives cannot delegate the responsibility of computer systems to computer executives. The administrative executives have to acquire some insight into the computer system development in order to be able to follow the development cycle from design to operational introduction of the system. Otherwise they expose the system to be handled to people who have other interests (generally computer and technical interests) than theirs and who have no ability to carry out an administrative change. It appears that, in this situation, the first occuring difficulty causes the abandoning of the system. Nevertheless, to conclude with an optimistic remark, MUPALU showed that the design and implementation of a model merging a spreadsheet and a knowledge-based module, seems to be a solution adapted both to the problems posed and to the decision makers.

REFERENCES

GIFFARD A., 1989, "L'aide à la décision à l'échelon local ou régional : le cas de la Formation Professionnelle", Institut de Recherche sur l'Economie de l'Education, Université de Bourgogne.

JELASSI T. , 1990, "Du présent au futur : bilan et orientations des systèmes interactifs d'aide à la décision", in L'administration et les nouveaux outils d'aide à la décision, D. Bourcier Ed., Economica, Paris.

KEEN P. G. W. , 1987, "Decision support systems : the next decade" , Decision Support Systems 3 , pp. 253-265.

KEEN P. G. W. and SCOTT MORTON M. S. , 1978 "Decision Support Systems" Addison Wesley, Reading.

KEENEY R.L. , 1988, "Value-Driven Expert Systems for Decision Support", Decision Support System n° 4, pp 405-412

KEENEY R.L. , 1992, "Value-Focused Thinking", Harvard University Press, Cambridge MA.

KLEIN M. and METHLIE L. B. , 1990, "Expert Systems, a Decision Support Approach", Addison-Wesley.
LAURIERE J.L., 1988, "Intelligence Artificielle, Représentation des Connaissances : le cas SNARK", tome 2, Eyrolles, Paris
LEVINE P et POMEROL J.C., 1989, "Systèmes Interactifs d'Aide à la Décision et Systèmes Experts", Hermès, Paris.
POMEROL J.C. et BARBA-ROMERO S. , 1993, "Choix multicritère dans l'entreprise", Hermes, Paris.
POMEROL J.C. et RETOUR D., 1990, "L'introduction et l'utilisation des systèmes experts dans le tertiaire", Aditech, Paris.
SIMON H. A. , 1977, "The new science of management decision", Prentice-Hall, Englewood Cliffs
SPRAGUE R. H. jr. and CARLSON E. D. , 1982, "Building Effective Decision Support Systems", Prentice Hall, New Jersey.
WHITE III C. C. , 1990, "A Survey on the Integration of Decision Analysis and Expert Systems for Decision Support", IEEE Transactions on Systems Man and Cybernetics, vol SMC 20 n°2, pp 358-364

Decision Support in Public Administration (A-26)
P.W.G. Bots, H.G. Sol and R. Traunmüller (Editors)
Elsevier Science Publishers B.V. (North-Holland)

A GDSS methodology for personnel planning in rheumatology

M.T. Smits[a], Th. J.B.M. Postma[b], C.A.Th. Takkenberg[a], S. Terpstra[c].

[a] School of Economics, Tilburg University, P.O. Box 90153, 5000 LE Tilburg, The Netherlands.

[b] Economic Faculty, Groningen University, P.O. Box 800, 9700 AV Groningen, The Netherlands.

[c] University Hospital, LRP, Oostersingel 59, 9713 EZ Groningen, The Netherlands

Abstract
Manpower planning in the field of health care on a national level is a regular item on the agenda of policy makers. Recent examples are the quantities of dentists and ophtalmologists in the Netherlands. This paper decribes a methodology for manpower planning in health care, applied in the field of rheumatology. In health care, important decisions usually have a multi-level and multi-actor character: different actors with different mental models, goals and power interact in a bargaining process, dealing with various problem situations on the regional as well as the national level. A group decision making approach is advocated, where interactive model building stimulates shared meaning and communication. The Group Decision Support System methodology to support manpower decision processes is described in this paper, and some early results are given in the form of conceptual models and a simulation model. A GDSS is recommended for supporting manpower planning activities in health care, especially the use of Delphi procedures, workshops and simulation models.

1. INTRODUCTION

In the Netherlands, but also in other western countries, manpower problems in the field of health care are recurrent subjects for policy makers. Recent examples in the Netherlands are shortages versus surpluses in the quantity of dentists and continuing shortages in the supply of ophthalmologists. The Dutch Ministry of Welfare, Health, and Culture therefore is interested in a systematic approach of manpower planning in the field of health care. For this specific research the motive was the perceived shortage of rheumatologists.

This paper describes a GDSS methodology for manpower planning in health care. This methodology is applied in the field of rheumatology. The methodology is based on the concept of political rationality: different actors with different mental models, goals, languages, and power interact in a bargaining process, each with incomplete and imperfect information. A group decision making approach is advocated where interactive model building stimulates shared meaning and communication. In health care, important decisions usually have a multi-level and multi-actor character. Modelling complex manpower decision processes in the field of health care requires insight at both a detailed and at a more aggregated level. Manpower planning research in this field needs to be aware of several levels of aggregation and the relations among levels (see table 1).

LEVELS	ORGANIZATIONS/INSTITUTIONS
International	World Health Organization European Community International Professional Associations
National	Government Departments Advisory Boards National Professional Associations
Regional	Provincial boards Regional Public Health Service Cooperations of hospitals or physicians Sickfunds, insurance companies
Local	Hospitals Universities Departments Physicians

Table 1: Levels, organizations, and institutions in Dutch health care

This table gives only an overview of the different relevant levels, organizations, and institutions. For instance, if we zoom in and have a more detailed look at the Dutch advisory boards, we observe more than five relevant boards. In the field of rheumatology, at the hospital level, more than 10 different participants may work together in the rheumatology care system. Because of the multitude of possible interactions it is of no use to enumerate all types of participants in the Dutch health care system. It is better to think of networks or relation patterns of participants. The Dutch health care system can be characterized as a multi-level and a multi-actor system, with coalitions, negotiations, and political decision making [1,2,3]. Moreover the environment of the health care sector at the macro-level is dynamic and often turbulent: developments in politics, economics, law, technology, medical ethics, demography and epidemiology must be taken into account. There are many decision makers and advisory boards dealing with the preparation and implementation of laws, procedures, and rules concerning facilities, tariffs etc. in the health care system. The role of the central government for instance, is to set rules and minimum standards for the quality of health care, the accessibility of the health care system to everyone, the control of costs, the protection of health and health education.

The methodology we describe can be compared to general stages in the process of computer modelling. Mitroff [4] mentions a general scheme of problem solving: first a conceptual model of the problem situation is developed. This means that important variables and their relations are determined, in most cases supported by flowchart techniques, resulting in a qualitative model. In the next phase, data are collected and incorporated in the model, so the model turns into a formal empirical model. In the last phase, attention is paid to the development of solutions of the model and the implementation of the solution.

We describe a methodology for interactive modelling to let a group of different experts agree on a model for health care. Human players perform and mediate this process, e.g. by making interviews with the different parties involved. Our research approach consists of a combination of a Delphi study, a workshop and a scenario approach, and is based on a study of recent publications in the field of manpower planning and publications on the epidemiology of rheumatism [2]. The Delphi study and the workshop are interactive means to generate consensus on models and data. The scenario approach is based on discrete event and system dynamics simulation models.

2. OVERALL OBJECTIVES AND APPROACH: CHOOSING THE GDSS-METHODOLOGY

2.1 Levels of aggregation

Reality can be viewed very aggregated or more detailed. At first sight, manpower planning for health care at the national level requires an aggregate (national) model, but these models may be too abstract: at an aggregated level, variables of the detailed level are frequently lost. In our opinion the choice of the level of description and analysis in modelling for manpower planning in health care is an important one.

When using detailed regional models, we have to restrict ourselves in general to a partial view of a system. This is caused by both technical constraints of the computer support system and cognitive constraints of the participants. For example, it is practically impossible to construct empirical (operational) models of health care at the national level that account for flows of individual patients and detailed decisions of medical specialists. Even if such models could be constructed, the analysis of its dynamic behavior would be bounded by our cognitive system.

When using aggregated models we often assume that the model is sufficiently representative for all subsystems. This assumption has to be tested and forces the researcher to analyze a sample of subsystems in more detail.

We suggest an approach that starts with the development of a general conceptual model. This model is the nucleus of the research approach. Our research clearly shows that the individual decision making and practice of rheumatologists in different regions varies considerably. So, for detailed models this conceptual model must be adapted to assure a sufficient resemblance between models and reality. Next the detailed (regional) models can be combined to develop an aggregated (national) model. This approach also includes different modes of simulation: on a detailed level discrete event simulation (with an object oriented approach) can be used and on a higher level continuous models (e.g. based on system dynamics) can be applied. The consistency between the detailed models and the aggregate models must be checked. The remarks given above about levels of decision making, participants, and levels of aggregation lead us to the following methodological approach.

2.2. The GDSS-methodology used in the rheumatology case

The methodology chosen and further developed in this study is of the policy-Delphi type: a Delphi approach is combined with a structured workshop to construct models of the problem situation. These activities involve experts in model building as well as experts in the field of health care. The steps in table 2 describe the recommended methodology. Relatively new in this approach is the modelling on two levels of aggregation, combining discrete event simulation and continuous simulation; the motivation was given in the previous. This methodology is based on empirical and theoretical research [4-7].

Steps	Activities
1.	- Formation of a research group and a steering committee. - Literature study on manpower planning methods and the epidemiology of rheumatology.
2.	- Development of a conceptual manpower planning model. - Development of a questionnaire for Delphi interviews.
3.	- Delphi procedure with a sample of specialists.
4.	- Regional analysis of some selected geographical areas. - Development of a simulation model on a regional scale (discrete event modelling) and on a national scale (continuous simulation modelling).
5.	- Workshop with representatives of all parties involved. - Discussion and demonstration of the conceptual and simulation models.
6.	- Adjustment of the models. - Validation of the models.
7.	- Exploration of the future through scenario analysis. - Application of the GDSS in negotiations with parties involved in the health care process.

Table 2. GDSS-methodology recommended for health care manpower planning.

The steps of table 2 are explained by using the rheumatology case. First a *research group* of about four members was formed. The members were researchers with knowledge of model building and the health care field, knowledge of planning processes in general and knowledge of simulation and decision support techniques. The task of this group was to analyze the problem area and to build the model. The research group regularly reported to a *steering committee* or reference group, consisting of approximately 15 members, in which all relevant parties were represented: rheumatologists, other adjacent specialists, patient interest groups, and several political, scientific and advisory institutions. The research group carried out a *literature study* aimed at getting knowledge of the specific health care field, specific epidemiological data, general demographic data, institutions, organizations and finance with respect to rheumatology.

Next the research group developed a conceptual model of the demand and supply of rheumatology health care. Another model described the relation networks of rheumatologists, the physician-general practitioner, and other relevant disciplines in the rheumatology care network. The research group developed a *questionnaire* as a guide and framework for the structured interview with rheumatologists for the Delphi procedure. The questionnaire is meant to elicit the respondents opinions on some concepts and relations in order to check the preliminary conceptual model, aiming at adjustment and improvement of the model. Also the reactions and answers can be used to obtain values for the variables in the model.

The *Delphi procedure was executed* in a large sample of rheumatologists in the Netherlands, namely 31 specialists out of a total of about 80. The specialists were selected on criteria based on (i) geographical distribution over the country, (ii) gender, (iii) type of hospital, i.e. academic, or general, or specialized rheumatological care institutions, (iv) type of appointment, i.e., as employee, or as partner in an own enterprise, (v) age and experience. Using the Delphi results some geographical areas are selected and analysed. Also data are collected from different sources (e.g. ROME-project, NZI publications) and databases (e.g. S.D.R., SIG). A regional model is developed for the northern part of the Netherlands and a national scale model for the whole country.

To evaluate the steps 1 to 4 a one day structured workshop is held with participants-experts of different expertise fields. Participants of this workshop are among others medical specialists, rheumatologists, general practitioners, politicians, insurance company representatives, scientists, and patient group representatives. The conceptual model of demand and supply in health care is discussed and preliminary quantitative models are presented. The workshop is used as an evaluation of steps 1 to 4, and to indicate important variables and outcomes of the models. A major part of the workshop consists of role plays on policy decisions concerning rheumatology health care: the participants are divided into groups and have to present various statements, each group acting from a specific point of view. This may result in the formation of networks and insight in group decision processes. Also new facts and data can be obtained to adjust the simulation models in step 6. Based on the acquired knowledge up till now, an educated guess can be given of the desired numbers of rheumatologists in the coming 20 years.

In step 6 the derived models are adjusted and validated. The validation of the models is an important item in this phase. In the previous phases this was done by the different experts involved, mainly based on face validity: how well do the models fit their views on the rheumatological practice. This check mainly concerns the completeness of the models: 'are all important variables and relations incorporated?'. In the final step scenarios are developed, discussed, and changed as input for and part of policy making.

The above mentioned steps do not necessarily follow a purely linear sequence. Some steps can be passed through simultaneously, also earlier steps can be repeated. The same steps for manpower planning, policy and decision making processes can be applied in other fields of health care.

3. THE GDSS APPROACH IN THE RHEUMATOLOGY MANPOWER PLANNING CASE

When sketching our methodology as above, it might seem that modelling cycles play a central role. In our opinion the main effect and most important result of the methodology is not the development of simulation models as such, but the process as a whole, which stimulates the parties involved to develop a common model (shared meaning) and to discuss which variables, relations and values are important. The benefits of interactive computer policy modelling might not include optimal decisions on the desired number of rheumatologists or expected numbers of patients with rheumatic disorders. We expect the main effect of this group decision support system to be an improved and strong social basis for the decisions reached by the participating groups. The main effect is an improved decision process and shared meaning among all parties involved, which may result in better decisions.

In paragraph 3.1 some of the results of the GDSS process are described briefly, as examples of the output of the interactive modelling process. In paragraph 3.2 some aspects of the interaction process itself are described.

3.1 Some results of the GDSS process

For manpower forecasting and planning in health care a taxonomy of planning models is described by Reisman et al. [8]. Based on this taxonomy, the manpower planning model in the field of rheumatology can be described as follows. The planning horizon is about 15 to 20 years, and planning is done on both a national and regional level. Both objective and subjective data are used in the planning process, and scenarios are applied for strategy evaluation. The demand for rheumatology care depends on epidemiological and demographical developments: the incidence and prevalence of rheumatology in an aging population are part of the scenarios. Different groups involved in policy making in health care participate in the decision processes.

One of the first conceptual models developed in step 2 of the GDSS-methodology is presented in figure 1. This figure shows a conceptual demand and supply model for rheumatological care. Scenario's can be developed for future numbers of patients with rheumatic disorders and for future numbers of rheumatologists.

Another conceptual model describes the network of formal and informal relations in the field of rheumatology health care. The Delphi research showed that rheumatologists take a central place in this network, next to general practitioners, other specialists, paramedics, nurses and others. Occasionally this means that one rheumatologist operates actively within a network of over 50 general practitioners and related providers of health care.

Based on the knowledge acquired in the first steps of the GDSS methodology a simulation model was build for the rheumatological care in the next 15 years. This preliminary model can be used to demonstrate possible effects of changes in 11 important parameters derived from the previous steps. After we change a parameter the model calculates the number of rheumatologists needed during a period of 180 months (= 15 years), the developments of queues of patients waiting for rheumatological treatment, and several other dependent variables.

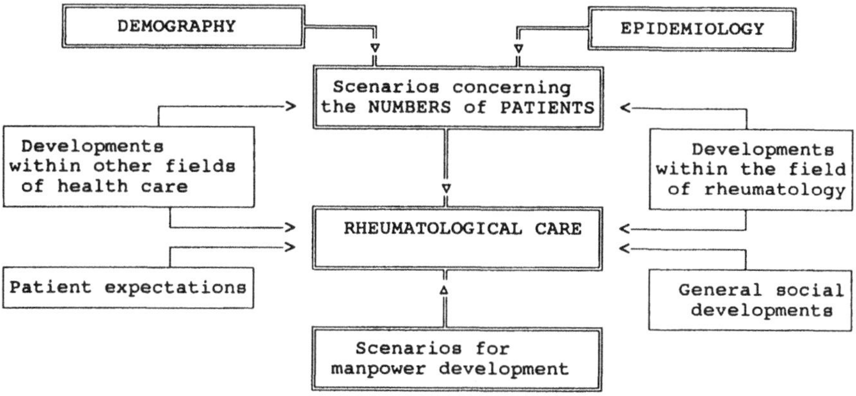

figure 1. A conceptual model for the demand and supply of rheumatological care.

An interesting conclusion of the simulation model is the saturation of individual rheumatological practices. After several years the rheumatological practice gets saturated with patients, so hardly any time is left to see new patients. This conclusion results from the Delphi interviews as well as from the experiments with the simulation model. From previous studies of the care of cancer it is known that no (or much less) saturation effects occur in the practices of cancer specialists. This might be due to the relative short period of time that cancer patients are treated by their specialists. Another considerable influence on the workload of rheumatologists comes from 'auxiliary services', so-called specialized nurses in rheumatic disorders. This was experienced in the northern part of the Netherlands.

A workshop was held to discuss the conceptual and simulation models with all parties involved in the rheumatological health care in the Netherlands. Participants concluded that it is necessary to involve many different participants and disciplines in the health care manpower planning process and that a network of people and organizations is indispensable. Furthermore they concluded that the coordination of rheumatological health care needs to be concentrated on the higher level of knowledge and experience, namely the level of rheumatologists, not the level of the general practitioners.

During the coming years the demand for rheumatological care will increase due to changing demographic patterns: more elderly people with rheumatic disorders. Also due to the relatively low death rates of rheumatic patients, the demand for care will increase, and practices of individual rheumatologists will tend to saturate. These effects must also be taken into account in manpower planning for other chronic diseases (e.g. asthmatic diseases, diabetes).

3.2 Analysis of the interaction process

For a more detailed analysis of the interaction process in interactive modelling it is important to look at the different players and their different roles in the process of model building, their interaction patterns, the progression of the building process and the control of the process.

Representatives of the different parties were involved in the health care planning process. Each party has a specific role, interest and view on the complex health care system (see also [9]). For instance, the policy makers are more interested in continuity and consistency of rules and laws, the insurance companies are interested in the balance between premiums and expenses, the patient representatives are concerned about the quality and accessibility of care for a specific disease, the specialists deal with the total workload, the quality of care and their private entrepreneurship. The GDSS-methodology leads to scenarios that are discussed and accepted by all parties involved. The system must be able to produce the specific output or information for each individual party.

Figure 2. Schematical presentation of 'shared meaning' of three individuals before and after a GDSS process. Each rectangle indicates a mental model. The amount of 'shared meaning' is denoted by *.

An important phase in the model building process is the workshop with representatives of all parties involved, whereby all participants are confronted with many statements, detailed as well as general, concerning the problem area. During the workshop, among others, a role play is done, in which role changes are a key instrument: for instance politicians and doctors have to play the role of patient representatives etc. Based on the reactions of the participants we have indications that the mental models of the different parties gradually change and show more overlap after the process. We assume that during the whole process the shared knowledge and the shared mental models of the participants grow or change. This is tentatively represented in figure 2.

The members of the research group are the mediators of the process: they do the Delphi interviews and mediate the workshop. Therefore they must have knowledge of model building and the health care system, modelling techniques and must have skills in communication, reflection and negotiation. The model building process progresses due to the participation of the parties in the interview sessions and the workshop.

4. CONCLUSIONS AND FURTHER RESEARCH

In the Netherlands manpower planning in the field of health care is mainly a political process: a multi-goal and multi-actor phenomenon. The GDSS approach has proved to be useful to support group decision making processes in this field. We recommend a GDSS-methodology for supporting manpower planning in health care, especially the use of Delphi procedures, workshops, and simulation models.

The GDSS methodology described in this paper comprises a few cycles of interactive modelling with representatives of several parties involved in the specific problem area. This process results in conceptual and simulation models of the problem situation. Furthermore due to multiple interactions between the parties involved, the project group and the steering group a form of consensus, 'shared meaning', is reached. This is in accordance with the findings of Watson et al. [10] in an experimental study on the intended and unintended consequences of the use of GDSS. Further research in this field is however necessary to arrive at more general conclusions.

Further research in the field of manpower planning for rheumatology should consist of follow-up studies at regional levels, construction and testing of a working GDSS-methodology, and further validation and extension of different simulation models. Also the implementation of GDSS, or Negotiation Support Systems [11] can be studied in other areas within the field of health care. More research is needed to elucidate or to quantify the amount of shared meaning between the parties involved before and after the GDSS process.

5. REFERENCES

1. N.A.A. Baakman: *Kritiek van het openbare bestuur* (Eng.: Criticism of the public

administration). Doctoral Dissertation, Thesis Publishers, Amsterdam (1990).

2. C.A.Th. Takkenberg, M.T. Smits, Th.J.B.M. Postma, S. Terpstra: *Mankracht-raming in de Gezondheidszorg* (Eng.: Manpower planning in health care), Stuur-groep Toekomstscenario's Gezondheidszorg (STG), Rijswijk (1992).
3. Th.J.B.M. Postma, M.T.Smits, S. Terpstra, C.A.Th. Takkenberg: *Personnel planning in the field of health care: an example in the field of rheumatology.* Proceedings of System Dynamics, 515-524, Utrecht (1992).
4. I.I. Mitroff: On managing science in the system age: two schemes for the study of science as the whole systems phenomenon. *TIMS Interface*, vol 4, nr 3 (1974).
5. J.A.M. Vennix: *Mental models and computer models.* Doctoral Dissertation, Nijmegen University (1990).
6. W.J. Scheper: *Group decision support systems.* Doctoral Dissertation, Tilburg University (1991).
7. M.B.M. van der Ven: *A Group Decision Support System for transfer pricing in the pharmaceutical industry.* Doctoral Thesis, Delft University (1989).
8. A. Reisman, M.H. Song, F. Ikem: A taxonomy for manpower forecasting and planning. *Socio-Econ. Plann. Sci.* Vol 25: 221-231 (1991).
9. R.E. Quinn, J. Rohrbaugh: A spatial model of effectiveness criteria: towards a competing values approach to organizational analysis. *Man. Science*, 363-377 (1983).
10. R.T. Watson, G. DeSanctis, M.S. Poole: Using a GDSS to facilitate group consensus: some intended and unintended consequences. *MIS Quarterly*: 462-477 (1988).
11. M.T. Jelassi, A. Foroughi: Negotiation Support Systems: an overview of design issues and existing software. *Decision Support Systems* Vol. 5: 167-181 (1989).

Decision Support in Public Administration (A-26)
P.W.G. Bots, H.G. Sol and R. Traunmüller (Editors)
Elsevier Science Publishers B.V. (North-Holland)

The MacPolicy Project: Developing a Group Decision Support System based on the Delphi Method.

Dirk Kenis and Lucas Verhaegen

Leisure, Future and Policy Planning Unit, Free University of Brussels (V.U.B.), Pleinlaan 2, 1050 Brussel, Belgium.

Abstract

This article gives a description of 'MacPolicy', a Group Decison Support System based upon the principles of the successful human sciences research method 'Policy Delphi'. This method facilitates consensus-seeking and exactly defines existing controversies in a computer conference. It is very well suited to handle policy planning or other tasks involving different stakeholder groups or different perspectives on the matter.

Our concept has the following features:

- it provides a structured discussion, using an iterative consensus seeking questioning technique with anonymous information feedback. As such it can be used as a front-end for different single-user Decision Support Systems.
- it is a database-mailing system that enables users to send and store questions, reports, opinions and critiques.
- it contains statistical tools, mainly based on the existing package 'Judges', to analyze collected data.
- Multicriteria Decision Aid tools are incorporated.

The MacPolicy project aims to raise the quality of most group decisions. Without pretending to be an alternative for every meeting, it is a well structured alternative for the solution of complex problems, or when timing or distance is problematic.

Keyword Codes: C.2.1; J.4; K.4.1.
Keywords: Computer-Communication Networks, Architecture and Design; Social and Behavioral Sciences; Public Policy Issues

1. INTRODUCTION

Rather than one expert making the choices with a Decision Support System on one computer, a Group Decision Support System allows several experts to use the computer to communicate with each other in order to obtain a better solution. The MacPolicy Project can be defined as an effort to the construction of such a system. It consists of different research projects at three research centers at the two Free

Universities of Brussels: the Flemish Vrije Universiteit Brussel as well as its French speaking sister, the Univeristé Libre de Bruxelles. The involved research centers are: the Programming Technology Lab under direction of Professor Theo D'Hondt; the Leisure, Future and Policy Planning unit which is directed by Professor Livin Bollaert; and the Statistics Institute at the U.L.B. represented by Professor Jean-Pierre Brans. The project is also supported by Apple Computer and SoftCore, a Belgian software company.

The Macpolicy project is an interdisciplinary research project. We would like to stress that it is not a group of human scientists telling the computer scientists what they should program. On the contrary, it is an equal collaboration where both parties try to get some grip on each others ways of thinking and stimulate each others creativity. There are several reasons for this close interdisciplinary approach. First of all, we believe it is a good way to develop software in general: the interactivity of the interface and the user-friendlyness of the software are important aspects of a G.D.S.S. and can benefit from interdisciplinary design. Secondly, there is an important groupwork-aspect to G.D.S.S., and although communication mediated by computers and a network differs thoroughly from face-to-face communication, this is typically a human scientist's domain. Finally, the underlying process structure of the MacPolicy software is derived from the Delphi method, a social sciences research technique that of course is best handled in close collaboration with social scientists. These elements all show that the field of G.D.S.S. lies on the intersection of the exact sciences and the humanities, and thus calls for an interdisciplinary approach. The need for such an approach has been stressed by many authors on G.D.S.S.

This brings us to the question of intentions: what is MacPolicy about and what is it aiming for? MacPolicy is a G.D.S.S.-prototype that enables people to communicate with each other over a computer network in a structured fashion. It can be used especially for policy planning or for many other group decisions or decision preparation phases.

In a first phase the aim of the MacPolicy project as a whole is the development of software for an experimental G.D.S.S.-room at the V.U.B. What we will try to prove by means of experiments is that the quality of group discussions can be raised if the group uses an adequately structured sequence, like Delphi, Nominal Group and other techniques provide, to discuss problems, side effects and possible solutions, and that such a technique can be supported by a computer system in a beneficial way. At this time a software prototype has been developed and tested on a small scale. Large-scale experiments are planned to take place in spring 1993.

In a second phase MacPolicy aims at the realisation of a meta-tool for network applications enabling Computer Supported Cooperative Work (C.S.C.W.). In this perspective the development of a G.D.S.S. can be seen as a benchmark application. In the following parts of this paper we will take a closer look at this attempt to make the difficult transition to a C.S.C.W. application via G.D.S.S. In order to do so we will start with a brief description of the first stage in this evolutionary process: the manual Delphi method. In a second section the next step, the computerization of this method, is handled. The following section describes a MacPolicy session and how this flexible G.D.S.S. adds new possibilities to the old Delphi method. This is followed by a consideration about the possible effects of the computerized Delphi method (as a new entity) on meetings. Next we take a look at the possibilities and challenges regarding C.S.C.W. Finally, a brief description of the technological requirements is given.

2. THE DELPHI METHOD AS A STARTING POINT.

The original Delphi method is a forecasting technique, meant to determine the probability and the future time of a certain event to happen, especially in the domain of technical topics. To do this, it uses opinions of a panel of experts in the field concerned. The actual technique consists of a structured discussion between these experts, whereby a convergence towards a certain degree of consensus is stimulated. A special trait of the first Delphi method is the way this discussion is held: not around a table but by means of a written questionnaire. Thus, the participants do not have to meet each other: they write down their points of view and answers to the questions asked and mail the questionnaire back to the team that is conducting the Delphi research. Based on these answers, a new questionnaire is constructed and sent to the experts again, together with eventual new information and accounts of statements of the different panel members. This process can be repeated several times. In this way a more or less common background of knowledge is built, against which points of view are explained, problems are clarified, priorities are determined and consensus is looked for.

Since its appearance in 1963 the Delphi method evolved into many variations and modifications. Whereas the original Delphi was used as a research technique for future forecasting, many derived variants of it with different objectives appeared very soon. The latter are rather hard to define because of the multitude of variations existing today. They are most often used in policy preparation phases, although they can be used for other goals as well. For reasons of convenience we will classify these variants together under the common denomination 'policy Delphi' to distinguish them from the original forecasting Delphi. It should be noticed that, when using the term 'policy Delphi', we are not specifically referring to the variant developed by M. Turoff (1,2).

Regardless of the goals aimed at, the difference between most policy Delphi's and the forecasting Delphi lies mainly in three points that are interrelated. The first point is the composition of the expert panel. In the traditional Delphi, this panel is a rather homogenous group of people having a comparable amount of knowledge about the research subject and having about the same qualifications. The homogenity of the panel is not surprising because the research subjects are very often of a technical nature, with questions of the "When will colour TV be realized?" - type to be answered. All - or as much as possible - aspects and problems relevant to make a realistic forecast ought to be considered, and the consensus among the collegues/experts is meant to give validity to the forecast.

In the case of a policy Delphi however, such a homogenous panel would'nt succeed in tackling a policy problem in a satisfactory way. Policy matters usually contain such a variety of aspects and perspectives that it takes very different kinds of specialists to cover up all the relevant scientific fields. These fields are not only technical any more, but also financial-economical, organisational, sociological, psychological, jurisdictional, etc... Thus, in a policy Delphi the expert panel will be a heterogenous group of specialists on very different fields, possibly having very different ways of looking at a proposed policy measure. Van Houten (3) calls this principle 'problem representativity', as opposed to 'field representativity' in the forecasting Delphi.

A second point of difference lies in the definition of "an expert" in a Delphi research context. This relates in a logical way to the point mentioned above. The function of the expert in the forecasting Delphi, with its aura of unquestioned scientific accuracy, changes completely in the policy Delphi, where there is not one but a whole range of ways to represent a problem. Here the expert does not necessarily need to be a highly qualified scientist who is able to make quantifiable estimations, but rather someone who knows a lot about one of several aspects of the issue discussed. His knowledge can be of a very practical and not only a theoretical nature, since practice is a very essential element of policy. Turoff (4) puts it this way: "A policy question is one for which there are no experts, only advocates and referees". This is especially true nowadays, in what is usually called the post-industrial society, where a growing complexity and interdependence emerges and policy makers more and more need to deal with the interests of different stakeholder groups. Policy Delphi's allow several stakeholder group representatives to participate in policy preparing processes in a highly qualitative and democratic fashion.

A third change in the policy Delphi's compared to the traditional one concerns the consensus seeking aspect. It is not difficult to understand that the necessity to reach consensus is left behind in the policy Delphi. Originally it was integrated in the method to give as much validity as possible to quantitative forecasts, but in a policy Delphi with respondents adhering sometimes radically opposing points of view, consensus may be hard to reach. "Then what's the use of organizing such an energy-consuming research if you can't reach agreement?" is an often heard criticism. The use is that one gets relatively fast a clear survey of the points where agreement exists en where it doesn't, and if the latter is the case, what the disagreement exactly is about. One may not forget that Delphi is a method for the support or preparation of policy making, not for policymaking itself.

3. INTO THE COMPUTER NETWORK.

Policy Delphi methods are being used since the early eighties at the 'Policy Consulting Services' (P.C.S.) unit at the Free University of Brussels, where they became a source of inspiration for the MacPolicy project. This experience in the field - mainly policy planning research on behalf of non-profit organisations and governmental institutions - was of great value in the process towards developing a G.D.S.S., since theoretical as well as practical knowledge on the process structure were available within the P.C.S. team, that worked closely together with the software developers.

The initial idea was to automate the Delphi communication structure, i.e. to implement it on a computer network with multiple personal workstations for the panel members. The substantial advantage was perceived to be a huge gain of time, since a handwritten policy Delphi with different subsequently constructed and substantial questionnaires takes about one year of work for a full-time researcher. A computerized version of the method, offering the possibilities of synchronous answering and immediate analysis of data, would make it possible to finish it within weeks or even a few days. But many more advantages are lying enclosed in the combination of Delphi and computer power, as can be read in the work of Hiltz and Turoff (5), pioneers in this field. Using the basic elements of the Delphi methodology as a guide, we will describe the transformation towards a computerized Group Decision Support System, the way it has been done in the MacPolicy Project..

The original forecastings Delphi as well as the younger policy variations share three basic features that form their methodological essence and distinguish them from other methods of group interaction: anonymity of the participants, iteration with controlled feedback, and statistical group response. Taking a closer look at these characteristic elements of the Delphi method, it becomes clear that it is very well suited to be translated into a computer application that enables group decision support.

3.1. Anonymity

The participants of a Delphi - the experts - are not made known to each other. In this way one can not identify a specific opinion with a particular person. This anonymity has several advantages compared with a face-to-face meeting:

- the influence of one or few dominating persons is neutralized
- the phenomenon that people don't want to change an opinion once they have publicly defended it loses its importance
- there is no deformation of individual opinions caused by pressure to conform to the group's thinking.
- it becomes difficult to have 'hidden agenda's'.

Through these effects, anonymity enables Delphi participants to have a more qualitative and rational discussion. In G.D.S.S. literature it is a known subject as well. Research (Jessup, Connolly & Galegher (6); Beauclair and Jelassi (7); Nunamaker et al. (8)) suggests that it has a positive influence on the quantity and on the quality of ideas uttered in a G.D.S.S.- meeting, enhances creative and disinhibited expression, and gives participants the feeling that negative feedback is not directed against themselves but against the content of their opinions.

Anonymity seems to have a negative influence when it comes to taking up responsabilities in the end. A solution to this might be to maintain anonymity throughout the Delphi process, but to drop it once the discussion has ended and engagement is wanted, as suggested by Jelassi and Beauclair (9). The implementation of optional 'degrees' of anonymity in the G.D.S.S. is not expected to cause much problems, except that it calls for a deontological code about its use: once G.D.S.S. participants are told that their communication is anonymous, it wouldn't be very moral to suddenly reveal names. It is clear however that the computer is an excellent medium for various anonymous communication processes.

3.2. Statistical group response

The status of the opinion of the group is usually expressed statistically in the manual Delphi research. Once the results from the second round of questioning are gathered, statistical distributions of the answers on each question can be made and sent to the respondents again together with the next questionnaire. Thus the participants are enabled to see and eventually re-position themselves within the spectrum of the group opinion. This statistical group response stems from the traditional Delphi approach, where mostly a quantitative estimation like a date or a number is asked. In this case the group's response is often represented in terms of a median and an interquartile.

In MacPolicy the statistical group response can be found back again in a form that is adapted to the advantages of computer use. Respondents are asked to answer open-ended questions, and are free to do so using as much words as they like. The problem of how to connect this textual information with statistical information is solved by presenting the answers of all participants and asking to express one's agreement with every answer on a five-point Likert scale. When all participants have made a rating, the software automatically calculates and provides every group member with statistical information about the group opinion based on the Likert scale scores. Users are able to change their personal opinion in any following round; the software then automatically adjusts the statistical distribution of the opinions within the group that are represented by histograms.

The MacPolicy software also provides a set of more sophisticated statistical tools by means of which the operator will be able to analyse the group's answers or any other data fast and easily.

3.3. Iteration with controlled feedback

The conventional Delphi procedure is fairly simple. The operator(s) designs a questionnaire and sends it to the panel members. The answers of this first round questionnaire are summarized by the monitor team, thus forming the basis for the construction of a second round questionnaire, that is sent to the respondents again. This process can be repeated until consensus is reached or until clear motives about disagreement are obtained. The respondent group is usually given at least one opportunity to re-evaluate its original answers after examination of the response of the group as a whole, the arguments for and against that were uttered and eventually the extra information that was provided concerning the problem discussed.

This iterative structure isn't hard to implement on a computer network and thus carried out easily by the MacPolicy system. It provides intelligent questionnaire forms that travel fast between users and operator, handles and distributes information efficiently, and also keeps it accessible at all times for any user by means of a transparent database.

4. A MACPOLICY SESSION IN A NUTSHELL

We know the ingredients for the MacPolicy application now; in this section we will give a brief description of a G.D.S.S. session. This session normally takes place in a decision room. Adapted communication between participants and operator for distributed settings are subject to further research.

The medium of interaction is the questionnaire. This questionnaire is constructed in advance and in a professional way by one or more communication specialists, after they have informed themselves thoroughly enough about the group or organisation and about the problem to be discussed. One of these specialists - or another qualified person who doesn't have any connection to the group using the system - can also function as an operator during the computer session. The operator has specific tasks: he or she creates the questionnaire forms on the computer and sends them over the network to the workstations of the panel members, who type in their answers and arguments and send the forms back. The operator can make summaries of answers if the same arguments are stated by multiple respondents. In order to do so his or her computer terminal has an interface that slightly differs from the other user interfaces, but which is just as easy to use by means of buttons that can be clicked with the mouse.

The spectrum of opinions uttered by the users is sorted, listed and sent to the participants again by the operator for a second round of questioning. This time the respondents are asked to rate the different answers to the first questionnaire on desirability, feasibility or agreement using five points-scales. They are free to write down some arguments for their point of view in a special text field. When they have finished this, the new information gets centralized again in the database and is accessible to the operator and the user - nevertheless, anonymity is maintained.

From this moment on - when the purely textual information has been linked to a numerical score - the operator is able to use several statistical tools to analyse the gathered data. These tools mainly depart from the package *Judges*, developed by B. Marechal (Université Libre de Bruxelles) and G. Colson (Université de Liège) and are recently integrated into MacPolicy. With the aid of *Judges* and on the basis of the information from the five points-scales, the MacPolicy operator can find out :

- who in the group has the same view (i.e. highly correlated scores)
- if existing subgroups (on the basis of profession, sex, age, etc...) have opposing views
- which ideas have reached a certain degree of consensus (hierarchical clustering of items)
- around which ideas disagreement exists
- which people in the group have an opposed point of view and why
- which is the range of resolutions that can be built, after clustering the items the group agreed on.

This and other information can be used in the MacPolicy session itself or kept in the database as documentation for the group. It can also be used by the operator as a basis for the construction of new (often consensus seeking) questions.

In a next round of questioning each participant gets on his screen an overview of the arguments given for every item, as well as a histogram of the distribution of the ratings of the group, and finally also a graphic display with a distribution of the ratings in the form of box-plots with a grey zone between the first and the third quartile, and a black bar representing the median. A position-mark shows the own score of the previous round to each respondent in the graphic displays. After reading the different arguments, some users will change their mind; they always have the opportunity to give a different rating using the five points-scale. The box plots and histograms are updated when they appear again in the next round. A process rule that can be implemented if wanted is the following: when somebody rates beyond a certain range and thus has a more or less 'deviant' opinion, he or she can be asked to consider the arguments on the item again and a) review the previously given rating in favour of the dominant group opinion, or b) stick to his or her first rating but give an extra argumentation for this point of view. In this way the 'Maverick' gets enough opportunities to convince the other group members.

This iterative process can be repeated several times, eventually with new questions added, until sufficient data are collected. In a real situation this will most often mean: until consensus is reached, or until the points of disagreement can be formulated clearly and there are no more significant changes of opinion over subsequent rounds. Another possibility is to stop after an agreed number of question rounds.

5. POSSIBLE EFFECTS OF THE COMPUTERIZED DELPHI METHOD ON MEETINGS

The Delphi method tries to be an answer to some dysfunctional and restricting aspects of normal face-to-face meetings. Mediation by computer also influences communication, and this may be an advantage or a disadvantage in trying to reach the goal of the communication - Nunamaker et al. (10) call this the influence on the 'process gains' and 'process losses'. We will take a brief look here at some eminent dysfunctional characteristics or process losses of face-to-face communication that are eliminated or weakened by the Delphi technique, or rather by the use of the three main features of its communication structure: anonimity, iteration with feedback, and statistical group response. The following list (Gustafson et al. (11); Dalkey and Helmer (12)) is not exhaustive:

- the hasty formulation of preconceived notions, and an inclination to close one's mind to novel idea's, often induced by too little time for reflexion;
- a 'central tendency' effect, where groups tend to follow a limited train of thought;
- a tendency to reach decisions speedily, before all problem dimensions have been considered;
- a tendency to defend a stand once it is taken: winning an argument often becomes more important then reaching a better conclusion;
- especially when no chairman has been appointed, the influence of a dominant personality can grow beyond proportion;
- group pressure for conformity and the implied (spoken or unspoken) threat of sanctions from the more knowledgeable and/or powerful members;
- the amount of time and effort spent by the group to maintain itself;
- the often overwhelming and distracting effect of superfluous and irrelevant information in group meetings;
- the difficulties of getting together a large group of experts due to time restrictions and geographical distances;
- the larger the group, the more difficult it becomes to reach equal participation;
- when the meeting consists of members of the same peer group, they can have a common bias.

Nunamaker's (13) list of effects that reduce normal process losses by the use of his own G.D.S.S. is very similar to the effects mentioned above. This is not a surprise since it also provides anonimity of the participants and a synchronous communication structure. Effects mentioned by him that are due to the use of the computer as communication medium are:

- a certain degree of depersonalization or deindividuation. This is most likely mainly caused by the "narrowing" of the communication to the verbal aspect only. Other sources of information that normally guide people to form an image of the conversation partner - para-verbal language, body language, visual appearance - are left out. This depersonalization is considered an advantage since it

promotes free and disinhibited expression of thoughts.
- the risk of failing to remember things is eliminated by the presence of a group memory in the form of a database;
- the speed and the redundancy of information of the computer medium are an advantage, but can also be a disadvantage for people not used to work with the computer. This is why the MacPolicy system tries to be as user-friendly and easy to handle as possible, providing a simple user-interface with screen-buttons that are triggered by a click of the mouse.

An additional advantage of 'computerization' regarding the iterative structure is the minimalization of the risk that the process must be ended prematurely; extra questioning rounds can be added as often as is considered to be necessary. In the manual Delphi it sometimes happens that, before a satisfying conclusion can be drawn, the process has to be stopped due to a lack of time or money.

6. ACTUAL EXPERIENCES WITH MACPOLICY

The MacPolicy system has not reached its final version. A prototype has been developed and tested with several groups, varying from testcases with fictive problems and some members of the research team as participants, to real-life problem cases and real experts who to try to solve it. During this period the software was constantly being refined and adjusted, based on this experiences. At the moment this article is being written, the prototype is still a prototype, but is fit to be used in a large-scale experiment, planned to take place in spring '93.

In this experiment we will try to evaluate the decision quality and the satisfaction of the participants to the discussion, compared with the 'normal' face-to-face meeting, presided by a chairman and without the application of any communication technique. In this way, we want to escape the danger of being incapable to distinguish effects when using the Delphi communication structure and the computer mediation as separate variables. The design of the experiment will be based on the theoretical framework of Pinsonneault and Kramer (14). Their taxonomy contains the categories "personal factors", "group structure", "task characteristics", "situational factors" and "technological support" that together give form to the "group process", which in its turn determinates the results, subdivided in "task related" and "group related" results. The basis for this framework stems mainly from a study of 12 articles containing empirical research on the influence of GDSS on goup processes and outcomes. Pinsonneault and Kramer aimed to integrate the dispersed concepts used by these authors, thus establishing a more complete framework.

7. FROM G.D.S.S. TO C.S.C.W.

As mentioned in the introduction of this paper, the G.D.S.S. is also meant as a benchmark application towards a system that enables Computer Supported Cooperative Work (C.S.C.W.). In general, a growing tendency can be seen towards systems developed for real collaboration by multiple users working as a team, slowly leaving behind the narrower G.D.S.S. - approach with its limitation to decision making.

The Delphi sequence implemented in the MacPolicy G.D.S.S. is not the only possible communication sequence to be implemented in such a system. Using an object-oriented programming environment that allows flexible and tailorable applications (see further in this paper), the step towards the implementation of other structured communication sequences becomes less difficult to take. When we only consider the computerized Delphi process, it is remarkable how many variations and optional rules could possibly be integrated in the MacPolicy system, as is shown in this list:

- anonymity could be made variable: among panel members only, among the whole group including the operator, throughout the whole process or not...
- subpopulations of respondent groups could be created, eventually interacting with one another in a serial or parallel way;
- using time constraints;
- allowing face-to-face discussions between some or all participants, at certain predefined moments or on request...

This list is only tentative; the effects of it on the communication process would make a serious job for a researcher to evaluate. It also wouldn't leave much of the original Delphi structure. A logical evolution of this trend would go towards the domain of workflow and document management. Still we have to be very careful not to become over- optimistic: scientists may know little about what an effective use of G.D.S.S. might be, about C.S.C.W. we know even less at this time. The G.D.S.S.-room can therefore be seen not only as a laboratory for the study of decision making but also for collaboration in general through network-communication. In this way we hope to learn how decision makers act and react in such an alternative 'meeting' and how this network interaction can be adapted and ameliorated for C.S.C.W.

An interesting point to mention still is that the MacPolicy G.D.S.S. can be used very well in combination with, or as front-end application for, other single user Decision Support Systems. In this case the questions in MacPolicy are structured around finding a consensus of input data for this DSS application. In this way virtually each DSS can be implemented in our G.D.S.S. A good example is the Multiple Criteria Decision Aids, for which the criteria as well as the alternatives can be generated by means of MacPolicy. A project has recently started to incorporate a Multi Criteria Decision Aid, Promethee (the software PROMCALC and GAIA, developed by Prof. J.P. Brans), in this environment.

8. TECHNOLOGICAL REQUIREMENTS

When thinking about the technical requirements to the realisation of the G.D.S.S.- and C.S.C.W.- concepts outlined in this paper, it becomes clear that requirement number one is flexibility. We were not looking for an application but rather for an environment, as no definite, in all cases optimal structured communication or G.D.S.S. could be found to exist. This has to do with the multitude and diversity of actions the system must be able to support: the creation of question forms, the sending and receiving of messages, the analyzing of data, the storing of very different kinds of information, the editing of interactive graphical displays, and last but certainly not least: the handling of the interface by computer laymen - because that is what most users will be.

Giving priority to this latter consideration, the first prototype that was constructed used Hypercard as an interface. This offered some advanced cutting and pasting abilities with predefined fields, buttons containing code, and an easy to use modular scripting language. However, the performance of Hypercard on a local area network was very poor: for instance, it took minutes to get a card sent from the database to the users.

Thus, an advanced programming environment with some Hypercard characteristics like an attractive and interactive interface as well as the different user levels was necessary. Our colleagues from the Programming Technology Lab opted for SmallTalk '80, an object oriented language that suited our purposes best. One of the great advantages of SmallTalk is the wide range of possibilities the end user will have at his/her disposal to create a unique communication sequence as well as an personalised interface with, if desired, advanced audio-visual features, suited to the specific needs of the user. This flexibility and tailorability may be too complex to handle in an adequate way for non-specialists. This is why we consider implementing different user-levels with progressive complexity and modeling possibilities, with a maximum of functionality at every level. It should also be possible to have specific standardised, ready-to-use SmallTalk programs available, comparable with HyperCard stacks.

The actual instances of the various software tools to be used in the proposed system as a whole are thus as follows:

- SmallTalk '80 as the programming environment in which different user programs can function
- an object-oriented database (Gemstone) that will be totally invisible to the eyes of the end-user, except for the net-result that objects (documents...) are accessible across workstation boundaries
- a conventional relational database
- a document-server providing access to non-conventional data such as sound, structured graphics, facsimiles, animations etc... will also be integrated in the system. This server is developed by SoftCore, the software company that supports the MacPolicy project.
- interconnection shall be realized through a TCP/IP network.

More information about the technology used in this system can be obtained at the following addresses:

Michel Tilman
Vrije Universiteit Brussel
Programming Technology Lab - F 730
Pleinlaan 2
B - 1050 Brussel

Phone: +32-2-641 34 91

For other information about this project please contact:

Dirk Kenis & Lucas Verhaegen
Vrije Universiteit Brussel
Policy Consulting Services - L 406
Pleinlaan 2
B - 1050 Brussel

E-mail: lverhaeg@vnet3.vub.ac.be

REFERENCES

1. Turoff, M.: The design of a Policy Delphi. In: Technological Forecasting and Social Change, 1970, nr. 2, p. 149-171.
2. Turoff, M.: The Policy Delphi. In: Linstone, H.A. en M. Turoff (eds.): The Delphi Method. Techniques and Applications. 1975, London.
3. van Houten H.J.: Policy-Delphi: de implementatie van een multi-actor onderzoeksontwerp. 1985, Subfaculteit Andragologie, Amsterdam.
4. Turoff, M.: The design of a Policy Delphi. In: Technological Forecasting and Social Change, 1970, nr. 2, p. 149-171.
5. Hiltz, S.R. and M. Turoff: The network nation: human communication via computer. 1978, London.
6. Jessup L.M., T. Connolly and J.Galegher: The effects of anonimity on GDSS group processes with an idea generating task. In: MIS Quarterly, 1990, vol. 14 nr. 3, p. 313-321.
7. Beauclair R. A. and T. Jelassi: An integrated framework for Group Decision Support System design. In: Information & Management, 1987, nr. 13, p.143-153.
8. Nunamaker, J.F., A.R. Dennis et al:Electronic Meeting Systems to Support Group Work : Theory and Practice in Arizona. 1990, University of Arizona, Tucson.
9. Beauclair R. A. and T. Jelassi: An integrated framework for Group Decision Support System design. In: Information & Management, 1987, nr. 13, p.143-153.
10. Nunamaker, J.F., A.R. Dennis et al:Electronic Meeting Systems to Support Group Work : Theory and Practice in Arizona. 1990, University of Arizona, Tucson.
11. Gustafson, D.H., R.K. Shukla, A. Delbecq and G.W. Walster: A comparative study of differences in subjective likelihood estimates made by individuals, interacting groups, Delphi-groups and nominal groups. In: Organizational Behaviour and Human Performance, 1973, nr. 9, p.280-291.
12. Dalkey,N. and O. Helmer: An experimental application of the Delphi Method to the use of experts. In: Management Science, 1963, sept., p.458-467.
13. Nunamaker, J.F., A.R. Dennis et al:Electronic Meeting Systems to Support Group Work : Theory and Practice in Arizona. 1990, University of Arizona, Tucson.
14. Pinsonneault, A. and K.L. Kraemer: The effects of electronic meetings on group processes and outcomes: an assessment of the empirical research. In: European Journal of Operational Research, 1990, nr. 46, p. 143-161.

Decision Support in Public Administration (A-26)
P.W.G. Bots, H.G. Sol and R. Traunmüller (Editors)
Elsevier Science Publishers B.V. (North-Holland)

Participatory Information Systems

– Supporting the decision process in public sector information systems

Åke Grönlund and Bai Guohua,
Umeå University, Institute for Information Processing
S-901 87 Umeå, Sweden
email gron□cs.umu.se

Abstract

Technical development and widespread computer knowledge have changed the preconditions for organizations. The development has led to a situation of choice between a centralistic and a decentralistic way of employing IT. This choice is of particular importance when it comes to public sector information systems, since issues of democracy, openness and participation in decision making are vital in that context. In this paper, we delinate an "Information Network Paradigm", which takes the clients' information needs as the starting point for the design of information systems. This paper also describes and discusses one project in this vein, the CO-project at Umeå university. The "Feedback Learning Stategy" is introduced as a way of involving users in system redesign. The "LiveBetter" is a prototype system designed to meet the communication and self-service demands raised by this strategy. LiveBetter includes some tools for redesign activities among users.

Keywords: The CO-project, Decision Context, Feedback Learning Strategy, The Information Network Paradigm, Participation, Participatory Information Systems, Redesign Activities.

1. The setting – new preconditions for IS

Information system use in the public sector is entering into a new era in several ways. The enormous growth of the public sectors in most industrialized countries has encountered economic constraints. A restructuring has begun, at the end of which one can expect considerable role-changes on the part of civil servants as well as on the part of their "customers", the citizens. The increasing internationalization of business, the loosening of the ties between the individual and the public authorities by abolition of national monopolies are examples of changes in the conditions. At the same time IS technology and user skill is improving rapidly. Technical achievements include the possibility of distributing data by means of computer networks, graphic interfaces and ever increasing computing power at the desktop. The humans are changing, too; there is a new generation of expert computer users currently playing at our schoolyards or just out of school. Altogether this introduces new possibilities as well as new demands to information systems intended to serve the citizens. The citizen of tomorrow will be more independent than the one of today. He will have to – and demand possibilities to – find his way to public information more by himself, by use of several information sources, many of them on-line databases accessible through various public computer systems. The new civil servant will be a generalist, providing help and guidance whenever expertise in information finding is providing help and guidance whenever expertise in information finding is needed. The new public agency will be more of a service centre and less of an information delivery agency. Much of this development is already emerging in various ongoing projects in Sweden. This paper describes and discusses one such project, the CO-project[1] at Umeå university.

When public service is concerned, issues related to democracy, influence and justice are crucial. Therefore participation in design and *re*design of information systems is important. The process of deciding on design of public service has to include the citizens. When information systems become publicly accessible, so must the struggle with redesign of the information systems. In this paper, the "Feedback Learning Stategy" is introduced as a way of involving users in system redesign. The "LiveBetter" is a prototype system designed to meet the communication and self-service demands raised by this strategy. LiveBetter includes some tools for redesign activities among users.

In the first part of this paper we will take a look at some concepts fundamental for the topic. The first is "participation", which has been on top of the agenda in the IS design field for many years. What has motivated the struggle for participation? How should it be conducted? The second is "decisions". How are decisions made? This is to ask questions like "how do people think and work?", searching into the psyche of the individual. But it is also to ask "how do people interact?" and "how do we *want* decisions to be made", which leads us into the field of social settings. The concept "decision context" will be introduced to discuss such issues.

Part two outlines the concept "participatory information systems" as systems aiming at improving decision quality.

Part three introduces the IS development model "Feedback Learning Strategy" as a way to organizational development by means of participation in redesign activities.

The last section presents "LiveBetter", a prototype public service system implementing the Feedback Learning Strategy.

In the next section, we will describe the setting for this paper in terms of two conflicting "paradigms" for information processing. These will be only briefly described, they are debated under various labels in other places, but we think that they are useful as a picture of the problems we are focusing on.

Two "paradigms" for information processing

The word "paradigm" should be reserved for major changes in the view of the world. It hasn't always been. In this section we will discuss two views of how information should be treated within and especially "without" – regarding the interface towards the citizens – organizations in general and public agencies in particular. The word "paradigm" may seem too much in this context. Aren't we just discussing another trend in

---

1 CO is for "CO-constructive systems development", which is a project sponsored by the Swedish Board for Technical Development (NUTEK) and several companies such as Volvo, Apoteksbolaget (The Swedish Pharmacy Company), the Municipality of Umeå and others.

the business world or even just within the IS society? We don't think so. Even if we are unable to pursue this line of reasoning here, we are convinced that the implications of what we will be referring to as "the information network paradigm" includes views of the character of man and – because of that – views of societal organization that are truly incompatible with those currently prevailing. The issue has been raised many times before, for instance in (Pitt, & Smith, 1984). Will IT lead to decentralization of organizations or to more centralization? As (Booth, & Pitt, 1984) claim, there is no deterministic way in which IT itself will lead to one or the other. IT holds a potential for both. In the following, we will pursue the decentralistic view as the one we want to achieve. We are thus not predicting a paradigm change, we are working towards one.

Let us now briefly describe the two information processing paradigms, which we will call The "Information Delivery Paradigm" and The "Information Network Paradigm". The paradigms concern the interface between an agency and its customers. The problem is: How should information exchange between the two be conducted?

The Information Delivery paradigm

The Information Delivery (ID) paradigm is the traditional view of how government agencies should conduct their information exchange with the outer world. In this view, the organization somehow possesses all the relevant information. It also has a *de facto* monopoly on how to organize this information. A client with some information problem may pose a *question* to the agency, represented by its front personnel (see Figure 1). If the question can be answered by investigation in the data banks available to the clerk by the use of the implemented search functions it will be answered. If not, the question will "die". The client will not be able to push it further with that clerk. An attempt to do so would only result in raised voices and an unpleasant situation. He will have to go somewhere else, with no guarantee whatsoever that the result will be better. If he is lucky, his question will fit into some other agency's question categories. Otherwise the same thing will happen over again. In the ID paradigm, the right to formulate problems is restricted to the information owners. Every attempt to formulate problems in other ways will be considered "foul": the questions will not be understood, or they will simply be ignored because trying to answer them would cause too much trouble. In a sense, therefore, the ID paradigm is an authoritarian paradigm. It also causes problem in dealing with an ever changing environment. What if the "unanswerable" questions in fact are the most important ones?

The Information Network paradigm

The Information Network (IN) paradigm (see Figure 2) is the opposite of the ID paradigm in the sense that it is less concerned with the internal efficiency problems of the agency. The IN paradigm focuses primarily on the information needs of the clients. The IN paradigm assumes that the main objective of a public agency is serving client information needs, and thus it should be very sensitive to the the questions posed by the clients. These question must be well taken care of, since they are indicators of the client information needs. Thus client questions comes first, organization comes afterwards. The role of the agency is to help the individual find his way to information needed to solve his problem. From being an information deliverer, the clerk turns into a *facilitator*. He is to help the client building his information network, which may be very differently organized than the public agency. This network may include data bases, it also may include persons, experts in various field pertinent to the issues at stake.

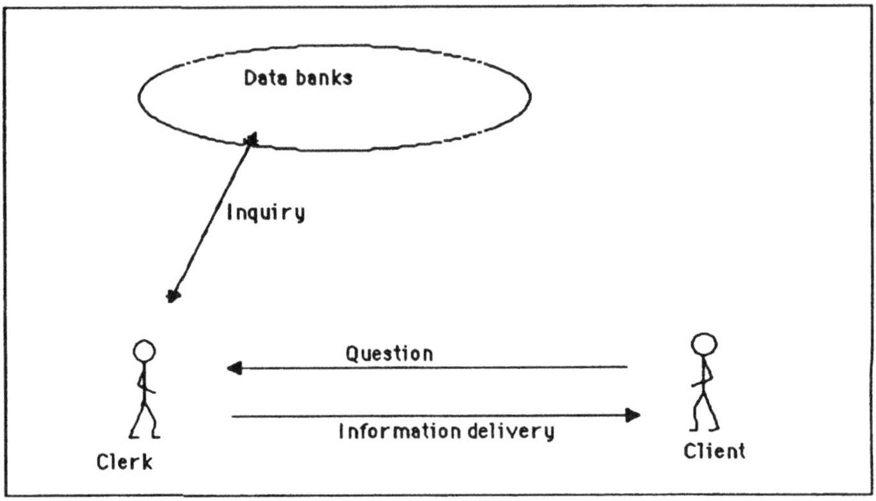

Figure 1: The "Information Delivery Paradigm".

It is important to note the word *indicators* in the above said. Client questions are *indicators* of information needs. It may well be that clients pose "wrong" questions in the sense that they are badly formulated, do not really cover the problem perceived, have to be transformed to be compatible with available data etc. Another trap is the number of questions. It is not at all clear the the most common question is the most important one. It is for instance very common that people don't pose a question because they know it will not be answered. Experiences like the one described in the previous section have taught them the uselessness of posing unanswerable questions. Therefore, an unusual question may well be of greater interest to those interested in the development of the agency because it touches at the limits of the agency's capacity. Being able to answer it might significantly increase the agency's capability.

But despite of all these problems, the bottom line of the IN paradigm is that *client's questions are seen as indicators of the social situation that the agency has to meet in some way in order to fulfill its mission.*

The rest of this paper will be devoted to proposing a IS development strategy – and some tools supporting this strategy – based on the IN paradigm.

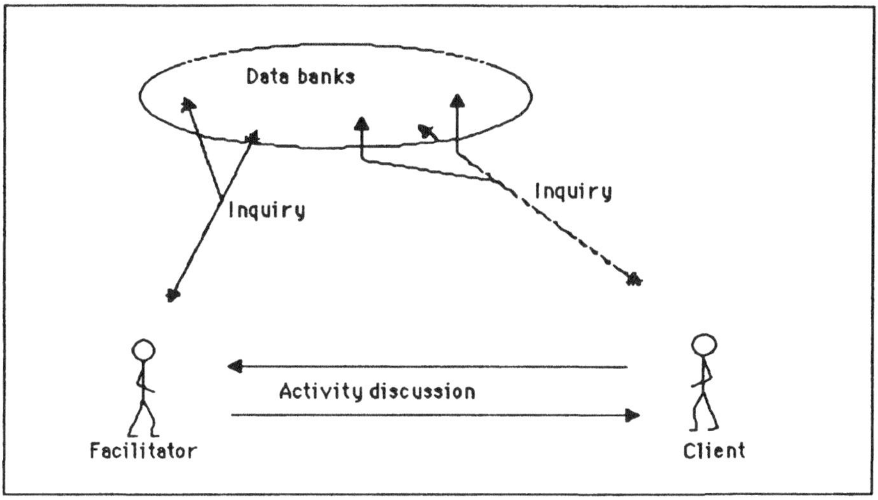

Figure 2: The "Information Network Paradigm".

New demands for IS development

The IN paradigm, as described above, imposes new demands on design of information systems. A larger and more diverse population of users changes the design problem to one of *re*design since you cannot possibly involve everyone at the design stage. Openness – as for data as well as for procedures – and adaptivity to changes in opinions are aspects crucial especially to public sector information systems. This makes it more important than ever to consider the issue "how do people work?", which in this context translates into "how do people use the public information systems?", because the only place you can elicit signals for IS redesign is precisely at work or in use. A lot of research has been done regarding this issue in the field Decision Support Systems, and we believe that research is relevant even in a wider context. For instance, (Jones, & McLeod, 1986) claim that the traditional way of viewing decision-makers' work styles and information requirements is generally wrong. They find that decision-makers retrieve data from many sources, many of them informal. Those sources often contain "low quality data", that is data on particularities, as opposed to the highly aggregated data usually considered the only concern of decision-makers. Furthermore, these information sources are often used in a seemingly random way, or perhaps it is better to say "non-modelled". It seems that the use of these sources has the very specific purpose to find the unexpected. The authors conclude that the concept of DSS has to be conceived in the "broadest possible" sense, and, more specifically, that a DSS has to

- be able to tap the proper sources, and
- match the information sources, including informal ones. This means an information source containing casual data must appear differently than one containing statistically significant data. This may seem prosaic, but computers tend to make everything appear alike, at least to

non-experts. They also generally make data look more reliable that it in fact is.

Also, there is the concept of "tacit knowledge". Even though it may not always be completely or forever tacit, it seems clear that some knowledge can be achieved only in the process of "doing", which may be interacting with other people or using artifacts[2]. This calls for new approaches to system development. Evolutionary approaches seem to be the only possible way to get to know about how users actually think about their work (Sandevall, Hägglund, Gustafsson, Jonesjö, & Strömfors, 1983), (Heng, 1987). If one accepts this epistemology, it becomes necessary to include the users not only in systems design, but also in *redesign*.

Participation

Participation in design of information systems has been a major theme over the past twenty years. Participation has been urged for several reasons, such as acquisition of knowledge, smoother implementation of computer systems, and user emancipation. The struggle for participation has so far taken place within the factory or office walls. We are today facing a new generation of computerized information systems that have tentacles grasping at the world outside those walls. Examples are publicly accessible or inter-organizational information systems. Design of such systems have to consider new groups of users, groups that cannot be reached the traditional way, since they don't belong to one specific company. Participation in design of such systems can thus not *only* be sought the usual ways. In this paper, a major theme is that in design of public information systems participation at the design phase is not enough. Public information systems are part of social systems that keep changing and therefore call for ongoing IS *redesign*. Therefore, participation has to include *participation in redesign*. Such redesign is urged for and conducted through innumerable decisions made by all persons involved with the system. *Redesign activities* are activities that are integrated in the use activities and contribute to the constant evolution of the information system. The inclusion of such activities is crucial to the survival of public sector information systems.

During the last few years a lot has been said about participation in the process of designing information systems. Starting with the socio-technical shool in the early 1970's, the users of information systems have been at the focus for systems design for twenty years. Especially renowned for the development of "participatory design" today is the so called "Scandinavian school" (Bansler, 1987). During the last fifteen years, academics of this school have participated in several systems development projects in which on top of the list of objectives has been found the issue of enhancing and improving user participation (Whitaker, Essler, & Östberg, 1991). The reasons for this strive towards user participation has been twofold. On the one hand, user knowledge has proven to be as attractive as elusive. How can such knowledge be retrieved and used in the systems development in order to build technically better systems? On the other hand, the worker's position in the power struggle at the workplaces has been at the agenda. Participation in IT systems

---

2 (Lundeqvist, 1982)

development has been seen as a means of strenghtening the user side in this struggle.

At the international scene, too, participation has become a top issue. In the last few years, some researchers have dealt with the problem of organizational survival in a world of rapidly changing conditions for business (Mitroff, 1990, Engelbart, 1990). This work seems to have rendered quite some interest among practitioners (Johansson, 1991). The suggestions are for companies to build monitoring and redesigning functions into their organizations. An example is Engelbart's "Bootstrap initiative" (Engelbart, 1990).

Regardless of the motives for participation, an observation is that the efforts have been directed towards the design phase of system development. While early systems development methods typically have called in the users at late stages – test, education and implementation – a common feature of the newer "participatory" methods is the notion that the sooner the users are called in the better. This view has by now spread to the practitioners in the field.

There are however problems with participation. Not only does it make the design phase more expensive by including more people and thus prolonging and making more uncertain the work. Also, it has been found that users don't always know what they want. This may seem ironical, but it is not. Information systems typically radically change the work situation for those involved. User expertise, be it tacit or explicit, is inevitably closely knit to their current work situation. Thus it is not likely to be directly applicable to a system which is intended to produce a radically different situation. Furthermore, users have learned by experience that computer systems tend to replace people, that is themselves. Therefore the normal user tends to be restrictive in suggesting changes in work routines and organization.

It is clear that many systems development projects have created more problems that they have solved. The typical problems are at the individual level ergonomically unsatisfactory workplaces, which combined with an increased work pace has led to physical diseases for many workers. At an organizational level conflicts between workers and management or between groups of workers have been common (Ehn, 1988). There seems to be limitations to the usefulness of participation. Participatory design seems to be successful only within the limits of consensus on the definition of system quality.

It is obvious that organizations have to change. This will often lead to people losing their jobs, some jobs being extincted. These are from the individual's point of view negative effects that immediately come to mind in the face of systems development projects. The positive effects – new jobs being created, routine jobs being replaced with more skilled or less routine ones – are often not as immediately visible to the workers. There is still a fear for computerization. Maybe one reason for this can be found in the way systems development is performed.

Participatory design, participatory prototyping, participatory business modeling are all concepts aiming at involving the users at early stages of systems development, participatory business modeling being the most radical in this sense (Whitaker, et al., 1991). This seems a natural way to go. Obviously to be able to influence the strategic decisions taken at early stages of projects you have to be there. But what if these decisions are not the starting point? What if there are important events *before* these decisions, events that in fact influence the decisions much more than what is said at committee meetings or done in project groups? If this is true, the belief that if you only participate in project groups you are guaranteed *real* influence seems disputable.

The crucial issue here is obviously how decisions are made. But are they really "made"? Often decision makers tell us that they "had no possibility to make another decision". Are such statements just excuses for poor guts? If they are not, how can it be that such situations occur? In the next section, we will take a look at the concept "decision".

Decisions

There are two aspects of decisions that we want to discuss in this section. These are the *decision context* and the *decision maker*. The latter of the two is widely debated. It seems that there is considerable consensus today on a shift of view from seeing the decision maker as "the rational man" towards perceiving him as more multi-rational[3], intuitive and emotional.

We would like to introduce the concept *decision context* in order to widen the view of decision making. We claim that decision making is a social process, involving many people and several views and conflicts between views. Decision making takes place within a social order that is much more complex than one may be led to believe when reading literature on for example decision support systems. This social order involves a lot more than a decision maker and his personality. Let us now elaborate some on this.

The decision context

A traditional view is that the goal of administration is to maintain some sort of equilibrium. (Simon, 1957) refers to this equilibrium as the point, or area, where three types of actors – customers, entrepeneurs and employees – keep the organization going in a way that satisfactory fills their respective needs, expectations or wishes. In order to maintain this equilibrium, innumerable decisions are made by all actors. The scope of a particular decision may be wide or narrow. What makes them all similar is that they are made within a social context. This context is delimited by the common area of interest, that is the area in which the equilibrium is maintained. Simon emphasizes strongly the notion of decisions as a *process* as opposed to a "decision point"[4]. He subdivides this process into

---

3 For a thorough discussion of rationality in design work, see (Stolterman, 1991), where it is concluded that there are several rationalities involved in design work. Very often, one of these rationalities is over-emphasized in design methods, which leads to methods that do not match reality, or simply do not work.

4 I am referring only to Simon here, but in fact ideas very similar to his, although using a different terminology, can be found in many other places, such as (Churchman, 1968) and (Forsgren, 1988).

three stages: intelligence, design and choice, words in which he puts a generally accepted meaning. *Intelligence* thus refers to the military way of using the word; it is what you do to find out about something, typically a social situation. *Design* is what you do when inventing action alternatives, among which you finally *choose*. Simon refers some evidence that decision makers spend a large part of their time on intelligence activities, even more on design, but very little on choice.

When trying to support decisions then, it seems interesting to think about what might be going on during these first two stages. When viewing decision making as a social process, the picture would look something like this:

- A *social situation* exists. In this social situation,
- *actors* come forward either by their own initiative or by organizational authorization.
- *Features* of the social situation begin to "show", that is become explicit. Such features are not objective, but biased according to the view of each observer. (Compare "intelligence" in (Simon, 1960)).
- *Action lines* are delinated. (Compare "design" in (Simon, 1960)). At this stage many activist groups may be involved, each developing lines of action promoting their interests.

• *Decisions* concerning the further development of the social situation are made. These decisions are made by authorized decision making bodies or individuals. The decisions are distinguishable points in the history of the social context, but they are most often decisions *pro forma*. The "real decision" was made earlier in the process up to the decision point. Nevertheless, these decision points are important, since they generally terminate a discussion by fixing a state. By doing so, they set the rules for the future and thus assigns responsibility for problems to come to some specified decision maker(s).

One may wonder whether we are not missing an important point here, which would be:

- *Evaluation*. This would be where the results of the decision is reviewed in order to prepare for next decision. This point, however, may not be distinct from "intelligence", since no decision is "first". They all depend on previously made decisions. Consequently, intelligence includes evaluating the effects of previous decisions. Therefore, we will not in the following consider evaluation separately.

If decision making is a social activity, what, then, is a *good decision*? How can we judge the quality of a decision? This is the theme of next section.

Decision quality

What is a "good decision"? Let us first restrict the question by saying that the types of decision we are discussing are such that do not only concern the organization itself, but also – and most of all – some people outside the organization. The decision is hence supposed to produce some (good) output to a client[5]. We are thus discussing quality of decisions and actions in a wider scope than that of the specific organization that makes the decisions and performs the actions. The problem is that the *real* outcome, the effects of a decision, may not show within years. Decisions may also produce ambiguous results, which are open to interpretation. Is there a way of judging decisions by process?

To keep to the Simon terminology, one could say that a good decision is one that gives the decision maker the greatest advantage while maintaining the organization's equilibrium. Which, then, are the ingredients of this equilibrium? In the social setting surrounding the decision, there are various actors. Those are individuals, but they are also most often part of some group. This group belonging is crucial to the individual's values and loyalties, which in turn form the (moral) base for any decision he makes. The actors possess some amount of power in that the ability to in practice influence a certain decision is not equally distributed among the actors. This power may stem from a number of conditions, such as economic wealth, personal charisma or large number. The actors also possess some knowledge about the social situation which makes them more or less able to predict possible consequenses of a decision. This knowledge is always incomplete. It is also unevenly distributed.

The social situation around a decision can thus be viewed as a game between values, a power game or a prediction game, or all of this simultaneously. Group belonging form the values and guides the actions of individuals. A decision made within a specific group but concerning also other groups is thus likely to have a bias whenever the interest or values of the decision making group conflict with those of other groups concerned by the decision. Similarly, decisions may be biased by the relative power – in all the respects mentioned above – among groups. Apart from the equality problems this arises, it also leads to the problem of "tunnel vision": a chain of perspective biased interpretations may lead to a decision that is significantly different than a chain of only slightly different interpretations (Dreyfus, & Dreyfus, 1986, p 165).

In the context of such "inter-group" decisions, the measurement for the quality ("goodness") of a decision has to be searched for beyond the group or organization that actually makes the decision. According to the situation sketched above, the quality of a decision would be the highest possible if:

- Loyalty bias[6] is kept to a minimum;
- Power bias is kept to a minimum;

---

5 Compare Churchman's concept of "measure of performance" and his distinction between "functional analysis" and "structural analysis" in, for instance, (Churchman, 1968).

6 This is referred to as "valuational bias" in (Simon, 1957, p 15)

- Rationality of the decision is seen in the broadest possible sense[7], that is
  - Including the largest possible number of "stakeholders" (openness);
  - Evaluating the largest possible number of alternatives (wide scope);

It is clear that organizations differ in the sense that they have different relations to their clients. Some organizations have a strong authoritative character while some at the other end of the scale have a "beggar" character. An organization of the first type is the tax authorities, the second kind may be a charity organization. What is to be considered "minimum" and "the broadest possible sense" is thus not at all obvious.

The decision maker

It should be clear from the above said that we want to modify the traditional view of a decision-maker as a person of high ranks making wide scope strategic decisions in an organization. While not excluding such persons, we consider a decision maker *anybody making a decision pertinent to the organization's activities*. This adds to the number of people, but it shouldn't make obsolete the research made on how decision makers work. Most of this is probably relevant even if we include other actors under the label "decision maker", since most of it concerns social and psychological issues applicable to humans in general. Work styles, preferences, social behaviour that have been observed and analyzed when studying "decision makers" may as well be related to "people". In the following, we will be referring to some of this work.

The studies of decision making, and in the IS community the concept of Decision Support Systems, have so far mostly been directed towards the fifth phase of the decision making process as described above, the choice between already defined lines of action. Decision support has been thought of as tools for the "brooding man on horseback who suddenly rouses himself from thought and issues an order to a subordinate" to borrow Simons ironic description (Simon, 1960, p 1). If we widen this view to encompass everybody making decisions pertinent to the organizations activities, we enter into the field of social interaction. Public sector information systems are good examples of systems where this has to be done. Such information systems are supposed to be not only a tool for regulation of citizen activities, but also a means for the democratic government of society. We are thus talking about social situations where large parts of important communi-cation is conducted by means of computer systems. It is inevitable to con-template how the earlier stages of decision making may be affected by this.

How, then, do people work during these early stages of the decision making process? Let us first consider the problem of "intelligence", how you get to know your social situation. (Dreyfus, et al., 1986) compare the American[8] manager with the Japanese. They claim that the Japanese

---

[7] Compare Ivanov's concept "data quality" (Ivanov, 1972)

[8] The Dreyfuses are comparing America to Japan, but one could easily replace America with Europe, because the ideas of leadership are very much the same on both sides of the Atlantic.

manager is better than the American because of his background. He will typically stay with the same company during all his career, and will thus by the time he becomes a top manager be familiar with every aspect of his company. He will be an "expert" in terms of the Dreyfus & Dreyfus five-stage skill acquisition model. The American manager, on the other hand, is typically "transplanted" into the organization. He has learned the job in some other organization. When starting a new job as top manager in a to him unfamiliar organization, he will be regressing to "competent executive at best" (Dreyfus, et al., 1986, p 160). In the Dreyfus*2 model, the situational – social – knowledge is what makes the difference between good and excellent.

What can we learn from this, except that you should stay on your job if you hope to become an expert? We think that one thing vital to IS development is the importance of constant learning. You can always learn something new, and you should make much effort to do so. In the FLS, to be presented in chapter 3, we have taken this as a starting point when introducing the concept *redesign activities*. Redesign activities must include a lot of sensivity concerning aspects of and changes in the social situation. To speak with Simon once again, constant good intelligence is crucial. How, then, should intelligence be conducted?

In intelligence work there are facts, but also intuition. The role of intuition seems to have been neglected in the era of "scientific management", but on the other hand it doesn't seem unfair to say that earlier it has been overestimated. The argument that such intuitive decision making is superior because "it has worked before" cannot be taken too seriously, since it is obvious that today almost any decision has wider implications than were usually considered earlier. As an example, today any decision concerning industrial activity includes not only economical factors, but also consideration of environmental effects and physical risk to workers.

What, then, is the role of intuition? Where does it come from? And how to maintain it? How to avoid the tunnel vision you are likely to develop when getting to deeply enmeshed in a situation? Dreyfus & Dreyfus calls it "deliberative rationality" when a (expert) manager uses mathema-tical models (which represent novice or at best competent understanding) to get *help* (that is, yet another view, nothing more) in understanding a problem. This is to be distinguished from "calculative rationality", which is a novice (that is, less conscious) way of using the same tool. Dreyfus & Dreyfus' main criticism against current use of mathematical models for decision support is that in creating such models you force experts to think like beginners, since you have to make them rationalize their acts and thoughts, assign numbers to their intuitive actions and "abstract from experiences new and more subtle rules for making decisions, rather than merely to remember the outcome so he can recognize and make the correct response to similar situations in the future" (Dreyfus, et al., 1986, p 170). The experts cannot do that, the very point is that they don't know the rules they "use". Also, if the intuition is *experience-based* rather than *rule-based* there is no reason to believe that rules created from such knowledge are universal, that is, can be extended to new cases. It seems that intuition is an as important as elusive thing. Obviously you cannot grasp it, but wouldn't it despite of that be possible to *use* it? After all, we all seem to do that all along, only we don't know exactly *how*.

When in a hard situation decision makers tend to look for *real-life stories* rather than for more data (Dreyfus, et al., 1986, p 166). They even prefer gossip, speculation and hearsay to the abstracted information in reports. This is because the manager normally works in a "calculated chaos" (Carlsson, 1991, p 111), while unable to find time to himself go through all reports and data available he is heavily dependent on other peoples judgement, opinions etc. The nature of his work is primary oral and social (Mintzberg, 1973).

Much has been said in criticism of decision support systems, and it seems obvious that people don't calculate in a mathematic-like rational way. But saying that doesn't solve the problem how to support decision making. According to what has been said above, there is no fixed boundary between a "DSS" and an "IS". A lot of people make decisions based on data coming from computerized information systems. Even if the systems do not include specified *decision* models, they certainly model *the context for decision making*. If we consider the social context important for decision making, then we have to look into how this context is modelled by computer systems employed in the business. In the following section, we will delinate a new class of information systems, deliberately built for dealing with the decision context in a participatory manner. We are going to use the name "participatory information systems" (PARTIS) for such systems.

2. Participatory information systems

We have said above that the decision making context, the social system that surrounds the formal decision makers and makes up the setting for their decisions, is not only crucial for, but in fact *is* the decision making. We have also said that computerized information system make up an often very important part of that social system. It seems very safe to predict that the computerized part will increase, as for the number of systems as well as for the number and sophistication of functions implemented in them. There are some situations when the discussion about decision context and participation becomes particularly interesting. Such situations are:

- *Where man-to-man communication has been replaced* by computers as intermediaries. Examples include the autobank, the bankomat, job information at the self-service jobcentre.
- *Where man-to-man communication in the "manual" system does not occur or is scarce* because of practical obstacles that computerization may remove. Examples include contacts between individuals and people in government agencies other than the "front-personnel", electronic markets such as MiniTel and TeleGuide[9].

In such cases the organization of redesign activities within the normal activity system becomes an important challenge. When computer systems are introduced in such areas, the social context will inevitably change, and thus the preconditions for decision making. New ways of inquiring for, discovering and responding to signals in the social system will have to

---

[9] The Swedish version of France's MiniTel.

be developed. It may be proper to remark that redesign activities are certainly not restricted to the implementation of proper tools in a computer system. Organizations as a whole must be included. My point here is that the computer system cannot be *ex*cluded.

In a situation where important parts of the business are taking place by the use of computers *instead of* face-to-face communication – which the increasing use of anything from automatic tellers to electronic mail points at – we face new problems. How to conduct the business in a new social setting? To which extent can the factors/features pertinent to decision making be described and modeled, communicated and developed by use of some computer system? To which extent can they *not* be controlled by the "center" of the company? This is to ask: how will the IT development change the terms for organization? And how should this potential be taken care of at the organizational level? This is the problem of participation, the conflict between the wish to engage users (in a wide sense) in IS develop-ment and the wish to maintain central control over the business. It is the conflict between decentralizational and centralizational forces within the field opened by information technology (Pitt, et al., 1984). This is the point where we focus our attention, one result of which has been the development of the "Feedback Learning Strategy" (FLS) (see sections 3 and 4). Let us now introduce our definition of a participatory information system:

A participatory information system (PARTIS) is one that aims at improving decision quality by sweeping in relevant parts of the decision context. It does so by soliciting for contributions by all actors in the social system surrounding the decision making.

A PARTIS, by definition aiming at providing decision makers with a broader scope of information than what can be processed by mathematical models must include proper tools for "informal" information processing.

The problem is not just one of supporting communication and "less-structured" (in terms of relevance for the decision making) data. In terms of the decision model above, a PARTIS must be able to:

- Describe a social situation in multiple ways and by multiple "describers" (actors).
- Support discovery and description of "features" of the social situation. This is not the same as the previous point, since in this case we are concerned with the general problem facing any individual belonging to any group to distinguish relevant features of a situation.
- Provide means for resolving conflicts and contradictions emerging within the activity system.
- Support activities to redesign the information system.

It is important to note some specific problems pertinent to this approach. It is conventional wisdom that programmed activity tends to drive out non-programmed activity. The organizational implication of this is that it is important to make special arrangements to provide for non-programmed activities if they are considered important. In the case of participatory information systems, special arrangements has to be made for "discovery" as opposed to "routine" in order to catch emerging new features of the social situation. This problem has been a starting point for the FLS. In particular, we find the following areas interesting:

- Encouraging participation,
- supporting multiple perspectives,
- maintaining neutrality between perspectives until the choice stage,
- supporting data structuring at several levels,
- developing tools for data transition between structure levels, and
- supporting use at different levels (skilled/unskilled users, client/administrator users etc.).

Many of these areas include problems that cannot be solved by a computer system. Let us take a look at one that can, the data structuring problem.

The data structuring problem

A PARTIS by definition involves a large number of people, people at various levels of a business, people of various skills, people working with different tasks and therefore facing different problems and working in different ways. The data structuring problem is thus one of *representing* data in various ways to different users, but also one of *transferring* a problem representation from one description level to another. Consequently, our PARTIS will have to consider the following structure problems:

- Levels of data structure,
- levels of use,
- types of use, and
- types of decision problem.

Let us elaborate on these structure problems.

Levels of data structure

The obvious problem with data structuring is that some data very easily can be transferred into numbers and then used for calculation while other, equally important, data does not lend itself to such operations. A simple classification would be:

- High level structuring: statistics.
- Medium level structuring: "Hard" but not complete data.
- Low level: Personal communication, such as letters and messages. Opinions, emotions.

This classification, though common and simple, may obscure the fact that any given data item may belong to all of these three categories, although *not at the same time* or *not at the same place*. What is unstructured now, may be structured later. What is structured in one use situation may be unstructured in another. What is structured now may be *re*structured later. The problems to be approached are:

- How to avoid too early structuring of data without too heavily restricting the system's useability?
- How to imposing *one* structure on data without preventing the imposal of *another* structure? That is, how to prepare for restructuring?

These problems are discussed in (Sandevall, et al., 1983), who propose a "stepwise structuring" method. Sandevall et al point out that very simple data structuring is often enough. In a similar vein, we believe that even very simple ways of multi-level structuring and equally simple ways of supporting transformation between structure levels could be most useful. In the FLS, we propose a simple model for such a structure in three levels for a public service system.

Levels of use

The Dreyfuses introduce a five-stage model for skill (Dreyfus, et al., 1986), ranging from "novice" to "expert". This model explains how persons at different levels of skill treat "tools" of various kind. The higher on the scale, the more conscious the use of the tools and the more independence from the tool. Computer manufacturers, too, have recognized the importance of intelligibility of screen layouts, interaction media etc, since problems at that level very easily prevents any further use. Very generally speaking, user interaction with a complex information system could be seen as somewhere on a scale reaching from "casual user level", which means just browsing, to "expert level", which includes search model experiments, extensive communi-cation with other actors, that is planned activities directed towards a clear goal.

Though neither new nor controversial, this point is a crucial one in that to be able to meet other demands in the PARTIS approach, system feasability for use at various levels of skill in computer use is a prerequisite.

Types of use

A PARTIS typically includes a number of different categories of users. In accordance with (Simon, 1957), but borrowing the terminology primarily from (Forsgren, 1988), the main categories of use would be:

- Client use, use by the customers, the final information users. Typically this would mean exploratory use in order to find out as much as possible in order to solve a problem.
- Administrator use. This would typically mean administrative routine work and pertinent problem solving.
- Organization decison maker use. Mainly use at intervals in order to supervise and improve the business.

Support for these activities apparently requires different tools, as for functionality as well as for complexity of use.

Types of decision problem

Decision problems, in terms of participatory information systems, differ in their social scope. They can be:

- Consistent, involving only people sharing the same interests, values or loyalties.
- Inconsistent, involving several groups with conflicting views, values and/or loyalties.

There is obviously a continuum here since decision problems can be more or less inconsistent.

In this chapter, we have discussed general requirements for participatory information systems. In next chapter we will introduce the Feedback Learning Strategy, which is our approach to – some of – the issues raised here.

3. The Feedback Learning Strategy – redesign based on use

The Feedback Learning Strategy was developed as a way to capture the issues that have been discussed in the previous sections and assimilate them into IS design. It should be noted that the FLS is not just a systems development method. It is a method for redesigning organizations according to the "Information Network Paradigm". The focus is on computer systems because of their strategic importance in the organizational information processing. IS redesign is thus a vehicle for organizational redesign.

The traditional way of developing an IS normally looks something like this:

problem analysis – modelling – prototyping – interface refinement – use

Once the system is in use, there is little preparedness for changes. The assumptions behind such a development strategy are:

- The features of the use context that are distinguished at the development stage are stable for a long period (in fact all the use period), and
- The users can formulate all their relevant knowledge in a way that can be understood by the designers prior to system design.

As for the first point, it is today conventional wisdom that this is not so. As for the second point, experiences from many IS development projects show that communication problems between designers and users during the design stage are common and often lead to serious system problems (Svensson, & Qwerin, 1986). The reason is often simple. Users are experts in use, designers are experts in design. This is to say; user knowledge does often not easily translate into designer language and vice versa. Therefore, the point to look for user expertise is in use (see Figure 3). But how to do that?

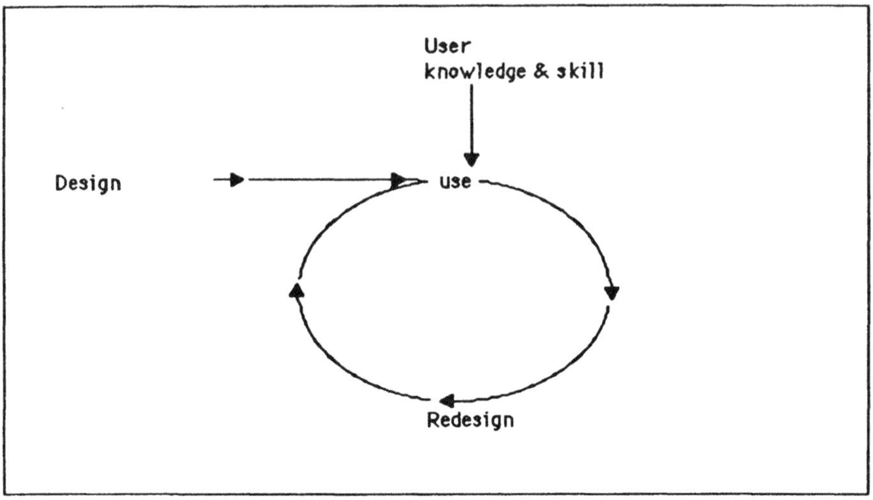

Figure 3: "Design is once, Use is forever". User knowledge is knowledge about the use situation, user skill is skill to act in that context. Therefore, information systems redesign must be based on what happens in the use situation.

One important point in this context is the concept *tacit knowledge*. Coined by Polanyi (Polanyi, 1967), much referred to and dicussed (Göranzon, 1984), (Göranzon, 1990), (Lundeqvist, 1982), (Ehn, 1988), the term refers to knowledge that cannot be verbalized, at least not easily. Riding a bike is an example of such knowledge. Four-year-olds know how to do it, but explaining the physics about it takes a lot of theoretical knowledge. The same applies to a larger or smaller extent to any skilled work.

Another related foundation for the FLS is the notion of the human learning process as not only an intellectual one. Recent work, not least in the Scandinavian system development tradition[10], has focused much on the human process of learning. Even though the theoretical foundations seem somewhat ambigous, this work sheds a new light on systems design. In this tradition, the suggestion is that humans learn not only by analyzing data, but also by *using artifacts* and by *interacting with other humans in practice*. This practice includes "doing" as well as *language-games.*. The FLS suggests that user and designer must work together in both these ways to construct a dynamic feedback system which could absorb energy from the environment so as to keep the system adaptive to changes.

Following the lines of thought outlined above, the general idea behind the FLS strategy is:

- Consider the end-users the most important decision-makers,
- try to support the decisions they have to make,
- try to learn from their activity, and

---

10 (Ehn, 1988)

• use the gained knowledge to redesign the business.

By the term *Participatory Information Systems* we have named systems that provide for user involvement in systems redesign based on everyday use. Such systems will have to include some kind of forum for redesign activities in close connection with the core activities within the system (see Figure 4).

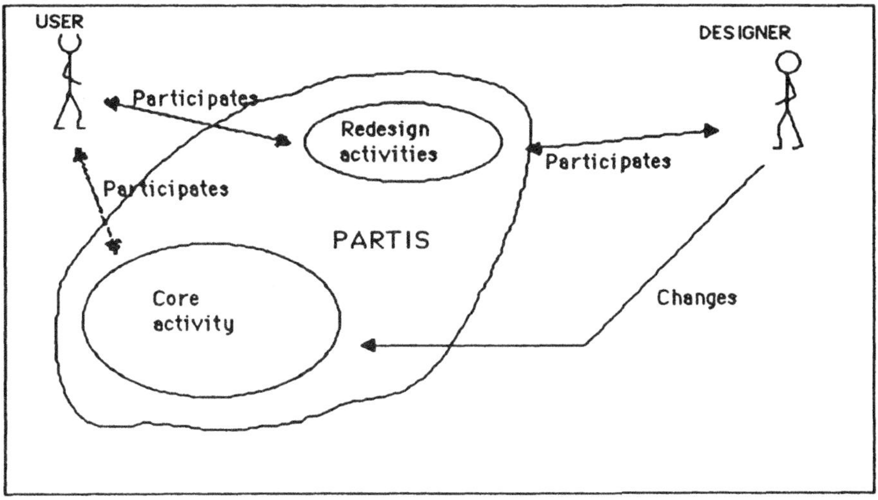

Figure 4: A participatory information system (PARTIS) is one that provides for its users to participate in redesign activities integrated with the core activities.

It is obvious that a system which encourages and supports user involvement also must adapt to user demands in some way. Involvement must lead to some action or reaction, otherwise nobody will bother to get involved. Therefore, what we propose is in fact a model for continous redesign of the computer system and by that creating incentives for organizational redesign as a way to support the organizational view of the Information Network paradigm. The FLS approach to system redesign is based on:

- decentralisation of some *redesign activities* to users,
- tools for collecting *peripheral data,*
- tools for interpreting and structuring such data, and
- setting up a *forum* where redesign activities can take place.

Before proceeding, let us interpret the meaning of these four foundations:

Peripheral data

Within the Information Delivery Paradigm (p 3), data collection is performed such that anything that does not fit into the predefined categories is ignored and never considered again. If the purpose is adapting to changing conditions, it appears to be a good idea not to throw away such data, but rather keep it until you know what to do with it. We call such possibly useful data "peripheral", since it is not – yet – at the core of the activities, it may, however, affect them, now or later.

The only persons that can tell about such peripheral data are the users. So, how can we elicit useful information from the everyday use of the system? One way is, of course, statistics. We can collect data on system use from within the system (how often certain functions were used, etc.), or from without (like questionnaires on utilization and user appreciation of the system). But the problem still remains; we will only be able to collect data based on predefined categories. In our prototype system, we have integrated mail and bulletin board features with the core system (housing brokerage) in order to be able to collect data that does not – yet – fall into any defined category. The purpose is to exploit the advantage of "being there" in situations when things happen, as opposed to making inquiry afterwards, in order to:

- spot unanticipated situations, and
- trace new trends.

But this is only the first step. If we manage to "grab the data at the scene of the crime", we need to take some action based on what we have found. We need to organize redesign activities.

Redesign activities & tools

Incentives to change pop up in the everyday use of the system, and it is a good strategy for collecting data to get as close to the source as possible. Applied to this context, this would mean that if the user is given some means of immediately noting and/or forwarding information about events or situations that are important for use but somehow go beyond the current system domain, then this information very likely is the best available as feedback on the system status. Within the IN paradigm, it is this information that provides motivation and energy for the system adaptiveness. It is also this information that should guide the direction of adaptation. To provide for production of such information the users should not only "operate" the system, but also have some tools and some authority to:

- identify critical situations, and
- react to such situations.

This is recognized by Heng (1987), who claims that evolutionary approaches to DSS development, though already the most successful approach, must be improved by incremental features of prototypes and easy-to-use updating facilities. To provide for this at an organizational level, a *forum* has to be set up[11], where redesign activities can take place. In that forum, within the terminology of the IN paradigm, actors meet for a dialogue on system quality and improvement (see Figure 5). "Actors" include the companies front personnel (the "facilitator") experts in relevant fields ("resource persons") and managers.

---

[11] Compare the "Open Hyper document" in Engelbarts Bootstrap Strategy (Engelbart, 1990).

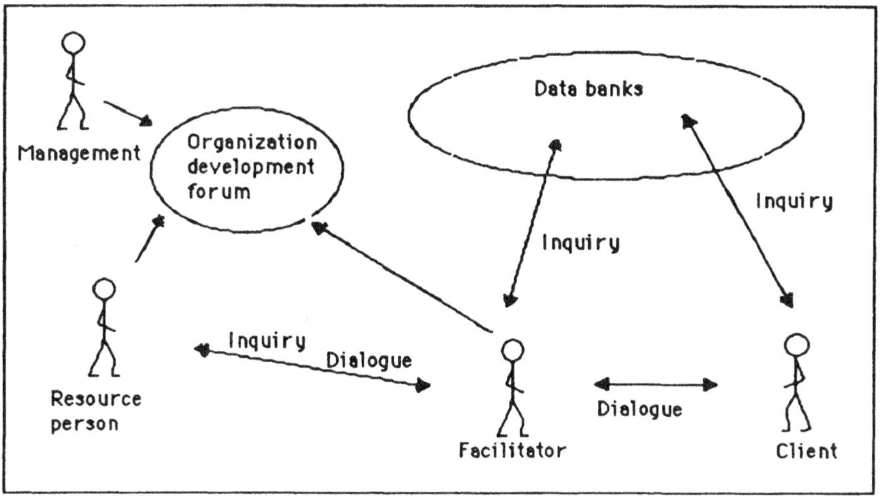

Figure 5: The "Extended Information Network Model" includes a forum for redesign activities.

The forum

A forum for redesign activities has to be widely accessible to actors in the activity system. It also has to include proper tools for collaboration. The mission for such a redesign forum is to provide users possibilities to:

- notify on situations that the system cannot cope with,
- communicate on system use, thus improving user competence,
- propose changes, like the addition or removal of features, functions, rules and so on, and
- discuss such proposals.

However, it is obvious that redesign activities at user level mainly concern operational use. At the strategic level, redesign activities in the FLS context include:

- scanning redesign activity among users,
- participating in discussions, and
- implementing changes judged necessary.

The first two points are motivated twofold. First, there is the generally recognized need for user education all through the systems life. Second, if the importance of "low quality" data and more random or personal search activities is such as concluded by (Jones, et al., 1986) and (Dreyfus, et al., 1986), then these activities must be supported by computerized tools in cases where IS replace humans. The third point is motivated by the obvious reflection that if the evolutionary approach is to work the time span from notification to reaction can not be too long (Heng, 1987). Tools for such activities are not yet commonly available, even though some are about to enter the market. However, much activity is going on. Different approaches to the problems include the following:

- Discussion structuring. This has been the focus of much research (Eherer, & Jarke, 1991) (Conklin, 1987) (Halasz, 1988), but also some software products implementing some findings have entered the market (Lee, & Brookes, 1992), (CMS., 1992).
- Semantic enhancement of searching in free text databases (Wendlandt, & Driscoll, 1991);
- Maintenance of rule-bases (Coenen, & Bench-Capon, 1991); and
- Stimulus agents as a way of creating a challenging arena for decision making (Anghern, 1992).

It seems the first point, how to organize discussions in an efficient and stimulating way is the most difficult problem, since it includes not only technical obstacles but also – and as it seems most of all – problems related to organizational culture (Lee, et al., 1992).

Embryonic development

In the FLS, we view a system as composed of two subsystems; "users" subsystem and "designers"[12] subsystem. The system should be developed in an evolutionary way, starting with an "embryo". This means the designers will implement preliminary tools and evaluate the system based on performance. During system use, a user will sooner or later find the limitations of the original system. He may then need some information, models or functions which the present system can not provide. Requirements like this are just the motivation or "energy" for system adaptiveness. To capture these requirements then becomes a most vital issue for system development. We will thus have to support this process somehow. In our strategy we do this by introducing the concepts *latent feedback*, *manifest feedback* and *communication* (see Figure 6). "Manifest" feedback refers to such data that can be used immediately in system updating, while "latent" is the label for data that is considered important at least by somebody but cannot be immediately integrated in the system. Therefore, such data has to spend some time being treated in the "communication" box before it can possibly be used in system redesign. In next section we will take a brief look at the implementation of this strategy in the prototype "LiveBetter".

4. "LiveBetter" – Some tools for participation

In this chapter, we will discuss some tools for communication and feedback, that is tools facilitating interaction between users and designers. The examples are selected from "LiveBetter", a prototype system for housing brokerage developed at Umeå University in cooperation with the municipal housing agency. The setting for the system is the following; The municipality of Umeå provides help for the citizens in finding or exchanging apartments, the agency "Bostadsförmedlingen" (Apartment brokerage service). This service is much used, and to avoid spending tax money doing things people can do

---

[12] By "designer" we here refer to *those responsible for the design of – smaller or larger parts of – the business.* This may mean everybody from a clerk to an executive or all of them at the same time. We thus *do not* refer to computer experts per se.

themselves, the idea was to provide a self-service means for people to go about their own business as much as possible. It seemed much of the client's information needs could be fulfilled by just allowing them access to the agency's data. There are, however, also more problematic cases.

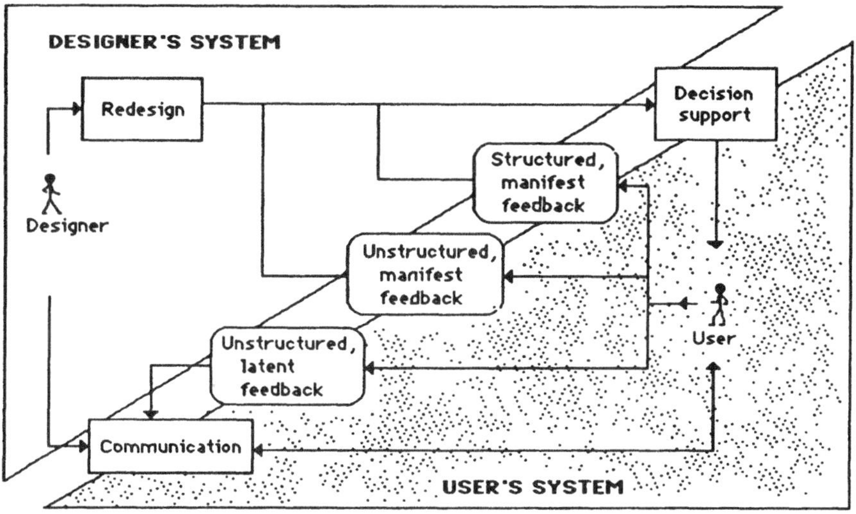

Figure 6. Latent and manifest feedback. A schematic view of the FLS. From (Grönlund & Guohua, 1991).

For instance, due to the Swedish social security system, persons with "social needs", like singles with children, may have special priority to houses owned by the municipal housing company. Issues like this requires communication between the agency and the client in order to find out the specifics of the situation, the regulations etc. To cope with such problems, the communication parts of LiveBetter was developed.

In Figure 6, the general framework for the FLS was outlined. Now, let's expand the "Communication" box (see Figure 6) a little. Communication is conceived in three categories: (1) user-user, (2) designer-designer and (3) user-designer. There are obvious differences among the three, the following are just examples:

- While the first two concern communication among peers, the third concerns actors at two different levels. This may arise problems of understanding, but also problems of dependence. For instance, a client seeking social service may not want the agency to know too much about him.
- While some users are casual, some are regular. When casual users are concerned, simple things like answering a message becomes a problem. The receiver may simply not be back to read an answer in a month.

To support communication in these categories, the LiveBetter system provides three types of tools: "message", "notice-board", and "letter" (see Figure 7). In accordance with the philosophy of embryonic development, and also considering experiences of hypertext systems for communication and discussion (Halasz, 1988), we have strived to keep the tools as simple as possible. Let us now briefly describe them.

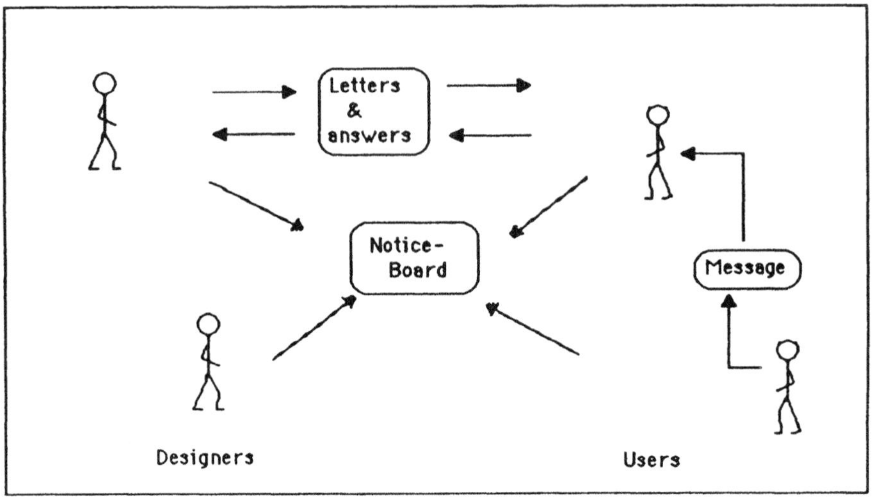

Figure 7: Tools for communication and collaboration; Messages, Letters and NoticeBoard.

Message

A "message" (Figure 8) is a communication means between users. The addressee is known and specified. A message is related to the advertisment; you can leave a message to any person that has made an advertisment. A message is therefore basically a one-way communication means, even though there are simple ways to circumvent this. No topic is specified. The format is plain text. No security is provided. The sender may remain anonymous. The purpose is to sort out simple issues concerning few people (usually two). A typical message would be "I'd like to make an offer for your flat. Please call me at 11 71 77 tonight after 6".

NoticeBoard

NoticeBoard[13] (Figure 9) was developed to support conversations around issues pertinent to, but not at the core of, the apartment exchange activity. This might include issues of regulations, special situations, reactions about the current ways to conduct the business and the like. This is, issues that cannot be sorted out immediately because they are complex or they concern several people.

NoticeBoard is a means for communication among users, among designers or cross-category. No individual adressee is specified. Messages are open to public access. The sender may be anonymous, or he may appear openly. Statements are protected, they can only be changed by the originator. Comments are not protected. An overview of subjects is

---

13 NoticeBoard is described more comprehensively in (Grönlund, 1992).

presented. This overview is sorted by actuality, which means most recently issued or commented subjects come first. At a higher user level, you can also build chains of subjects.

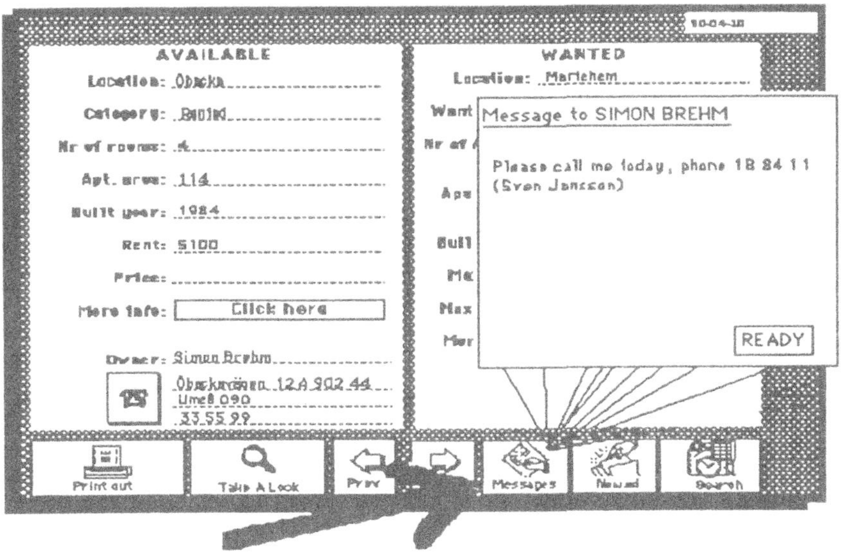

Figure 8. Message

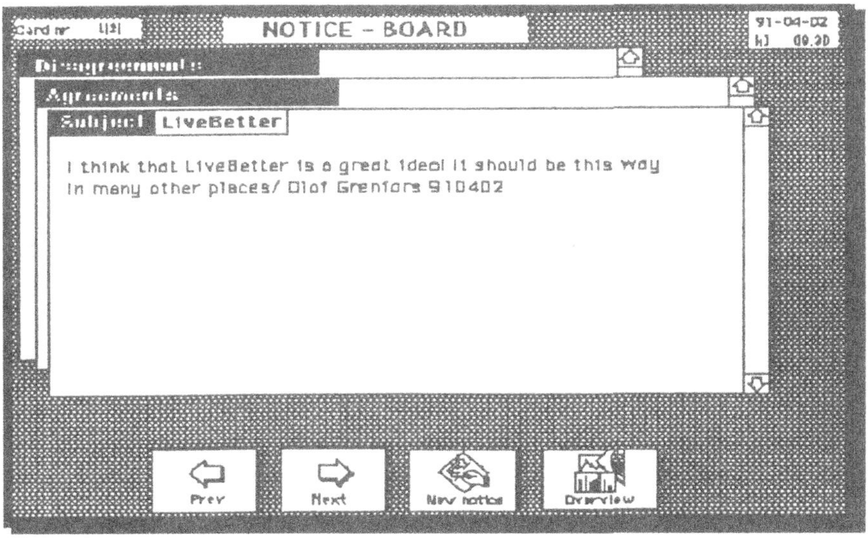

Figure 9: NoticeBoard.

Communication at NoticeBoard is set up as follows: A *subject* has to be specified by some originator (a user at any level), who then can state something about that subject. Other users can respond by *commenting* the statement under one of the labels "agreements" and "disagreements". Thus, a discussion can take place, which in time can provide some semi-structured information about user views of that subject.

Letter

A letter (Figure 10) is a communication means between users and designers. The addressee is known and specified. Addressees are people within the agency. Users can mail letters to these people, which have predefined mailboxes. The sender of a letter can specify how he wants his letter to be answered:

- "Private" means that the answer is sent as a private letter to a public mailbox protected by password.
- "Public" means that the sender considers the issue of general interest and wants it to go into a discussion at the noticeboard.
- "Not at all" is the proper label for plain notifications.

Figure 10: Letter.

An example – From peripheral to central data

We will now try to illustrate the way the above mentioned tools might be used to improve the knowledge structure in the system.

When we set up the search model that was supposed to help the users find suitable apartments, it some data seemed indipensable. We decided that (1) apartment area, (2) number of rooms, (3) construction year, (4) price, (5) rent, and (6) location were the essential variables. As obvious, the first five can easily be measured by a number, whereas the sixth can not. The search model was implemented such that if no exact match can be found, it is possible to search for apartments "close" to the preferences stated. "Close" was defined by the users by assigning relative weights to each variable by pointing at a linear scale from "not important" to "important", indicating weights from 0 to 1.

For the sixth variable, no "better" was defined, since we had only vague ideas about how to determine what it would mean. This means if the variable "location" is set to "important" and there is no exact match, no apartment at all can be found. Similarly, if "location" is set to "not important" by the user, it is not considered at all. Any residential area will do. This is not satisfying, since it seems clear that in many cases an apartment in residential area x may be as suitable as one in area y, whereas area z is definitely disqualified. In fact, area x may even be better, only the user did not know about that area when he set "location" to "y". It seems that we need some criteria to judge residential areas by. The problem is how to find the right criteria.

Use may help here. There are a number of possible scales by which we could attach numbers to the variable "location": Geographical proximity to the "best" area, number of residents, kind of residents (average income, profession, social status....), area design (green areas, playgrounds...), facilities (schools, shops, communications...), area location (distance to city center, to recreation areas...), area age, and so on.

The LiveBetter tools described in previous section can be used in the following way to acquire and/or distribute knowledge on this topic:

1. A user who gets annoyed at the systems limitation can send a letter to a system designer, stating that she is looking for a "children-friendly" area and needs a way to tell the system what she means by that (for instance nice playgrounds, not so much traffic, shool and nursery school nearby).

2. A system designer reacting to this message could set up a discussion at the notice-board on this topic, thus drawing other users attention to the problem. He could also suggest a few possible criteria, for instance those mentioned above, and encourage users to comment on these or suggest other. After some time there may be sufficient comments available to at least preliminary interpret general user opinions on the topic. The designer could then refine the search model, e.g. by introducing the concepts "Children-friendly area", "Retirement area" and "Stu-dent/yuppie area" as area categories, each concept reflecting some values on the scales suggested above.

3. If no changes are judged necessary by the designer, there is still a means available to the users to communicate on the topic. Using the message facility, they can describe their residential areas and their requirements in whatever terms they find suitable, thus enabling at least free text search. This message communication may then, if it after some time becomes voluminous and unstructured, lead to a new attack on the system designers.

The scenario described above could of course be reversed, i.e., incentives to change may origin at the designer level.

What has been described here is a kind of intelligence phase in knowledge acquisition. The aim is first to *detect* a potentially critical situation (the search model does not match use situation), then to *react* to this situation. Struggling with this is the terms of life for organizations devoted to the Information Network paradigm.

Conclusions

The changing of business towards a flattening of organizations and decentralizing much decision making is a top issue of today. If one takes this to the point, one faces the dilemma of centralization versus decentralization of the business. This has been described here as two conflicting paradigms, the "Information Delivery Paradigm" and the "Information Network Paradigm". Recognizing that information technology holds a potential for both paradigms, those concerned with organizational development face a choice about which way to go. Based on the information network paradigm, the "Feedback Learning Strategy" has been introduced as a way to organi-zational development. This is done by means of developing "participatory information systems", information systems that aim at improving decision quality by increasing user involvement.

The concept "Participatory Information Systems" as outlined in this paper is an idea that has not yet been much tried in practice. The CO-project is however engaged in some interesting experiments, involving several large Swedish companies, where at least parts of the strategy is applied. Even though the empirical work is yet scarce, it is already clear that some problems will have to be dealt with. In particular these problems are:

- Organizational redesign versus restrictions in user involvement.
- Discussion organization. This includes the discussion in general, but for our part particularly
- communication tools for the computerized parts of the discussion.

The first of these points is a long-term issue. It involves radically changed views as of what an organization is and how individuals should be allowed to act within the organization. As for the second and the third point, we hope to be able to further develop our prototypes, even though the possibilities for real-life testing is somewhat dependent on the development of the organizational issues.

References

Anghern, A. (1992). *Stimulus Agents.* Transactions of DSS 92, the 12:th International Conference of Decision Support Systems .

Bansler, J. (1987). *Systemutvikling, teori og historie i skandinavisk perspektiv.* Lund: Studentlitteratur.

Booth, S., & Pitt, D. (1984). *Continuity and Discontinuity: Information Technology as a Force for Organizational Change?* In D. C. Pitt Smith, B C. (Ed.), The Computer Revolution in Public Administration. (pp. 17-40). Brighton: Wheatsheaf Books Ltd.

Carlsson, S. (1991). *Ececutive Behaviour.* Uppsala 1991: Almqvist & Wiksell International.

Churchman, C. W. (1968). *The Systems Approach.* Delta, New York.

Corporate Memory Systems (1992). *CM/1: A Tool for Organizational Learning.* Corporate Memory Systems Inc.,

Coenen, F., & Bench-Capon, T. (1991). *A Graphical Interactive Tool for KBS Maintenance* . Berlin: Springer-Verlag.

Conklin, Jeff. (1987). *Hypertext: An Introduction and Survey*. In COMPUTER, September 1987, pp 17-41.

Dreyfus, H. L., & Dreyfus, S. E. (1986). *Mind Over Machine. The Power of Human Intuition and Expertise in the Era of the Computer*. Oxford: Basil Blackwell Ltd.

Eherer, S., & Jarke, M. (1991). *Knowledge Base Support for Hypermedia Co-Authoring* . Berlin: Springer-Verlag.

Ehn, P. (1988). *Work-Oriented Design of Computer Artifacts*. Umeå: Arbetslivscentrum.

Engelbart, D. C. (1990). *Bootstrapping Organizations Into the 21:st Century. A Strategic Framework*. Bootstrap Project, Stanford University.

Forsgren, O. (1988). *Samskapande datortillämpningar. En systemteoretisk ansats för lösning av vissa förändringsproblem vid administrativ datoranvändning*. Umeå: Umeå universitet, institutionen för informationsbehandling.

Grönlund, Å., & Guohua., B. (1991). *Adaptive Decision Support Systems*. Umeå University, Institute for Information Processing.

Grönlund, Å. (1992) *NoticeBoard 2.0*. Umeå University, Institute for Information Processing.

Göranzon, B. (Ed.) (1984). *Datautvecklingens filosofi – tyst kunskap och ny teknik*. Malmö: Carlsson & Jönsson.

Göranzon, B. (1990). *Det praktiska intellektet*. Stockholm: Carlssons Bokförlag.

Halasz, F. (1988). *Reflections on NoteCards: Seven Issues for the Next Generation of Hypermedia Systems*. In Communications of the ACM, Vol 31, Nr 7, pp 836-852.

Heng, M. S. H. (1987). *Why Evolutionary Development of Expert Systems Appear to Work*. Future Generation Computer Systems, Vol 3, Nr 2.

Ivanov, K. (1972), *Quality Control of Information*. Royal Institute of Technology, NTIS no PB219297, Stockholm 1972 (dissertation).

Johansson, B. (1991). *Bootstrap Seminar by Douglas Engelbart at Stanford University, June 18-20, 1991*. Swedish Attaché of Science and Technology.

Jones, J. W., & McLeod, R. j. (1986). *The Structure of Executive Information Systems: An Exploratory Analysis*. Decision Sciences, 17(2, spring 1986),

Lee, D. L., & Brookes, C. H. (1992). *An Innovative Corporate Intelligence System at The M.W. Kellogg Company, Houston*. University of New South Wales, Sydney, Australia.

Lundeqvist, J. (1982). *Norm och modell: samt ytterligare några begrepp inom designteorin*. Stockholm:

Mintzberg, H. (1973). *The Nature of Managerial Work*. New York: Harper & Row.

Mitroff, I. (1990). *Can Appropriate Technology Help in the Battle Against Crises? Computer Software for Crisis Management*. University of Southern California, Los Angeles.

Pitt, D. C., & Smith, B. C. (Ed.) (1984). *The Computer Revolution in Public Administration*. Brighton: Wheatsheaf Books Ltd. (Custom 1.)

Polanyi, M. (1967). *The Tacit Dimension*. New York: Anchor Books, Doubleday & Company.

Sandevall, E., Hägglund, S., Gustafsson, C., Jonesjö, L., & Strömfors, O. (1983). *Stepwise structuring: a style of life for flexible software*. Anaheim: 1983 National Computer Conference.

Simon, H. (1957). *Administrative Behavior*. A study of Decision-Making Processes in Administrative Organization. . New York: The Macmillan Company.

Simon, H. A. (1960). *The New Science of Management Decision*. New York: Harper & Row, publishers.

Svensson, K.-E., & Qwerin, A. (1986). *Användaren är också expert*. Stockholm: TCO, SSI.

Wendlandt, E. B., & Driscoll, J. R. (1991). *Enhancing Text Retrieval Semantically* . Berlin: Springer-Verlag.

Whitaker, R., Essler, U., & Östberg, O. (1991). *Participatory Business Modeling*. (TULEA 1991:31). Luleå University, Sweden.

IFIP

The INTERNATIONAL FEDERATION FOR INFORMATION PROCESSING is a multinational federation of professional and technical organisations (or national groupings of such organisations) concerned with information processing. From any one country, only one such organisation – which must be representative of the national activities in the field of information processing – can be admitted as a Full Member. In addition a regional group of developing countries can be admitted as a Full Member. On 1 October 1992, 45 organisations were Full Members of the Federation, representing 62 countries.

The aims of IFIP are to promote information science and technology by:

- fostering international co-operation in the field of information processing;
- stimulating research, development and the application of information processing in science and human activity;
- furthering the dissemination and exchange of information about the subject;
- encouraging education in information processing.

IFIP is dedicated to improving worldwide communication and increased understanding among practitioners of all nations about the role information processing can play in all walks of life.

Information technology is a potent instrument in today's world, affecting people in everything from their education and work to their leisure and in their homes. It is a powerful tool in science and engineering, in commerce and industry, in education and adminstration. It is truly international in its scope and offers a significant opportunity for developing countries. IFIP helps to bring together workers at the leading edge of the technology to share their knowledge and experience, and acts as a catalyst to advance the state of the art.

IFIP came into official existence in January, 1960. It was established to meet a need identified at the first International Conference on Information Processing which was held in Paris in June, 1959, under the sponsorship of UNESCO.

Organisational Structure

The Federation is governed by a GENERAL ASSEMBLY, which meets once every year and consists of one representative from each Member organisation. The General Assembly decides on all important matters, such as general policy, the programme of activities, admissions, elections and budget.

IFIP ORGANISATION CHART

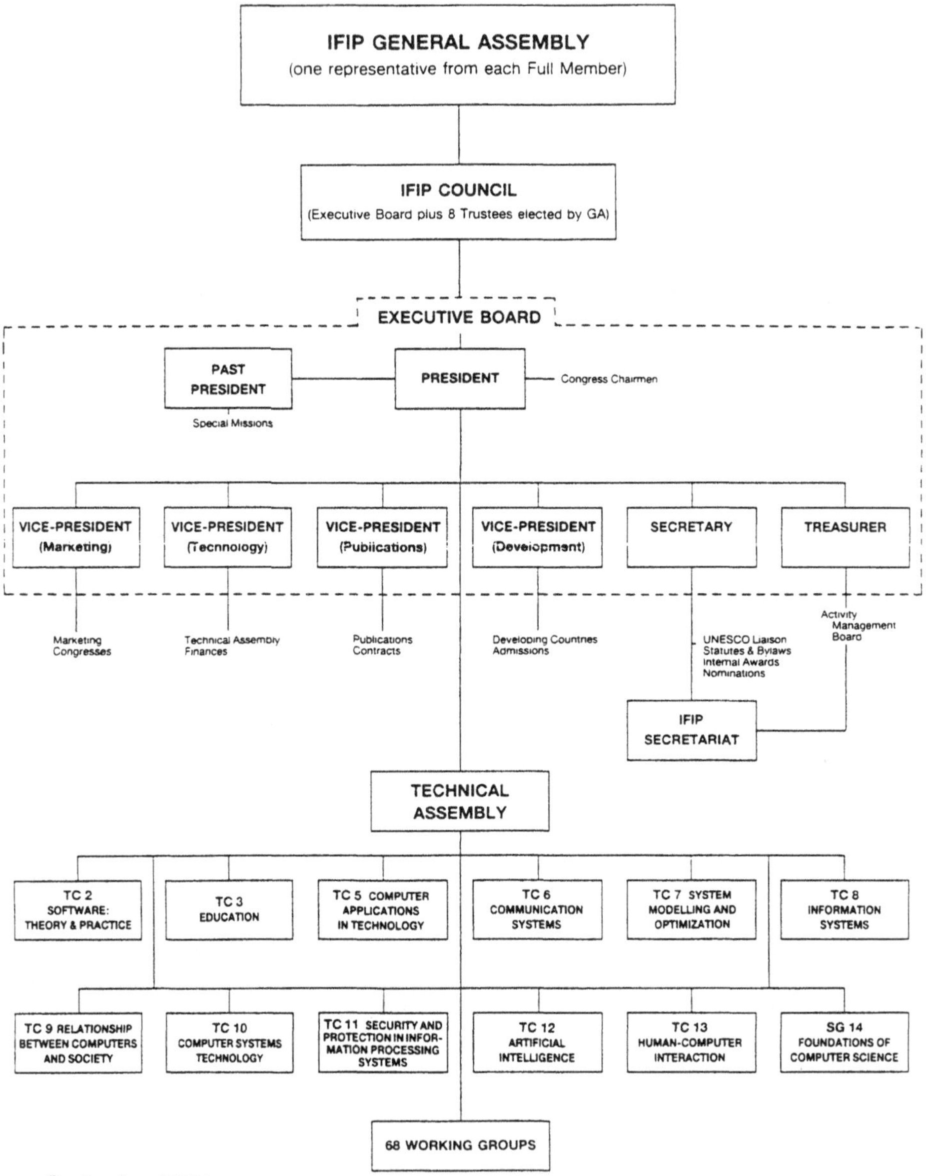

September 1992

The day-to-day work of IFIP is directed by its Officers: the President, Vice-Presidents, Secretary and Treasurer, who are elected by the General Assembly and together constitute the EXECUTIVE BOARD.

The COUNCIL, consisting of the Officers and up to eight Trustees elected from the General Assembly, meets twice a year and takes decisions which become necessary between General Assembly meetings.

The headquarters of the Federation are in Geneva, Switzerland where the IFIP Secretariat administers its affairs.

For further information please contact:

IFIP Secretariat
attn. Mme. GWYNETH ROBERTS
16 Place Longemalle
CH-1204 Geneva, Switzerland
telephone: 41 (22) 28 26 49
facsimile: 41 (22) 781 23 22
Bitnet: ifip@cgeuge51

IFIP's MISSION STATEMENT

IFIP's mission is to be the leading, truly international, apolitical organisation which encourages and assists in the development, exploitation and application of Information Technology for the benefit of all people.

Principal Elements

1. To stimulate, encourage and participate in research, development and application of Information Technology (IT) and to foster international co-operation in these activities.
2. To provide a meeting place where national IT Societies can discuss and plan courses of action on issues in our field which are of international significance and thereby to forge increasingly strong links between them and with IFIP.
3. To promote international co-operation directly and through national IT Societies in a free environment between individuals, national and international governmental bodies and kindred scientific and professional organisations.
4. To pay special attention to the needs of developing countries and to assist them in appropriate ways to secure the optimum benefit from the application of IT.
5. To promote professionalism, incorporating high standards of ethics and conduct, among all IT practitioners.
6. To provide a forum for assessing the social consequences of IT applications; to campaign for the safe and beneficial development and use of IT and the protection of people from abuse through its improper application.

7. To foster and facilitate co-operation between academics, the IT industry and governmental bodies and to seek to represent the interest of users.
8. To provide a vehicle for work on the international aspects of IT development and application including the necessary preparatory work for the generation of international standards.
9. To contribute to the formulation of the education and training needed by IT practitioners, users and the public at large.

Note to Conference Organizers

Organizers of upcoming IFIP Working Conferences are urged to contact the Publisher. Please send full details of the Conference to:

Mrs. STEPHANIE SMIT
Administrative Editor – IFIP Publications
ELSEVIER SCIENCE PUBLISHERS
P.O. Box 103, 1000 AC Amsterdam
The Netherlands
telephone: 31 (20) 5862481
facsimile: 31 (20) 5862616
email: s.smit@elsevier.nl

IFIP TRANSACTIONS

IFIP TRANSACTIONS is a serial consisting of 15,000 pages of valuable scientific information from leading researchers, published in 35 volumes per year. The serial includes contributed volumes, proceedings of the IFIP World Conferences, and conferences at Technical Committee and Working Group level. Mainstream areas in the IFIP TRANSACTIONS can be found in Computer Science and Technology, Computer Applications in Technology, and Communication Systems.

From 1993 onwards the IFIP TRANSACTIONS are only available as a full set.

IFIP TRANSACTIONS A:
Computer Science and Technology
1992: Volumes A1–A19
1993: Volumes A20–A40
ISSN 0926-5473

IFIP Technical Committees that are involved in IFIP TRANSACTIONS A
Software: Theory and Practice (TC2)
Education (TC3)
System Modelling and Optimization (TC7)
Information Systems (TC8)
Relationship Between Computers and Society (TC9)

Computer Systems Technology (TC10)
Security and Protection in Information Processing Systems (TC11)
Artificial Intelligence (TC12)
Human-Computer Interaction (TC13)
Foundations of Computer Science (SG14)

IFIP TRANSACTIONS B:
Applications in Technology
1992: Volumes B1–B8
1993: Volumes B9–B14
ISSN 0926-5481

IFIP Technical Committee that is involved in IFIP TRANSACTIONS B
Computer Applications in Technology (TC5)

IFIP TRANSACTIONS C:
Communication Systems
1992: Volumes C1–C8
1993: Volumes C9–C16
ISSN 0926-549X

IFIP Technical Committee that is involved in IFIP TRANSACTIONS C
Communication Systems (TC6)

IFIP TRANSACTIONS FULL SET: A, B & C
1992: 35 Volumes. US $ 1892.00/Dfl. 3500.00
1993: 35 Volumes. US $ 2340.00/Dfl. 3885.00
The Dutch Guilder prices (Dfl.) are definitive. The US $ prices mentioned above are for your guidance only and are subject to exchange rate fluctuations. Prices include postage and handling charges.

The volumes are also available separately in book form.

Please address all orders and correspondence to:

ELSEVIER SCIENCE PUBLISHERS
attn. PETRA VAN DER MEER
P.O. Box 103, 1000 AC Amsterdam
The Netherlands
telephone: 31 (20) 5862602
facsimile: 31 (20) 5862616
email: m.haccou@elsevier.nl

Printed in Dunstable, United Kingdom

91343652R00127